Between Reason and Irrationality

The Prose of
Valerijan Pidmohyl'nyj

Between Reason and Irrationality

The Prose of Valerijan Pidmohyl'nyj

Maxim Tarnawsky

UNIVERSITY OF TORONTO PRESS
Toronto Buffalo London

© University of Toronto Press 1994
Toronto Buffalo London
Printed in Canada
ISBN 0-8020-2993-0

Printed on acid-free paper

Canadian Cataloguing in Publication Data

Tarnawsky, Maxim
   Between reason and irrationality : the prose of Valerijan Pidmohyl'nyj

   Includes bibliographical reference and index.
   ISBN 0-8020-2993-0

   1. Pidmohyl'nyj, Valeriĩan, 1901–1941 – Criticism and interpretation. I. Title.

PG3948.P49Z84 1994   891.7'933   C93-094317-1

University of Toronto Press acknowledges the financial assistance to its publishing program of the Canada Council and the Ontario Arts Council.

This book has been published with the help of a grant from the Canadian Federation for the Humanities, using funds provided by the Social Sciences and Humanities Research Council of Canada.

To the memory of my father
Ostap Tarnawsky

Because I know that time is always time
And place is always and only place
And what is actual is actual only for one time
And only for one place

T.S. Eliot, 'Ash Wednesday'

Contents

INTRODUCTION
Valerijan Pidmohyl'nyj: Writing and Reality   3

CHAPTER ONE
The Early Stories: Shaping a Theme   21

CHAPTER TWO
Ostap Šaptala: The Structure of Prose   45

CHAPTER THREE
The Later Stories: Elements of Style   69

CHAPTER FOUR
Misto: The European Connection   105

CHAPTER FIVE
Nevelyčka drama: Philosophical Roots   145

CHAPTER SIX
The Last Works: A Final Synthesis   171

Notes   189

Bibliography: Works by and about
Valerijan Pidmohyl'nyj   201

Index   217

Between Reason and Irrationality

The Prose of
Valerijan Pidmohyl'nyj

INTRODUCTION

Valerijan Pidmohyl'nyj
Writing and Reality

A critical study of the works of Valerijan Pidmohyl'nyj, one of Ukraine's foremost literary figures, is long overdue. Although there is a sizeable body of writing about him and about his works, nowhere is his opus examined in a methodical and comprehensive manner. This study aims to fill that gap. In particular, it examines Pidmohyl'nyj's writings in chronological sequence, illuminating the development of theme, structure, and style. Pidmohyl'nyj's works trace a harmonious pattern of gradual development in each of these areas. Both intellectually and aesthetically, they give evidence of a writer who is learning, developing, adapting to new ideas, and reacting to new stimuli while at the same time never straying far from the basic methods and subjects that characterize his entire *œuvre*. The principal goal of this study is to map that artistic central core and to delineate its gradual evolution.

Given this aim, the study is necessarily modest in its methodology. It relies on the traditional tools of literary analysis, textual interpretation and literary–biographical commentary. This is neither fault nor virtue, but a matter of simple necessity, dictated by circumstances. Deconstruction, feminism, and semiotics depend on an established tradition of reading which they deliberately confront. Valerijan Pidmohyl'nyj's texts, like those of many Ukrainian writers, have been mostly neglected. There is no established reading of his works for a critic to deconstruct. There is no dominant view of his writing for a feminist to challenge. There have been many Marxist analyses of Pidmohyl'nyj, but none that a serious Marxist literary critic could endorse. The ineluctable traditional method serves well to establish the parameters within which Pidmohyl'nyj's texts can be read and against which iconoclasts can struggle.

Between Reason and Irrationality

One of the lessons of recent metacriticism in literature is the renewed appreciation of the importance of context. Subjectivity is an unavoidable characteristic of both reading and writing. The text can neither be realized without a reader, nor created without an author. The author is present in the text not as authority, but as a unifying subjectivity. The shadow (hologram) of the author links the disparate elements of a text into a single work. What is true of a single work is equally true of a writer's entire corpus. The body of a writer's work is held together by innumerable threads of style, structure, and subject. Of course, the nature of this subjective presence varies from author to author. The shadow of Balzac that unifies *La Comédie humaine* differs both in substance and in kind from the subjective reflection that runs through the works of Virginia Woolf. Yet in each case, there is something distinctly Balzacian or Woolfian that links the author's life's work into something more than a random collection of literary texts. William Butler Yeats offers an instructive example. From his early fascination with Irish mythology through his mature personal and political expression and his later mysticism, there is a constant mental framework, a consistent set of intellectual paradigms that link a variety of poetic subjects, styles, and techniques.

My study traces such a subjective shadow through the corpus of Pidmohyl'nyj's works. It also serves to introduce Pidmohyl'nyj to English-language readers, who necessarily know little about either the man or his writing. To this end much of this introductory chapter is devoted to a sketch of his life and of the literary and political reality of his times. But first, a few words are in order about Pidmohyl'nyj's writing and about the organization of this book.

For various historical reasons, Ukrainian prose did not develop as freely or as completely as did Ukrainian poetry. For a prose writer to appear among the major figures of Ukrainian literature is a distinction in itself. The relative absence of lyricism in Pidmohyl'nyj's prose makes his presence in those ranks even more exceptional. And the mixture of two cultural traditions, of two literary and philosophical streams, in his writing makes it truly outstanding.

Pidmohyl'nyj's works reflect the influence both of Ukrainian predecessors, such as Vynnyčenko, Kocjubyns'kyj, and Nečuj-Levyc'kyj, and of French realists of the nineteenth and twentieth centuries, among them Balzac, Flaubert, Maupassant, and Anatole France. Like many Ukrainian writers in the 1920s, a period of cultural renaissance in Ukraine, Pidmohyl'nyj was in search of new models on which to develop his own creativity. As a prolific translator of French prose into Ukrainian, Pidmohyl'nyj was intimately acquainted with the finest examples of western European realism.

The relationship between these two formative factors, the Ukrainian

Introduction

inheritance and the French alternative, is an unequal one. This book deals at length with the western European influence, but only occasionally mentions similarities with Ukrainian prose writers. This imbalance is conditioned by the discernible impact of these factors on Pidmohyl'nyj's works. As a Ukrainian writer, Pidmohyl'nyj is obviously and necessarily indebted to his Ukrainian predecessors, but this debt is general in nature and not subject to specific analysis. Pidmohyl'nyj consciously chose to model his writing on European models. Those models, specifically the works of the French realists, are the chief formative influence on his writing, and their impact is tangible and demonstrable.

From the collapse of tsarist Russia to the onset of Stalinist terror – roughly the decade of the 1920s – Ukrainian literature experienced a renaissance unprecedented in the millennium of its existence. Suddenly, a generation of young Ukrainians was permitted to believe that Ukrainian culture was a free and equal partner in the pantheon of world culture. After centuries of implicit and often explicit restrictions, Ukrainian literature exploded in a torrent of new-found freedom. Valerijan Pidmohyl'nyj was one of the many young writers caught up in the surging cultural floodwaters.

Much has been written about the political and institutional facets of the 1920s renaissance, but the aesthetic history of the period has yet to be told. Such a history would need to account for a broad spectrum of forms and subjects and an equally diverse range of formative influences. Without a general model of the aesthetic profile of Ukrainian literature in the 1920s, it is difficult to situate Pidmohyl'nyj concretely in the context of his own times. In general, however, it is fair to say that he differs from the majority of Ukrainian writers in the 1920s in at least three ways: his approach to literature is not political, his works are not lyrical, and his prose style, for the most part, is not subjective. While the bulk of Ukrainian literature in the 1920s revelled in its newness, Pidmohyl'nyj turned to traditional aesthetic models.

Pidmohyl'nyj's links to earlier Ukrainian literature are obvious but unilluminating. The subjects of his earliest stories show an unmistakable link to those of Volodymyr Vynnyčenko. The dehumanizing effect of sexuality, particularly on young men, is a frequent subject in the early works of both writers. Yet the young Pidmohyl'nyj is not deliberately copying anyone. There are echoes of Kocjubyns'kyj in his narration and of Nečuj-Levyc'kyj in his dialogue, but mostly there is the original, sometimes unpolished, creativity of a talented young writer.

Chapter 1 of this book focuses on the early writing and examines the themes to which Pidmohyl'nyj is repeatedly drawn, particularly the role of the irrational in human affairs. The origins of this theme can be sought in many areas, of which the tradition of the fantastic in Ukrainian literature is certainly one. But essentially, Pidmohyl'nyj is reacting to the events of the moment. His idea of chaos and order is stimulated largely by the destructive power of the revolutionary events he witnessed in the first two decades of the twentieth century. Like Pavlo Tyčyna, he sees the force of revolution as something awesome. This is especially evident in a brief fragment of an unfinished larger work, 'Na stepax,' in which an industrious young agricultural communist, comrade Vasyl', is saddened by the destruction of a landlord's estate as a result of the universal law of revolution – cleansing by fire, blood, and storm. The urbane young writer is both frightened and seduced by the raw power of human emotion, but nevertheless remains detached from it: Pidmohyl'nyj views the phenomenon through the eyes of a stranger. He is neither a populist champion of thatched roofs, as were Myrnyj and Nečuj, nor an apologist for the intelligentsia, as were Kocjubyns'kyj and Lesja Ukrajinka. For Pidmohyl'nyj, the irrational force in human affairs is an abstract phenomenon.

The stories in Pidmohyl'nyj's first collection established his credentials for writing; now he set about polishing his craft. After the instinctive successes of his first efforts, the learning curve slows significantly. In his stories from 1920 to 1925 Pidmohyl'nyj experiments with a variety of structures, styles, techniques, and devices in an attempt to move even farther from lyrical and evocative prose towards a neutral, objective technique that could sustain longer, more substantial efforts. The structure and style of the works from the mid-1920s are examined in chapters 2 and 3.

Chapter 4 considers the influence on Pidmohyl'nyj of western European realism, particularly as channelled through the writings of Guy de Maupassant. Maupassant's influence can be seen in three areas: subject, technique, and theme. It is most apparent in the novel *Misto*, which shows a strong resemblance to Maupassant's *Bel-Ami* in plot, narrative technique, and philosophical undertones. Love and the relationship between men and women are frequent subjects for both writers. Both often focus on the struggle that sexuality engenders within the individual psyche. Maupassant sees this struggle as a moral dilemma in which the individual must choose whether to embrace or resist the evil temptations of human nature, understood in terms of the Schopenhauerian will. The truly moral man struggles against sexual drives and base human instinct. In contrast to Maupassant, Pidmohyl'nyj presents the psyche in an existential battle between reason and irrationality, seen in a Nietzschean dichotomy. The conflict is no longer a moral dilemma, but an ontological one.

Both writers apply the objective method, a narrative technique based on the principle of an observing and observant spectator. Although the degree of

Introduction

which he also worries about the state of his friendship with his correspondent: 'Little boy Pidmohyl'nyj is very anxious (among other things, he thinks that he can bring joy to the whole country with his most thoughtful example. I think this is great self-deception). He writes to Kosynka that all the Kievites have rebelled against me and that the time is near when even Zerov will leave Xvyl'ovyj. Then I just laughed, but now I'm asking anyway: did I perhaps insult you somehow, comrade Zerov?'[10] The degree of insecurity in this letter bolsters the sense of a personal grudge against the 'little boy.' It also underscores the tenuous atmosphere of the times, when even Xvyl'ovyj is uncertain of his footing.

In this atmosphere it is small wonder that Pidmohyl'nyj felt the need to defend himself in an open letter to the editors of *Červonyj šljax*.[11] The attempt proved futile, however: the editorial comments that follow the letter speak of counter-revolution. Attacks continued, and only a few months later Pidmohyl'nyj wrote another open letter to the same journal, this time with Kosynka and Os'mačka as co-signers, in which the three writers protest their innocence and their treatment at the hands of ideological critics.[12] Once again, a sarcastic editorial comment followed the letter, but this time it conceded that 'non-proletarian' is not yet 'counter-revolutionary.' The final scene in this drama came in the form of an editorial statement at the end of the journal's first issue for 1924: it exonerates Pidmohyl'nyj and Os'mačka, and attributes the appearance of their works in *Nova Ukrajina* to the 'quick hands of the émigré publishers, who used various means to capture the young writers in their tentacles.'[13]

This reversal in the editorial position of *Červonyj šljax* was not serendipitous. The reason for it is evident in a comparison of the editorial board for issue 4–5 with that for issue 6–7 of 1923. The former lists Hryhorij Hryn'ko as editor; the latter lists Oleksander Šums'kyj as head of an editorial board that included Tyčyna, Hryn'ko, Blakytnyj, Pylypenko, and Xvyl'ovyj. This was an important change at *Červonyj šljax*; it signalled the early, tangible results of the official policy of Ukrainization.[14] It was also a token of Pidmohyl'nyj's improving fortunes. In the summer of 1923, while Pidmohyl'nyj and Kosynka were fighting for their right to be published in Soviet Ukraine, Vynnyčenko was sending them relief packages of food.[15] In 1924, the same issue of *Červonyj šljax* that contained the editorial exoneration also contained a story by Pidmohyl'nyj entitled 'Vijs'kovyj litun.'[16] The April-May issue contained an article by M. Dolengo (pseudonym of Myxajlo Vasyl'ovyč Klokov) devoted to Pidmohyl'nyj's works,[17] as well as an item in the 'Chronicle' section noting that Pidmohyl'nyj had finished a story entitled 'Trik-trak' and that a collection of his stories had gone to the printer.[18]

'Trik-trak' was renamed 'Sonce sxodyt" and appeared in *Žyttja j revoljucija* in 1925.[19] The collection of stories, Pidmohyl'nyj's second, was published in 1924 by 'Červonyj šljax' under the title *Vijs'kovyj litun. Opovidannja*, and was positively reviewed by Osval'd Burhardt in the August-September issue of *Červonyj šljax* for that year. Also in 1924 an excerpt from an otherwise unpublished work appeared in *Nova hromada*.[20] Perhaps even more significant was the announcement in *Červonyj šljax* that Pidmohyl'nyj, Kosynka, Antonenko-Davydovyč, Os'mačka, Plužnyk, and M. Halyč had formed a new literary organization.

This organization, 'Lanka' (later reorganized as MARS), comprised a group of so-called fellow-travellers. As such, it did not take part in the competition among Marxist literary organizations for the exclusive right to represent the Party in matters pertaining to literary policy. Indeed, there is no formal record of the organization's activities whatsoever. Its members, however, did play a very important role in the cultural and intellectual life of Kiev. The organization is usually associated with the journal *Žyttja j revoljucija*, although the relationship was, no doubt, informal.[21] Perhaps of the greatest significance, however, is the personal relationship between Pidmohyl'nyj and Jevhen Plužnyk that grew out of their collaboration in Lanka. In his excellent biographical introduction to Plužnyk's collected poems, Leonid Čerevatenko captures the spirit of the friendship:

> The tightest bonds united Je. Plužnyk with V. Pidmohyl'nyj. The similarity of their personalities was a factor here. They were both intelligent beyond all measure, observant – they noticed everything, witty – they remembered details, phrases, and as for their expressions …! And they both knew their worth. They perfectly understood their own place and significance in literature …
>
> But for all the similarity with V. Pidmohyl'nyj, these were very different people. They were both smart, disparaging, and sharp-tongued. And yet, Jevhen somehow never lost his innocent, bright childishness. For him there was always a line 'thou shalt not cross'! Meanwhile Valer"jan Petrovyč did not shirk from black scepticism and turned willingly to cynicism as a weapon.[22]

The years 1924–30 were good years for Pidmohyl'nyj. In addition to his writing and translating, he was active in publishing, working at times for the publishing houses Rux and Knyhospilka, as well as in the editorial offices of *Žyttja j revoljucija*. Pidmohyl'nyj's name does not often appear in connection with public events at this time,[23] although he did participate in the political struggle that has since come to be known as the Literary Discussion.[24] The discussion, in its public form, reflected the divergence between a utilitarian and an aesthetic view of the function of literature. The Party, of course, promoted a utilitarian view. Pidmohyl'nyj's views were made clear in his speech at the public debate on the future of literature that was held in Kiev on 24 May 1925: 'If a comrade, having tried his hand at writing a sonata, were to claim that it was a beautiful sonata because it had a beautiful ideology, no one would hesitate to tell him that this was musical nonsense, and no one would listen to the sonata. If this comrade were to take up painting, having as much talent for painting as many of our poets have for poetry, no one would go to see his paintings just because they were ideologically correct. But in literature, it's go ahead and write if you're literate.'[25] Pidmohyl'nyj's literary and personal prospects were good as long as the discussion continued. His creative output for the years between 1924 and 1928 was considerable. In 1927 alone, Pidmohyl'nyj published seven volumes of translations of French prose.

Pidmohyl'nyj's writing was undergoing a change during this period. Except for 'Z žyttja budynku No. 29,' written in 1933, his last short story was 'Tretja revoljucija,' dated 1925. Pidmohyl'nyj apparently had a particular inclination for the longer form and simply abandoned the short form in favour of the novel. Historically, it was, indeed, in the period 1925–27 that young Soviet Ukrainian literature as a whole finally outgrew its reliance on short forms, especially on lyrical verse and often-facile short stories. Moreover, the writer-hero of the novel *Misto*, in part an autobiographical figure, exhibits a similar progression from the short form to the novel.

Pidmohyl'nyj adopts urban settings and themes in his novels more often than in his stories. Perhaps this reflects his own re-orientation from the cultural model of a village to that of a city. This conjecture is further supported by the works Pidmohyl'nyj published in the interval between 'Tretja revoljucija' and *Misto*. The most unusual of these, by far, is the lexicon of business expressions Pidmohyl'nyj compiled with his friend Jevhen Plužnyk. Although she is not given credit in the book, Tajisa Kovalenko, Pidmohyl'nyj's intimate friend and Plužnyk's sister-in-law, was a third collaborator in this project.[26] It was published in 1926 by Čas, the publisher for which Pidmohyl'nyj worked, under the title *Frazeolohija dilovoji movy*, and later reissued in a revised edition in 1927. Mykola Stanyslavs'kyj gave it low marks in a review.[27] Leonid Čerevatenko, however, says that it was well compiled and that it was to be found decades later in institutional offices and on the desks of teachers and writers, with the title page and the names of the arrested and executed compilers removed.[28] In the preface to the recent reprint of this dictionary, Larysa Masenko calls it 'one of the most valuable achievements of Ukrainian lexicography of the 1920s.'[29]

Pidmohyl'nyj joined the editorial board of *Žyttja j revoljucija* in 1927 and, as an editor, was no doubt expected to contribute to the journal. Over the course of fourteen months he contributed two essays of literary criticism, a review of a collection of short stories, and a report on the visit of the writer Panait Istrati to Kiev. These four pieces reveal a growing interest in literary criticism. Before 1926 there had been no indication that Pidmohyl'nyj had any interest in criticism. His incomplete statement during the literary debate of 24 May 1925 addressed political rather than literary concerns. But the essays in *Žyttja j revoljucija* are clearly the work of someone interested in literature *per se*. The first of those essays is a study of the poetry of Maksym Ryl's'kyj,[30] and represents Pidmohyl'nyj's only known foray into the world of poetry. Pidmohyl'nyj sees Ryl's'kyj as a hopeless romantic. In the conflict between illusion and reality that inspires Ryl's'kyj's creativity, the poet chooses illusion, says Pidmohyl'nyj, but chooses it half-heartedly, always remaining aware that his choice is just an illusion. Vjačeslav Brjuxovec'kyj suggests that Pidmohyl'nyj uncharitably and dishonestly views Ryl's'kyj as a man unsuited to an era of revolutionary social change.[31] He thus implies, unfairly, that Pidmohyl'nyj was an ideological henchman of Stalinism. The fundamental dualism in Pidmohyl'nyj's thinking is always between reason and irrationality. Ryl's'kyj's poetry, he argues, is a deliberate flight from reason.

Pidmohyl'nyj's second essay in *Žyttja j revoljucija* was another study of a single author. This time his subject was Ivan Nečuj-Levyc'kyj, a major figure in nineteenth century Ukrainian prose. It is likely that the essay grew out of Pidmohyl'nyj's work on a two-volume collection of Levyc'kyj's stories, which he edited for Čas. In his preface to the collection, Pidmohyl'nyj stressed the social and economic realism of Levyc'kyj's stories.[32] In the essay that appeared in *Žyttja j revoljucija*, however, he focused on the personality of the author, which, he argued, reflected the essential features of an Oedipal complex.[33] The psychoanalysis offered in this essay is naïve and tendentious. Levyc'kyj may have been everything Pidmohyl'nyj says he was, but this essay will not convince serious readers. Its real significance lies not in what it tells us about Levyc'kyj, but in what it reveals about Pidmohyl'nyj. His interest in and familiarity with Freudian psychology, despite Jevhen Plužnyk's friendly jibe that he had not read what he was agitating for,[34] offer a major clue to understanding his own works. His application of this tool to literary analysis, together with the nature of his review of Tymofij Borduljak's stories[35] and his piece on Istrati,[36] give evidence of his growing interest in the technical and psychological analysis of literature.

Introduction

Pidmohyl'nyj's interest in questions of theory and aesthetic judgment, which would culminate in the creation of an opinionated writer as the protagonist of his first novel, is also apparent in the preface to his *Problema xliba*, a retrospective collection of stories published in 1927 by Masa. The piece discusses the then-fashionable question of *sjužetnist'*, a term used to describe thrillers, mysteries, science fiction, and other types of popular fiction that rely heavily on plot structure. In both form and substance Pidmohyl'nyj's prefatory epistle rejects plotting as inappropriate to his own temperament as a writer. The tone of the piece is playful but the interest in theory that it reveals is real.

The preface was written in 1926 in Gurzuf, a town in the Crimea just up the coast from Yalta. A resort town, Gurzuf has a history of famous visitors, among them Pushkin, Chekhov, and Mickiewicz. Whatever its literary significance, the fact that Pidmohyl'nyj found himself at this resort can be taken as an indication that his personal and literary fortunes were improving. This is not to say that his personal life was not uncomplicated at this time: In 1926 Pidmohyl'nyj separated from his wife to pursue a new romance. Vasyl Chaplenko depicts the young couple's troubled marriage in a biographical story dedicated to the writer's memory.[37] Subsequently, Pidmohyl'nyj reconciled with his wife, and they had a son, Roman.

By 1928 Pidmohyl'nyj was a well-known writer, an important figure in the literary life of Kiev, a respected translator, and the subject of a number of essays and reviews. Reviewers were unanimous in the opinion that he was an exceptionally good translator. His literary skill as a writer of short stories was also highly regarded, but in this area praise was almost always qualified by reservations about his political loyalties. The keepers of ideological purity were particularly offended by the story 'Tretja revoljucija,' in which the anarchist revolutionary Nestor Maxno appears as a central character. But the political attacks against the story were more concerned with denouncing Maxno, who was still alive in Paris and apparently perceived as a threat, than with Pidmohyl'nyj, whose fault consisted of depicting Maxno without horns, tail, or cloven foot. At the tender age of twenty-six, Pidmohyl'nyj was a literary success and ready for his next big step. That step was taken in the first half of 1928, with the publication of his first novel, *Misto*.

For Pidmohyl'nyj and, indeed, for Ukrainian literature, the novel's publication was an important event. In the timid and often orchestrated literary life of Kiev in the 1920s, *Misto* generated excitement. The novel aroused genuine interest and sparked a controversy of significant dimensions. Some measure of the magnitude of its impact can be gleaned from Olena Zvyčajna's review of the 1955 émigré edition of the novel[38] as well as from her own, less-than-inspired novel about life in Kiev in the 1920s, which devotes an entire chapter to its protagonist's reaction to *Misto*.[39] A more objective yardstick is the fact that the first printing, of 4,000 copies, was followed by a second, of 5,000, in 1929. There was even a Russian translation of the novel,[40] as well as plans to translate Pidmohyl'nyj's works – no doubt including *Misto* – into Czech.[41] All this was accompanied by a chorus of reviews and analyses in newspapers and journals. The novel became a subject for public discussion. On 2 March 1929, an assembly was held at the Instytut narodnoji osvity (Institute of People's Education, formerly the university) in Kiev, at which three speakers discussed the current literary situation. *Misto* figured prominently in all of the presentations.[42] The very next day a representative of Molodnjak, the Komsomol literary organization, led a group of Komsomol members at the Kiev film studios in a discussion of *Misto*.[43] But these two events pale in comparison with what had taken place at the All-Ukrainian Trade Union Congress, held 1–8 December 1928. The official report on the cultural activities of trade union organizations used Pidmohyl'nyj's novel as its centrepiece example of the current state of Ukrainian culture.[44] Of course, most of the public discussion was organized specifically to condemn the novel. But the fact that the authorities considered such attacks necessary or prudent attests to the popularity of the novel – which was also evidenced by the trade union libraries' relatively high circulation figures for the book.[45]

With his first novel generating such excitement, Pidmohyl'nyj was enjoying the benefits of public attention. In the second half of 1928 the Ukrainian Commissariat of Education sent him, with a group of other writers, on a trip to the West. His itinerary took him to Paris, Prague, Berlin, and Hamburg.

By early 1929 Pidmohyl'nyj was back in Ukraine and preparing for another trip, this time to Moscow, as part of a delegation of Ukrainian writers invited by their Russian counterparts for a 'Ukrainian week in Moscow.'[46] Among the highlights of this trip was a visit by the Ukrainian writers to the Kremlin, and an audience with Stalin himself. One account of this meeting ends with the General Secretary leading the respectful Ukrainian writers in song while Pidmohyl'nyj and Antonenko-Davydovyč quietly leave.[47] Comrade Stalin had apparently failed to make much of an impression on the young writer.

Back in Ukraine, Pidmohyl'nyj's work continued as before. He submitted a short article giving his own view of his novel to a popular magazine.[48] A half-dozen volumes of his translations from French appeared during 1928–29, among them his best-known translation, that of Maupassant's *Bel-Ami*, entitled *Ljubyj druh* in Ukrainian. Work on the ten-volume edition of Maupassant and on a twenty-five-volume edition of Anatole France continued. Some letters from Pidmohyl'nyj to Il'ko Borščak, a Ukrainianist in Paris, and to Mykola

Introduction

Zerov have survived from this period. They are largely business correspondence dealing with the details of editorial plans and publishing arrangements.[49] Most important during this period was Pidmohyl'nyj's work on another novel, *Nevelyčka drama*, which he completed by early 1930. But the political climate had changed. The novel was serialized in *Žyttja j revoljucija*,[50] but it did not appear as a separate volume. Stalinism had set in. Pidmohyl'nyj was removed from his position as co-editor of *Žyttja j revoljucija*. In its 15 July 1930 issue, *Literaturna hazeta* mentions that Pidmohyl'nyj had been elected to the Kiev Writers' Committee (Miscevkom pys'mennykiv) and that he was the co-leader of a newly organized exercise group (fizkul'turna brygada) in the city's literature building. But these honours masked a precipitous decline in Pidmohyl'nyj's fortunes. His career as a writer was being curtailed.

Little is known of Pidmohyl'nyj's life after 1930. He moved to Kharkiv, where he continued to translate from French and Russian, publishing volumes of Anatole France, Diderot, Turgenev, and Gogol. He served as the foreign-literature specialist at the Rux publishing house. Although a request made in 1932 to publish his second novel was denied,[51] in June 1933, a month after the suicide of Mykola Xvyl'ovyj and two weeks before that of Mykola Skrypnyk, as Pavel Postyšev purged the Ukrainian Party apparatus and a famine devastated the countryside, Pidmohyl'nyj was allowed to publish a story in *Literaturna hazeta*. The story, 'Z žyttja budynku No. 29,' is largely an indictment of Soviet ideological terror. Čerevatenko explains its publication as part of an effort by the regime to ease up on its campaign of terror at that particular time.[52] Whatever the explanation, the appearance of the story was not a sign of Pidmohyl'nyj's improving fortunes. His father died in Vorzel' in 1933. One by one, his fellow writers and fellow intellectuals were being arrested. Yet Pidmohyl'nyj kept on writing. In 1933–34 he worked on a novella, *Povist' bez nazvy*, and, according to Jurij Smolyč, translated André Malraux's *La Condition humaine*, but neither work was published. Pidmohyl'nyj waited for the inevitable knock on his door.

On 1 December 1934, Stalin had Sergei Kirov assassinated in Leningrad. A massive campaign of terror had begun. On 8 December Valerijan Pidmohyl'nyj was arrested at the Zan'ky artists' colony near Kharkiv. The warrant for his arrest was dated 4 December. He was charged with membership in a terrorist organization. His career as a writer was over.

The story of Pidmohyl'nyj's life from his arrest to his death is a tale of the barbarity of the Soviet regime under Stalin. Yet it is only one of millions of such stories. Volodymyr Mel'nyk has told Pidmohyl'nyj's in frightening detail.[53] I summarize it here: Pidmohyl'nyj was interrogated and tortured for a month (two extensions of the ten-day limit on interrogations were granted). On 14 January 1935, having signed a confession to the state's fantastic charges, he was moved to Kiev, where he was kept for two and a half months. On March 27–28 he was sentenced to ten years in prison. He was sent to the prison camp on the Solovecki Islands, which occupied a famous monastery founded in the fifteenth century in the White Sea, and which became an infamous link in the Gulag Archipelago. Pidmohyl'nyj's wife and son left Ukraine and eventually settled in Alma-Ata. They did not return until after the Second World War. But Valerijan Pidmohyl'nyj never returned from prison. On 9 October 1937 a special commission re-examined his case. By order of that commission, on 3 November 1937, Pidmohyl'nyj was executed.

Pidmohyl'nyj's recently discovered letters from the Solovecki Islands to his wife, his mother, and his sister offer an interesting picture of his life in the camp. They are, as one would expect, documents of a highly personal nature, expressing the political prisoner's anxiety about the physical, material, and emotional well-being of his family. At the same time, however, they are the reflections of a creative artist. They offer a rare glimpse of the person who has been called the most intellectual and the most intelligent Ukrainian writer of the 1920s. In all, thirteen of the existing thirty-two letters have been published in *Vitčyzna*[54] and *Družba narodov*.[55] They were written in Russian (to accommodate prison censors) during the period from 16 February 1935 to 2 June 1937. The first two letters are from Kiev, shortly after Pidmohyl'nyj's arrest. The others are from the Solovecki Islands prison camp. Two letters are to his mother and sister in Kharkiv. The rest are to his wife and son.

The letters are often quite emotional in tone, particularly where Pidmohyl'nyj's son, Roman, is concerned. But they also give many indications of the writer's literary and intellectual activity. In the first of the published letters Pidmohyl'nyj writes his own literary obituary. He asks his wife to collect all of his published works and provides her with a list. Although incomplete, the list none the less provides new information for bibliographers. In subsequent letters Pidmohyl'nyj occasionally mentions his reading and writing. For example, in the letter of 6 July 1935, he says, 'With great satisfaction I have read here only one, unfortunately, volume of Plutarch's *Lives* (in an English translation). With Lycurgus, Solon, Numa Pompilius I recalled so clearly my childhood – the school, third or fourth grade' (*Vitčyzna*, 96).

In other letters Pidmohyl'nyj writes about studying English and translating Oscar Wilde's *The Picture of Dorian Gray* and two acts of Shakespeare's *Henry VI*. In September 1935 he writes that he has read nearly ninety books. Clearly Pidmohyl'nyj was striving to survive his sentence by immersing

Introduction

himself in intellectual activity. In addition to reading and practising his English and French, he was also creating original works. In a letter dated 13 April 1936, he tells his wife that he has been working on plans for a variety of new projects: 'I began, for example, to write a series of short stories, but I gave up on them (I finished one). Then I began a novella, but it was too light-hearted, even humorous. I wrote the first chapter and gave up. All this was very painful for me. I drew up plans for a novel about the 1930s, but I cannot write it because I do not have sufficient knowledge of the functioning and technology of a factory, which needs to be included' (*Vitčyzna*, 102). Later he speaks of a novel about collectivization:

> From the very beginning, when I arrived here, there arose in me a desire or rather a need to write about collectivization. This subject is very poorly covered in Ukrainian literature ... I have written two chapters and I'm ready to continue ... Right now I envision this thing as a 'full-length' novel with 32 chapters and 15 characters. I want to write it very simply, but I also want to avoid literary stereotypes. It will have a few basic threads, continuously developing. I will attempt to portray the people as well as the conflicts in their beliefs, feelings, and characters as clearly as possible without simplifying them. My assignment is to narrate as little as I can so that, to the degree that it is possible, even the details would be revealed in the action, both external and internal. As you can see, my intentions are very good. I've even chosen a title: *Autumn 1929*. (*Vitčyzna*, 102)

He also mentions another work: 'In 1935 I wrote a novella, which I sent to Kiev. It's a small thing, consisting of 20 chapters under the title *Budynok No. 32* [Building No. 32]. It's the life of the building in various cross sections, with many characters, but, in the final analysis, it's a story about myself' (*Vitčyzna*, 101).

Even allowing for the possibility that these letters were meant to calm anxious relatives and impress the prison censor with the prisoner's determination, diligence, and mental discipline, Pidmohyl'nyj is obviously trying to exercise his creativity. Furthermore, his descriptions and analyses of his projects give a good indication of the kind of writing he is planning. They also show what sort of writer and thinker he is – perhaps nowhere more than in the following requests, which he makes in a letter dated 7 March 1936:

> To Katja: (1) From the library get Spinoza's work *On the Improvement of the Understanding*[56] (there is a new Russian translation) and in the first 6–7 pages find the passage where the author says that he has not yet completely

freed himself from the passions of greed, sloth, and desire. Please copy the whole passage and send it to me. (2) Look in the album of postcard reproductions from the Tretiakov Gallery and find out whose work is the painting *Nekrasov Ill in Bed*. If possible, buy this postcard and send it to me. I think you can get it at the stationery, where they sell reproductions and frames. For Katja:[57] (1) Find out if this is correct Latin: *sancta simplicitas* (holy simplicity), and what is the first line of Cicero's oration against Catiline, that begins *quo usque* etc.?[58] (2) If possible, get a picture of the Xolodnohors'kyj bridge in Kharkiv, one that shows the figures at the beginning of the bridge. Perhaps Jura can take the picture himself, if no such card can be bought. Or let him write a description of the bridge and the figures, as well as how the bridge is illuminated at night and the view from the bridge in the direction of Merefa – this I ask him to do even if he does find a postcard. 3) What is the name of the tenor in the play *Zaporožec' za Dunajem*? The one who sings the duet 'Čorna xmara?' Her name is Oksana, what is his? (*Vitčyzna*, 99–100)

The intellectual portrait of Pidmohyl'nyj that emerges from these letters is one of an exceptionally erudite man with a wide range of cultural interests. As a writer he consciously emphasizes the techniques of realism, reducing the role of the narrator in favour of exposition through action (that is, showing rather than telling). He plans and structures his works carefully and requires a detailed knowledge of the material he describes. The impression given in his letters is borne out by his works, to which we now turn.

CHAPTER ONE

The Early Stories
Shaping a Theme

Like the images in a sixty-second movie preview, Pidmohyl'nyj's early stories, published in 1920 in the immodestly titled collection *Tvory: Tom 1* (Works: Volume 1), reflect and anticipate the themes and techniques that characterize all his later literary works. And, also like the images in the preview, those represented by Pidmohyl'nyj's early stories are incomplete, occasionally inaccurate, and partially misleading in their anticipation of the later works. Many of the themes, motifs, and techniques that appear in the early stories undergo a transformation before they reappear in the later works.

A notable characteristic of Pidmohyl'nyj's works, taken as a whole, is their remarkable unity of theme. His works cover a variety of subjects, including sex, war, famine, urbanization, science, national rights, and journalism. His heroes include writers, scientists, children, students, soldiers, and secretaries. The works are all set in contemporary Ukraine, but they encompass both the city and the village, the north and the south, the years of war and revolution and the years of the NEP and the first five-year plan. None the less, Pidmohyl'nyj's works are all fundamentally shaped by a single idea: in a sense, he is writing the same story over and over again. He is continually preoccupied with the conflict between instinct and reason. Philosophically, all his works are about this conflict. Between the early stories and the later works, however, his understanding of this basic dualism undergoes substantial changes.

In the stories contained in *Tvory: Tom 1* the young author is still far from the existential view of his theme that will appear in his later works. In these early stories the conflict between instinct and reason is depicted in a simple, literal representation. Instinct, in the form of male sexual libido, arouses young men and propels them into dramatic acts of self-assertion and self-discovery. Resistance to this force comes from the superego, that is, the youths' natural timidity and their socially and religiously conditioned guilt. The struggle typically ends with the defeat of the libido and a consequent loss of individuality and self-worth for the young men.

This model appears in a few variants among the stories in *Tvory: Tom 1*. It takes one of its simplest forms in the earliest story, 'Važke pytannja' (A Difficult Question), in which the young protagonist, Andrij, is led by his high-school friend Mykola to the apartment of a prostitute. The contrast between the two boys is the earliest version of Pidmohyl'nyj's basic dualism. Andrij is a naïve and sexually inexperienced boy whose values have been formed largely by parental, social, and religious influences. He is a champion of order and decency, as evidenced by his initial reason for calling on Mykola. After meeting Mykola's girlfriend, Halja, at a party the previous evening, he feels compelled to share with his friend his own negative impressions of the girl and, generally, to warn him about the dangers of love. The problem with Halja, he believes, is that she is too full of desire:

'Я тільки хотів сказати, що вона дуже жагуча. Ти спитаєш відкіля в мене такі відомости? Це, дорогий мій, по ній самій видно. Очі в неї, знаєш, так блискають і рот підозріло великий. І взагалі вся постать.... А хто жагучий, той мало постійний. Побаче чоловіка більш статечного з фізичного погляду ніж ти,—й прощавай, Миколко....' (*Tvory*,[1] 51–2)

'I only wanted to say that she has so much desire. You will ask how do I know that? That, my dear friend, is evident just by looking at her. Her eyes, you know, sparkle so and her mouth is suspiciously large. And her whole figure... And you know, the more desire, the less constancy. She'll glimpse someone more impressive physically than you are and it's "So long, Mykola."'

Of course, Andrij is masking his own desire in a characteristically Freudian compensation, but the fact remains that, except for one trip to the prostitute, he successfully represses instinct and allows socially conditioned consciousness to govern his behaviour. Mykola, too, is shaped by Freudian sublimations and repressions, but, unlike his schoolmate, he allows instinct to prevail and then finds arguments to justify his actions.

In a structural sense, the contrast between Andrij and Mykola reflects an incomplete dualism. In this story, as in most of Pidmohyl'nyj's early works,

The Early Stories

the underlying philosophical conflict is not between instinct and reason, but between instinct and repression. Schematically, this is X versus $-X$, rather than X versus Y. It is characteristic of Pidmohyl'nyj's early and middle periods that the focus of his intellectual attention is on the irrational in its various forms and manifestations. Only in some of the stories from the middle period and in his later novels does Pidmohyl'nyj divide his attention equally between the irrational and the rational.

The focus on the irrational in the stories in *Tvory: Tom 1* places them in a well established current in Ukrainian literature of the early twentieth century. In the nineteenth century, the irrational was represented in Ukrainian romantic literature in at least two forms: the fantastic, most obviously in Gogol but also in such writers as Kvitka, Kotljarevs'kyj, and Storoženko; and the personal or subjective, in such writers as Ševčenko. Significantly, the irrational in both these forms is part of a specifically Ukrainian context. Late in the century, particularly in the socially conscious realist novels of populist writers, the irrational has a different and less prominent role. In the works of such writers as Myrnyj and Nečuj, the irrational, usually in the form of uncontrolled instinct, is an evil force that preys on innocent individuals, eroding their moral values, unbalancing their personalities, and destroying their lives.

A more profound exploration of the role of the irrational in the human psyche is found in the works of Dostoevsky, which influenced both Myrnyj and Nečuj to some degree. Unlike those Ukrainian novelists, however, the author of *Notes from Underground* does not reduce the irrational to an extrinsic evil force, but presents it as the principal battlefield for the psychological conflict that is at the centre of his intellectual attention. The villain, for Dostoevsky, is rational humanism. The irrational includes both the moral values that must combat this evil and the psychological mechanisms that allow it to spread through the entire social organism. It is Dostoevsky's particular achievement that he focuses attention specifically on the irrational as a principal component of the individual psyche.

The influence of Dostoevsky, the demise of populism, the rise of modernist aestheticism, and the spread of Freudian concepts are among the factors that contributed to the growing importance of the irrational in Ukrainian literature in the first decades of the twentieth century. Although it usually went by a different name, the irrational is an important element in the works of many prominent Modernist writers. Myxajlo Kocjubyns'kyj often focuses on the alienation of the individual from the incomprehensible 'otherness' surrounding him, as he does in *Tini zabutyx predkiv* (Shadows of Forgotten Ancestors). In many of her plays – for example, in *Cassandra* – Lesja Ukrajinka explores the failures and inadequacies of reason. Volodymyr Vynnyčenko, particularly in his early novels, stories, and plays, tries to reconcile sexual instinct with the norms of civilized behaviour.

The influence of Vynnyčenko's depiction of the conflict between instinct and civilization is clearly evident in Pidmohyl'nyj's early stories. As in Vynnyčenko's works from before 1917, so in the stories of *Tvory: Tom 1*, the central force affecting the lives of the fictional characters is sexual desire. Of the nine stories in *Tvory*, seven deal specifically with a young man's sexual drive. Only 'Did Jakym' (Grandfather Jakym) and 'Vanja' are devoid of explicit sexuality. And in the case of the latter, as we shall see in the discussion that follows, it is only the explicitness that is missing. In the remaining stories, Pidmohyl'nyj depicts young men or boys whose budding sexuality puts them in conflict with accepted moral and social norms of behaviour. In 'Važke pytannja' the situation is reduced to its bare essentials: two young boys battle their own scruples to visit a prostitute. In his next story, 'Dobryj boh' (Merciful God), Pidmohyl'nyj adds more depth and complexity to the psychology of his young male protagonists. Viktor Xobrovs'kyj is a very religious young man with a peculiar notion of self-worth:

'Чоловік тільки тоді вартий чого-небудь, коли знайдеться жінка, котра покохає його й захоче зв'язати з ним своє життя на підставі цього кохання. Я маю дев'ятнадцять років і вже знайшлась така жінка. Виходить, що я маю людську вартість.' (*Tvory*, 118 / *Misto*,[2] 244 / BUL,[3] 28)

'A man is worth something only when a woman can be found who will fall in love with him and will wish to tie her life to his on the basis of that love. I'm nineteen years old and already such a woman has been found. It follows that I have value as a human being.'

After his girlfriend, Kusja, terminates an unwanted pregnancy, their relationship sours. When Viktor discovers an officer in her bedroom, he vows to commit suicide. But when he learns that his sexually active friend Jurko has contracted venereal disease, he abandons his plan and rationalizes breaking his solemn vow to take his own life by relying on God's mercy and forgiveness.

The juxtaposition of sexual desire and religious faith offers significant insight into Pidmohyl'nyj's understanding of the irrational. The device is also used in the story 'V epidemičnomu baraci' (In the Epidemic Ward), where Odarka Kalynivna, one of the nurses, is portrayed as a religious fanatic.

Religious fanaticism is key in 'Did Jakym' and 'Ivan Bosyj' as well. Characters with deep religious feelings are central in 'Vanja,' 'Syn' (The Son) and *Ostap Šaptala*. In all these stories religion is invariably a refuge from reality. Weak and frightened, human consciousness adopts religion to avoid the need to deal with reality on its own, often unpleasant, terms. For instance, in 'Dobryj boh,' Viktor first turns to religion after his 'miraculous' cure from a childhood disease. Pidmohyl'nyj explicitly emphasizes the anti-rational and anti-scientific character of Viktor's faith:

Хобровський вірив сліпо й грубо.
   'Кому ти кланяєшся?' насмішкувато питав Юрко, коли Віктор скидав кашкетку, ідучи повз церкву.
   Знову Юрко! Ой, чудак. Але веселий хлопець. Безбожний хоч куди. Як він було каже:
   'Вікторе, ти дурний. Я розумію таку віру в темному народі, але тобі її простить не можу. Головне діло, що ти по цьому питанню нічого не читав. Прочитай, тоді ти побачиш і почуєш, що Христос такий же Бог, як і ми з тобою, а божественного в йому стільки, як у всякій корові. Візьми в мене деякі книжки....'
   'Ти мене не переконаєш, я вже переконаний,' казав Віктор. 'Змалечку я хворів, дуже тяжко хворів. Навіть лікарі заявили, що надії на одужання немає. А як батько відслужив молебня, то мені поліпшало в той мент, коли служили молебня. І це мене переконало в Бозі. А ніяких глузливих опосмішок я не хочу чути. Та не однако хіба тобі, вірю я, чи ні?'
   'Чудно, що ти одужав від того, що батько відслужив молебня, а не від того, що твоя мати з'їла за обідом дві котлети замість одної.'
(*Tvory*, 119–20 / *Misto*, 244–45 / BUL, 28–29)

Xobrovs'kyj's faith was blind and tough.
   'To whom are you bowing?' asked Jurko, laughing, when Viktor would take off his cap while walking past a church.
   That's Jurko again! What a crazy guy! But he's full of laughs. Completely Godless, though. He used to say:
   'Viktor, you're stupid! I can understand such faith among the dark masses, but in you I cannot forgive it. The main thing is that you haven't read anything on the subject. Do some reading. Then you will see and hear that Christ is as much a God as you or I and that there is as much of the divine in him as in some cow. Let me lend you some books …'
   'You won't convince me, I'm convinced already,' Viktor would say. 'As a

child I was sick, very seriously sick. Even the doctors said there was no hope for recovery. But my father had a prayer service served and I got better just at the moment that the service was being served. And that convinced me about God. And I don't want to hear any sniggering remarks. Besides, what do you care whether I believe or not?'

'It's remarkable that you got better because your father had a prayer service served rather than because your mother ate two meat patties for dinner instead of one.'

Jurko's sharp remarks about Viktor's beliefs are used to highlight the complete irrationality of religious faith. The melodramatic account of a 'miraculous' recovery from an unnamed childhood disease also underscores the superstitious, medieval character of Viktor's religious feelings. Throughout the story, Pidmohyl'nyj is at pains to point out the inconsistency of Viktor's behaviour relative to his faith. When Kusja tells him she is pregnant he weighs only two options, abortion or mutual suicide, both of which he understands as sins. He even imagines a cartoon hell of boiling tar in cauldrons and red-hot skillets, with ugly devils wielding pitchforks. (The same image is repeated later in 'Vanja.') Eventually he settles on mutual suicide as the better choice. The possibility of accepting reality, even though it is unpleasant, does not occur to him. Nor does the possibility that Kusja might not want to die. Eventually, he is willing to accept as God's providence the fact that Kusja took care of everything herself and had an abortion.

Viktor's blind faith is only one aspect of the irrational in this story. Indeed, the central event in 'Dobryj boh' is the confrontation between religious faith and instinct. Throughout the story, sexual desire is depicted as a force beyond human control. Viktor characteristically blames everyone but himself for the consequences of his own actions:

'Ну, що ж! Бог простить. А як же я після того молився! Та й вийшло все проти моєї волі. Хіба в той вечір я йшов до Кусі з яким-небудь наміром? Ні, я йшов до неї посидіти, як сидів раніш.'...

'Я йшов без наміру. Це вона, вона всьому винна. Та й не вона, а просто жіноче бажання показатись напівубраною.' (*Tvory*, 120 / *Misto*, 245 / BUL, 29)

'Well, what can I say? God will forgive. And how I prayed afterwards! And everything came out against my will. On that evening did I go to her place with any intentions? No, I went to sit for a while, as I had sat on previous occasions.' ...

'I went without intentions. It was she, she who was to blame for everything. Not even she, but simply women's desire to show themselves half-dressed.'

The 'unconscious' aspect of sexual desire is also evident in Jurko, who claims that science itself says man is a polygamous creature (*Tvory*, 127 / *Misto*, 249 / BUL, 33). Even after local boys shoot him in a confrontation over a village girl, Jurko is still eager to return to the village to enjoy its happy, free, and natural atmosphere. In his role as a rationalizing hedonist, Jurko is a precursor of the poet Vyhors'kyj in *Misto*. Both characters serve to underscore the protagonist's response to natural instinctive stimuli. In 'Dobryj boh' Jurko's unfettered vitality, embodied in his licentiousness, convinces Viktor to spare his own life.

Such vitality, however, is not peculiar to Jurko. Three scenes of violence occur in the story. The first two are outside the immediate story line and are described indirectly. While chasing girls in the village Jurko is confronted by a mob of disgruntled village boys. He tries to protect himself with a pistol but is shot in the hand with his own gun. Later, he goes drinking with the village boys and is accepted into their company. After their relations have begun to sour Viktor and Kusja go to the movies to see a film that ends with five policemen finally subduing a criminal after a violent struggle. The criminal, apparently the protagonist, is handsome and appeals to Kusja, who expresses her sympathy for him. In both these incidents, violent instinctive behaviour is seen in a positive light. Not so in the third episode:

Почуття чогось гидкого й образливого заворушилось у йому. Насувалось чорне, волохате й холодне. Розпечений мозок відрікався розуміти, що тут коїться, чого не пускають. З напруженими м'язами, блискучими від обурення очима Віктор зробив крок уперед. (*Tvory*, 133 / *Misto*, 252 / BUL, 36)

A repugnant and insulting feeling stirred within him. Something black, hairy, and cold crept up on him. His fiery brain refused to understand what was going on here, why he was being refused entry. Muscles tensed, eyes shining with indignation, Viktor took a step forward.

The images suggest a wild animal. The cold, black, hairy, repugnant beast with flexed muscles and wild eyes is merely the natural Viktor emerging above the surface of his religious consciousness. He forces his way past Kusja and sees the officer hiding in her bedroom. In a flood of anger and desperation he draws his pistol and raises it to his head with a prayer for God's forgiveness and assistance. Kusja's maid screams, the officer lunges at Viktor's hand, and the bullet buries itself in the wall. This third scene of violence in the story is meant to be compared with the earlier two. Viktor's recourse to natural, instinctive violence differs from Jurko's and the criminal's in the movie in that he cannot accept, overcome, or forget his instinctive behaviour. His naïve emotional response is to consider the vow to commit suicide a binding obligation. He will not allow his sexual desires or his violent outburst to have an independent influence on his behaviour. Everything must be rationalized into his religious universe.

Pidmohyl'nyj associates the irrational with the forces of nature in many of his early stories. 'Vanja' shows the influence of nature on a young boy. 'Na seli' (In the Village) is built around the contrast between a 'natural' and an 'artificial' setting. 'Prorok' focuses on a similar contrast. Even in 'Važke pytannja' Pidmohyl'nyj is careful not to reduce the scope of the irrational merely to sexual instinct:

> Весняна ніч уже обхопила й заповнила місто. Всі будинки зробились сіроватими й здавались нижчими, ніж вдень, немов хотіли вони нахилитись до землі, з котрої підіймались свіжі пахощі маленької зеленої трави. Із відчиненого вікна линули на волю згуки роялю, – часом сумні, як журба, часом веселі, як сміх; на волі вони жваво розбігались геть навкруги, мов юрба рухливих діток, і помирали з тихим зітханням понад далекою рікою. Сновигали люди,—одні заклопотано-швидко, інші поважно-тихо, але всі вони здавались одноманітними й бездушними, бо легка темрява ночі згладила на обличчях їх носи, очі й губи й злила все в одну сірувато-синю пляму. (*Tvory*, 57–58)

The spring night had already encircled and filled the city. All the buildings had become grey and seemed lower than in the day, as if they wanted to bend over towards the earth, from which rose the fresh scent of short green grass. The sounds of a piano – sometimes sad, like worry, sometimes happy, like laughter – flowed to freedom from an open window; once free, they scattered briskly all around, like a crowd of active children, and died with a quiet sigh over the distant river. People were scurrying, some in preoccupied haste, others with quiet resolution, but they all seemed monotonous and soulless, because the soft darkness of the night smoothed the noses, eyes, and lips on their faces and blended everything into a single grey-blue spot.

The Early Stories

Clearly many of the features characteristic of the irrational in Pidmohyl'nyj's stories from the early 1920s are already evident here. The focus on the smell of the earth and the darkness of the night anticipate similar images in 'Povstanci,' 'V epidemičnomu baraci,' 'Syn,' 'Ivan Bosyj,' and other stories from the later collections. However, the image of music drifting from a window and scattering like children is a token of the young Pidmohyl'nyj's indebtedness to Vynnyčenko, who often uses music as a symbol of heightened emotion or passion,[4] and Ševčenko, to whom all the scattered children of Ukrainian literature eventually return. The image of urban scurrying echoes a similar image from the opening of 'Starec' (The Beggar), the first story in *Tvory: Tom 1*:

> Місто шуміло й хвилювалось, кипіло й реготало. Життя виштовхувало вдень на вулиці його тисячі, десятки тисяч людей, котрі заклопотано бігли, метушились, щось думали, обмірковували, сміялись, плакали, сподівались і, нарешті, помирали, – все це іноді тут же на вулиці а здебільшого під залізними дахами кам'яних мурів, що самі ж і утворили собі, аби ховатись на ніч для спочинку і кохання. Тих, що знесилені і виснажені хоробами і турботами, конали, якнайшвидше забивали в дерев'яний футляр, кидали в землю, а життя вигонило на опорожнене після них місце десятки нових людей, котрих родило кохання під залізними дахами кам'яних мурів.
>
> Ці люди, як і їх батьки, починали сновигати по вулицях міста, забували про те, що волею сліпого випадка родились, не думали про те, що так само помруть, і в шаленій метушні їли, пили, творили культуру, поглиблювали науку, будували собі нові мури, кували нові кайдани; жилава ж і костиста рука буття без жалю й радощів шпурляла їх на їхніми ж руками зроблене каміння, проти їх повертала їхню ж науку, здобутками їхньої ж культури виснажувала їх, а вони все так само заклопотано бігали по вулицях міста, сміялись, плакали, сподівались і покірно врешті йшли на страту. (*Tvory*, 3–4 / *Misto*, 286 / BUL, 70–71)

The city buzzed and worried, boiled and guffawed. During the day life pushed onto its streets thousands, tens of thousands of people, who ran around frantically, bustled, thought about something, deliberated, laughed, cried, anticipated, and, finally, died – all this sometimes right here on the street but more often under the metal roofs atop the stone walls that they themselves had erected in order to hide at night for rest and love. Those who died, weakened and exhausted by diseases and troubles, were wrapped in a wooden sleeve as quickly as possible and thrown into the earth, while into the places they had vacated life herded scores of new people, born from the love beneath the metal roofs atop the stone walls.

    These people, like their parents, began to scurry through the streets of the city, forgetting that they were born by will of a blind accident, did not think about the fact that they would die the same way, and, in a wild frenzy ate, drank, created culture, expanded science, built themselves new walls, forged new chains; without sorrow or joy the veined and bony hand of being cast them against the stones of their own making, turned their science against them, wore them out with the accomplishments of their own culture, and still they scurried as anxiously as ever about the streets of the city, laughed, cried, anticipated and, finally, meekly went to their end.

These two paragraphs are a clear statement of Pidmohyl'nyj's basic theme. Surely it is no accident that they occur on the first page of his first book. As Petro Jefremov points out in his review of that volume, for Pidmohyl'nyj people are slaves: 'The forces of nature, the demands of blind instincts, laws and customs developed by the citizenry – each of these things individually and all of them collectively demand their authority. And people have meekly bowed their heads before these authorities that exist within them and outside of them.'[5] Indeed, the human condition can be described as futile servitude. Its key ingredients are human instincts, especially sexuality; the human desire to accomplish, to create something, whether stone walls with metal roofs or knowledge and beauty; and the mercilessness of fate, the meaninglessness of individual existence. For Pidmohyl'nyj, the city is a particularly apt metaphor and emblem for this condition.

    The thematic motif of the city, particularly as contrasted with the village, is very important in Pidmohyl'nyj's works. Although much of the critical attention Pidmohyl'nyj received in the past was devoted to that motif, its role in his works has usually been misunderstood. As the two paragraphs from the first page of *Tvory: Tom 1* indicate, Pidmohyl'nyj sees the city as an emblem of the human condition. Yet the characteristic features of that condition, which I have called 'futile servitude,' are not an exclusively urban phenomenon. Significantly, there is no mention of the village and no suggestion of an urban–rural contrast in the passage quoted above. The juxtaposition of the city and the village, which occurs often in Pidmohyl'nyj's other works, most notably in the novel *Misto*, must be understood in both a philosophical and a sociological context. The manner in which the motif is developed in his earliest stories leaves no doubt as to which of the two contexts is primary.

    Among the stories in *Tvory: Tom 1*, city and village are juxtaposed in

'Prorok' and 'Na seli.' There are a few minor examples of the device in other stories, such as Jurko's and Viktor's girl-chasing trip in 'Dobryj boh,' but these occurrences are insignificant. In 'Prorok' the protagonist, Jevhenij Pereponenko, or Ženja, is caught in an internal struggle between reason and mysticism, between rationality and religious fanaticism. In his own mind the spirituality he senses is associated with the village, specifically with the sensuality of nature. After a particularly difficult evening in the country he decides to leave the village:

Яка ж важка боротьба! А все природа ця вродлива. Треба їхати в місто. Там життя шумить і кипить, своїх думок не так чути.
(*Tvory*, 67)

What a difficult struggle! And it's all on account of this beautiful nature. I've got to go to the city. Life rumbles and boils there, one's own thoughts aren't as audible.

In the city Ženja indeed finds life teeming, but with as many or more problems than he encountered in the village. Moreover, the essential nature of those problems has not changed. In order to avoid admitting his own defeat and disillusionment, Ženja turns into a Nietzschean prophet of his own superiority.

The situation in 'Na seli' offers a different perspective. Petro leaves town to find a peaceful place where he can study up on socialism without the distraction of his roommate. Pidmohyl'nyj is setting an ironic trap for Petro. The village is not an appropriate place to read up on socialism. Petro's decision to study in the village is based equally on his expressed reservations about the possibility of doing any serious work in the same apartment with his singing roommate and on the unexpressed notion that the village is a clean, healthy environment, uncontaminated by the evils of urban man, and, therefore, a suitable place to make an unprejudiced evaluation of socialism. People with so low an opinion of urban man should stay away from socialism; people with so exalted a notion of natural man should stay away from the village.

In the village Petro is sidetracked from his intellectual goal by the presence of a young woman, whom he meets at the home of his friend Olel'ko. Later he discovers that she is Olel'ko's fiancée. Once again, a Pidmohyl'nyj hero is checkmated by his own sexuality. And in Petro's final soliloquy Pidmohyl'nyj delineates some of the associations he draws between instinct and the village, on the one hand, and between reason and the city, on the other:

'Я ненавиджу тебе, пекуче сонце! Ти теплом своїм маниш до себе людей, вони виходять із самотних захистів до купи і, мов зачаровані, гублаться в юрбі, юрбою живуть, навіть сили свої віддають їй. Гарячими промінням та блиском яскравим ти, сонце, єднаєш тисячі людей, і вони, безглузді, забувши про волю давню, роблять однакові рухи, співають разом пісні своїй безсилості та приниженню.... День панує над людьми-рабами! Чого не збунтуються раби? Вони здолали б зірвати свого пана з неба, жорстоко пошматувать, відкинути геть та прикликати до себе запашну ніч із вільних степів, ніч теплу, ласкаву й таємничу. Ту ніч, коли видно, коли співає земля, коли прокидаються зорі...'

'О, як я сумую за тобою, ноче, що родиш казки дивовижні, коли все тихо навкруги, коли всі сплять!'

Потім добув іспід лави лантуха і почав з презирством шпурляти туди зі столу соціалізм – породження сонця. (*Tvory*, 162–3 / *Misto*, 308 / BUL, 93)

'Burning sun, I hate you. You lure people to you with your warmth. They leave their solitary shelters and come together, and as if enchanted, lose themselves in the crowd, live through the crowd, even give their strength to it. With your hot rays and bright reflection, sun, you unite thousands of people, and they, mindless fools, having forgotten their old freedom, perform identical actions and sing songs together in honour of their helplessness and debasement ... The day rules over people-slaves! Why don't the slaves rebel? They could tear down their lord from the sky, cruelly tear it to shreds, throw it away and summon to themselves the fragrant night from the free steppes, the warm, tender, and mysterious night. The night when one can see, when the earth sings, when the stars awaken ...'

'O, how I miss you, night, that gives birth to strange tales, when all is quiet, when everyone is asleep!'

Then he pulled his sack out from under the bench and began with disdain to throw into it all that socialism – offspring of the sun.

In this passage Pidmohyl'nyj clarifies the role of the motif of city and village by establishing a range of associations for each element of the pair. The polarity within this pairing is simply another instance of the general polarity between reason and irrationality. Petro's soliloquy adds the opposition of sunlight and the darkness of night. The night represents freedom, sexuality, sensuality, rebellion, individuality, and the natural forces of the steppe and the

The Early Stories

village. Daylight is associated with servitude, social and psychological restraints, materialism, utilitarianism, social values, and urban life.

Socialism, a system of social organization designed to optimize the common good, is, of course, a part of the daylight world of reason. Petro's rejection of it has nothing to do with the politics of the day. Pidmohyl'nyj sets all his works in contemporary time, and contemporary issues and problems are generally reflected in them. (Petro's desire to become better acquainted with socialism is a good example of this.) But Pidmohyl'nyj is also very skilful at manipulating those topical references into a larger philosophical argument. Any attempt to interpret his works must therefore take into account both the contemporary and the philosophical level. This is as true of his early works as it is of his later novels, which provoked a storm of criticism precisely because critics refused to acknowledge that the works operated on two separate levels. The sociological issues inherent in the relationship between rural and urban culture in Ukraine during the first three decades of the twentieth century are often reflected in Pidmohyl'nyj's works, but they are never the chief focus of his attention. The function of sexuality, religion, and rural sociology in the early stories is similar to that of science, literature, and urban sociology in the later works. One of the corollaries of the general thematic unity of Pidmohyl'nyj's works is the remarkable consistency with which he constructs philosophical arguments from topical elements in the plot.

The construction of plots in the stories in *Tvory: Tom 1* anticipates the techniques that appear in the later works. Pidmohyl'nyj's attention to structure is evident in the parallels he establishes on various levels within his stories. A simple example is the contrasting character that so often accompanies the young male protagonist. In 'Dobryj boh' Jurko acts as a foil to the confused Viktor. Vasyl' plays a similar role in relation to Oles' in 'Hajdamaka' as does Mykola in relation to Andrij in 'Važke pytannja.' In later works there will be Levko Verbun and Ostap Šaptala, Vasyl' and Serhij in 'Vijs'kovyj litun,' Ivan Danylovyč and Volodymyr Petrovyč in 'Sonce sxodyt',' Vyhors'kyj and Radčenko in *Misto*, and L'ova Rotter and Jurij Slavenko in *Nevelyčka drama*. Occasionally Pidmohyl'nyj expands the contrast to two characters, as in *Povist' bez nazvy*, or to a variety of contrasting pairs, as in *Nevelyčka drama*. Characters very often undergo a series of parallel incidents. In 'Starec',' for example, Tymiš experiences three violent rejections: when he first starts to beg and is refused, and beaten by two men; when his landlady takes away his food after counting his meagre earnings; and when Hal'ka refuses his sexual advances. A similar series occurs in 'Dobryj boh,' as we have seen, and in 'Hajdamaka' where Oles' is disillusioned first by the prostitute, then by the surrender of his fellow partisans, and finally by his mock execution and release by the Bolsheviks. The device of a series of similar incidents that are meant to be juxtaposed is, in fact, a cornerstone of Pidmohyl'nyj's technique in plot construction.

Despite these and many other examples of skilful construction, the stories in *Tvory: Tom 1* are clearly the work of a very young writer: they show a personal and literary immaturity in several respects. The earliest story in the collection was written in March 1917 in Katerynoslav, shortly after Pidmohyl'nyj's sixteenth birthday. The last three stories – two of which are merely two-page sketches – were written in September 1919, no doubt in a rush to provide the printer with enough material for a slim volume. Although some of the stories from 1919, particularly 'Vanja' and 'Na seli,' show a growing sophistication, the collection as a whole suffers from some of the sins typical of young writers, namely, overwriting, tendentiousness, and naïve psychology.

The depicted motivation of some of the characters in *Tvory: Tom 1* is characteristically immature, particularly as it relates to the conflict between sexuality and religious values that so many of the young men in these stories experience. Although the psychological conflicts Pidmohyl'nyj describes are not atypical for young men, his portraits lack the subtlety and flexibility that identify real people. Much of the psychology that defines Pidmohyl'nyj's early characters derives in some measure from contemporary psychological theory, but the author applies that theory with a heavy brush. The psychology of the characters in this collection is designed to illustrate particular philosophical problems. Ženja's internal debate, in 'Prorok,' about the existence of God is a case in point. The boy's ability to analyse his own thoughts and feelings is somewhat unusual. His overwhelming emotional response to an intellectual dilemma that he has fully verbalized puts him outside the realm of real nineteen-year-olds (and of many adults, for that matter). The difficulty here, and in many of the other stories in the collection, is that the young author does not distance himself sufficiently from his characters. One story in the collection, however, represents an outstanding exception to that rule.

'Vanja' stands out from among the stories in *Tvory: Tom 1*, and, indeed, from among all of Pidmohyl'nyj's stories, for a number of reasons. It is a story about a child, set in a peaceful rural environment, with no hint of the social or intellectual turmoil that so often forms the background for Pidmohyl'nyj's stories. Furthermore, it is, arguably, a fantastic tale, an uncommon genre for both Pidmohyl'nyj and Ukrainian literature as a whole. But what is most compelling about the story is its highly polished veneer of simplicity – it reads almost like a children's story – beneath which lies a rich and fascinating world of psychological complexity.

The Early Stories

Vanja, a seven-year-old boy, has started a garden in the steppe, in which he grows eggplant and melon. The boy's dog recently became rabid and had to be destroyed. To spare his feelings, Vanja's parents told him the dog had run away. When a friend finds the dog's corpse in the forest he tells Vanja, and the boys go into the forest to look at it. Thinking the dog is still breathing, they attack the corpse with rocks and sticks until their hands are limp with exhaustion. From that day forward, Vanja is haunted by the thought that the dog is hiding under his bed, waiting to attack and eat him. He is greatly disturbed by this fear until he finally musters up the courage to return to the place where the dog's corpse lies rotting. There, in an exertion of rational willpower, he overcomes his fear. That evening Vanja finally goes to bed without fear, and he is attacked by the dog.

Among the stories in *Tvory: Tom 1* 'Vanja' immediately stands out because it is not about sex. Only one other story in the collection does not involve sexuality, but it is not at all like 'Vanja.' 'Did Jakym' is a bitterly ironic anecdote about an illiterate peasant who mistakes a copy of Marx's *Das Kapital* for the Bible. The differences in subject and tone between 'Vanja' and the other stories in Pidmohyl'nyj's first collection are reflective of the story's uniqueness within the entire corpus of his works. But for all its singularity, there are important links tying the story to those among which it appeared. Moreover, these links, as we shall discover shortly, lead to further connections, which reveal an underlying structure that will allow us to re-evaluate our reading of the story.

With the exception of 'Starec'' and 'Did Jakym,' all the stories in *Tvory: Tom 1* are about young men or boys. Specifically, we know that Vanja is seven; Andrij, in 'Važke pytannja,' is seventeen; Ženja, in 'Prorok,' is nineteen; and Viktor, in 'Dobryj boh,' is also nineteen and attends the seventh grade of his gymnasium. Oles', the hero of 'Hajdamaka,' is a seventh-grader as well, although his behaviour suggests he is younger than nineteen. Petro, in 'Na seli,' is a little older: The fact that his friend is now an unmarried schoolteacher in the village, together with the way the two behave, suggests they are somewhere in their twenties. The age of the boy in 'Na imenynax' is also not specified, but he is young enough for the women in the story to discuss their little amours in front of him without blushing.

The majority of the stories in this collection are about young men. In 1920, when the volume was published, Pidmohyl'nyj was nineteen, so in writing about young men he was merely writing about that which was most familiar to him. Writers generally write about things with which they are familiar, but it is important to distinguish between general inclinations and meaningful preoccupations. Pidmohyl'nyj's is a case of the latter.

Between Reason and Irrationality

Pidmohyl'nyj's two focuses, on young men or boys and on sexual insecurity, are not unrelated. But even in the stories in which the focus is not on a young man, the central issues are problems typically experienced by young men. For example, the situation in 'Did Jakym' resembles that of a child with an adult. The old man does not hear the deliberate irony in Andrij's reference to Marx's *Das Kapital* as the new Bible but takes the comment literally, with childlike trust and naïvety. Similar trust is invoked in 'Vanja,' when the parents tell the child the dog has run away rather than admit that they had to kill it. In both stories it is qualities characteristic of children – ignorance, trust, and imagination – that motivate the actions of the protagonists.

The situation in 'Starec" is not quite that simple, but it too involves qualities generally associated with young men. Tymiš is thirty-four. He became a beggar three years earlier, when his leg was severed by a train. His disability puts him in a position of physical dependence not unlike that of a child, and this aspect of his situation is underscored throughout the story. The first episode in the story involves a learning experience for Tymiš. Having just been released from the hospital, he must learn that not all people are sympathetic to his plight. Significantly, the description of the scene puts an emphasis on the size of the two men whom he encounters. The bigger man, like a stern father, not only refuses to take pity on Tymiš, but even strikes the beggar, who has hurled an insult at the two passers-by. Another parent-surrogate is found in the character of the old woman who gave Tymiš alms on her way to church every day and on whose generosity he had come to depend. Her sudden death, which precipitates the tensions in the story, orphans Tymiš in the sense that he will now be expected to do more for himself. The situation in the house where he and a young woman live with the elderly landlady is also suggestive of a parent-child relation – that is, of a mother with two children – which would make Tymiš's passion for Hal'ka incestuous.

In 'Hajdamaka,' the character of Oles' is very deliberately juxtaposed with that of the partisan commander, Dudnyk. The commander is a confirmed Ukrainian patriot. In a skirmish with the Bolsheviks, he continues to fight even after his men have surrendered. For this, and because he is the commander, the Bolsheviks decide to execute him. He faces his executioners with quiet courage and, just before he is shot, asks his partisan followers not to forget him or their common cause, Ukraine. In contrast, Oles' is a very confused boy:

Другий учень був невисокий, худий і слабосилий. Він прийшов до гайдамаків того, що був зовсім розчарований у житті й навіть серйо-зно думав про самовбивство.... Коли він думав про своє життя й

The Early Stories

життя взагалі, то воно здавалось йому маленьким, нікчемним і тонким, як він сам. (*Tvory*, 92 / *Misto*, 259 / BUL, 43)

> The other student was short, thin, and weak. He had joined the partisans because he was completely disenchanted with life and had even seriously considered suicide ... When he thought about his life and about life in general, it seemed to him small, worthless, and thin, just like he was.

By his own admission, he does not know why he chose to join the partisans rather than the Bolsheviks. Yet, when the partisans surrender he is disgusted by their lack of heroics. When the Bolsheviks shoot the rebel commander, Oles' turns sentimental: he wants to go home and dreams about his favourite teacher in school. When he is taken prisoner to stand trial for treason, he collapses and, unable to walk any further, has to be carried by the Bolshevik soldiers. But during the interrogation, he is testy and impertinent. Even a mock execution fails to shake his resolute defiance. When, at last, the Bolshevik commander stops trying to teach the boy and orders him whipped and sent home, Oles' breaks down and cries.

The partisans in the story are not named, but it is likely that they are supporters of Petljura. They are fighting against the Bolsheviks for Ukraine. The partisans Pidmohyl'nyj will write about in his later stories are followers of Maxno; those in 'Hajdamaka' are not. Symbolically, Pidmohyl'nyj associates the Ukrainian cause with a confused and naïve boy, who very obviously does not understand what he is doing. There is, of course, the contrasting association with Dudnyk, but this is presented as something truly exceptional and hopeless. In effect, Pidmohyl'nyj describes a world in which ideals, whether heroic or puerile, turn out to be equally ill suited to reality.

This interpretation of 'Hajdamaka' helps to illuminate the role of youth in *Tvory: Tom 1* and, indeed, in Pidmohyl'nyj's works as a whole. The protagonists of these stories are typically people who must learn to accept reality. Whether it be the beggar Tymiš, who, like the characters in Samuel Beckett's world, struggles with the incompatibility of his desires and his body, or Petro in 'Na seli,' who discovers, as Hemingway's and Fitzgerald's heroes do, that guilt and innocence are the same thing, Pidmohyl'nyj's characters are invariably students in the classroom of reality, and the lesson is alienation. They are, for the most part, young, because this lesson is poorly suited to the old, who have either learned it already or, like Grandfather Jakym, are unlikely ever to learn it. And the lesson often focuses on sexual drives because they constitute a strong, natural human instinct that involves powerful psychological, ethical, and social reactions.

Moreover, it is important to note that the sexual problems depicted in this collection are all of a particular nature. To begin with, the situation is always seen from the male point of view. Of course, the author is a man, so this seems natural. In Pidmohyl'nyj's case, however, it is clear that the determining factor is not his sex, but his specific thematic interest. Pidmohyl'nyj is not interested in sexuality *per se*, or in its social consequences. He is not interested in its effects on women or on families. He is not even interested in the relationships between men and women. His interest is focused exclusively on male drives and male guilt.

In 'Starec',' for example, the narrator focuses almost exclusively on Tymiš, even after his attempted rape of Hal'ka. Her reaction, although clearly presented, is very narrowly defined, as rage. The story ends with the image of Tymiš lying prone on a bench, covering his head with his hands, while Hal'ka beats him with his crutch. It is his humiliation and guilt, and not the feelings of the woman that the narrator places at the centre of the reader's attention. Had Pidmohyl'nyj been interested in Hal'ka's feelings, the story could not possibly have ended here. As it stands, however, the thematic structure of the story is complete. Tymiš's view of the world has once again conflicted with reality. And once again, accommodating reality has involved a loss of self-esteem. The focus in 'Dobryj boh' is even more revealing. For a man whose self-respect is bound up so intimately with his sexual activity, Viktor is lucky to have such a malleable a conscience. Otherwise he might end up, like the student who declares his affections to the wife of his high school principal in 'Na imenynax,' facing consequences disproportionate to the perceived seriousness of his actions.

This last formulation leads us back to Vanja. If any character in Pidmohyl'nyj's first collection experiences consequences disproportionate to his actions, that character is surely Vanja. The guilt he feels after the first episode in the forest is entirely out of step with what actually happened. Vanja and his friend Myt'ka did not kill Žučok: The dog was dead when they found him. Although beating the corpse with sticks and stones may have been a shameful act, it could hardly provoke intense guilt. It is true, of course, that children should not be judged by the same standards as adults in such matters: A seven-year-old is likely to suffer guilt over actions that an adult would ignore. In fact, as we have seen in 'Dobryj boh' and 'Prorok,' Pidmohyl'nyj often depicts characters whose guilt is attributable in large measure to inexperience. But in both those stories the guilt is a reaction to a sexual encounter. In other words, although the guilt experienced by those young men may be irrational, it is psychologically comprehensible. Can the same be said of Vanja? What, then, is the actual cause of Vanja's fear and guilt?

The Early Stories

In the story, Vanja and Myt'ka are frightened from the moment they stop beating the corpse. Vanja thought he saw Žučok breathing, so Myt'ka suggested they stop his suffering and kill him off. The boys gather sticks and stones and start beating the corpse in a mounting frenzy:

Били доти, поки із тремтячих рук не повипадали киї. Гостре незадоволення від того, що ще хотілось бити, а сили вже не було, й невідоме їм доти захоплююче обурення опанувало їми. Ваня вже харчав від притоми, задихувався й ледве стояв на ногах; Митька тільки одсапував і раз-по-раз ковтав слину. Вони подивились один на одного й по невисловленій згоді зробили рух до Жучка, щоб схопити його, рвати на шматки, видерти очі і язика, кусати його тіло зубами, – але, глянувши на Жучка, спинились. Жучка не було: замість його лежав безформений рудо-сірий шматок м'яса.

'А-а-а-а ...' несамовито заверещав Ваня й подався навтьоки.

Слідом за ним побіг і Митька. Чипляючись за гілля, спотикаючись й знову підводючись, бігли вони, простягнувши вперед руки, щоб не вдаритись об стовбур якогось дерева, того що перед очима їх маячили чорнуваті плями і крапки. (*Tvory*, 36 / *Misto*, 279 / BUL, 63)

The beating continued until the sticks fell out of their trembling hands. Now, a sharp dissatisfaction – because they wanted to continue the beating but had no strength left – and a thrilling sense of disgust, which they hadn't felt before, overcame them. Vanja was gasping from exhaustion, gulping air and barely keeping himself on his feet. Myt'ka was only out of breath, swallowing hard from time to time. They glanced at each other and with unspoken consent started for Žučok, to tear him to pieces, pull out his eyes and tongue, grind up his flesh with their teeth – but catching sight of Žučok, they stopped. Žučok was no more. In his place there was only a formless, reddish-grey piece of meat.

'A-a-a-a!' yelled Vanja uncontrollably, and took to his heels.

Myt'ka ran off behind him. Tearing themselves from the clinging branches, tripping and scrambling up again, they ran with arms outstretched to avoid running into tree trunks. All they saw were blackish dots and splotches.

This passage contains a number of key elements. First, it does not offer a clear and direct answer to the question of the cause of Vanja's guilt. Pidmohyl'nyj has masterfully captured the indistinctness and ambiguity of a child's anxiety. From the aesthetic perspective, his treatment is realistic and skilful psychological portraiture. But from the perspective of clinical psychology, something seems to be missing. Why are the children so frightened by what they did? *Why* did they do what they did? To these and similar questions, the story offers no direct answers. All we know is that the children are frightened and ashamed as soon as they stop beating the corpse. Furthermore, it is important to note that both children experience these feelings. In the paragraph that follows the above-quoted passage, Myt'ka returns to Vanja the toy pistol he had named as the price of leading Vanja to Žučok. Although the remainder of the story focuses exclusively on Vanja, he is not alone in his guilt. Finally, we should observe that Pidmohyl'nyj has deliberately left the cause of Vanja's guilt uncertain. There are a number of opportunities in the story for the narrator or Vanja himself to explain the situation. In each case Pidmohyl'nyj offers only vagueness and confusion. In some of the nightmares in which Vanja imagines his punishment, his crime is killing Žučok; in others it is beating him. The narrator's description of Vanja's feelings offers no clarification:

Він почував, що було зроблено щось негарне. Це мучило його, тягуче смоктало, й він не втримався і заплакав. Заплакав і злякався, що хтось прийде сюди й побаче його сльози та й неодмінно вгадає, що робив він за півгодини перед цим. Ваня перестав плакати і, схопивши подушку обома руками, лежав тихенько притулившись до стінки, щоб його ніхто не помітив. Але в середині в його перерталась важкими клубками чорна туга й надушувала на тендітні груди маленької людини. Вані захотілось кудись серед чужі люди, щоб ці люди думали, що він гарний, добрий хлопчик. Потім стало жалко чогось такого, що немов би уже розбите було, ростоптане й чого ніяк не можна вернути. Ця жалість, переплітаючись і змішуючись з невиявленим жахом перед заслуженою карою, стиснула до болю груди, й Ваня заридав голосно, з великими перервами між хлипанням. (*Tvory*, 37 / *Misto*, 279–80 / BUL, 64)

He felt that something bad had been done. It tortured him, weighed on him. Finally, he could bear it no longer and began to cry. But the crying made him fear that someone would walk in and see his tears and then surely guess what he'd been doing a half-hour earlier. Vanja stopped crying, grabbed the pillow with both hands, and rolled over against the wall where no one could see him. But inside, dark boulders of grief were rolling onto the tender breast of this small person. Vanja wanted to go somewhere among strangers, where people would think he was a nice, good little boy. Then he felt a sorrow for something that seemed already to be shattered, trampled, never to be brought back again. This sorrow, mixing and blending with the suppressed terror of the punishment he deserved, clamped Vanja's chest in a painful grip and the boy burst into loud sobs punctuated by long pauses.

As readers, we accept this description as a reasonably appropriate and satisfying account of the events. There is a respected narrative method at work here, and there is no reason to argue with it. But a deeper meaning may lie hidden beneath the polished surface of the text. 'Vanja' is a well-constructed story. At first glance the events of the first half of the story, before the boys visit the site of Žučok's corpse, seem to have little to do with the events of the second half, yet a number of important parallels are developed between the two sections. The first half of the story consists of two episodes. One involves the story of Vanja's garden in the steppe. The other, which is much shorter, recounts the two days during which Žučok was tied to a stake on the front lawn in order to confirm his infection. Both episodes reveal important information about Vanja that can help us interpret his actions.

Vanja's first visit to the gully where he will plant his garden suggests a clear parallel to his trips into the forest to Žučok's corpse. Like the forest, the gully is a frightening place. On his first descent into it, Vanja catches his shirt on the branches of a tree. For Vanja, however, this is no tree but the feared man-eater who had captured Vanja. After a brief struggle, Vanja escapes the creature only to find himself on the far side of the gully, with the man-eater blocking his route home. After considering climbing out of the gully to go around the long way, Vanja picks up a stick and returns to the place where the man-eater had caught him. How happy he was to discover that the monster had fled!

The story of Vanja's encounter with the man-eater has at least two purposes. The first is to show that Vanja is an imaginative child, readily frightened by illusory evils. The second is to show that he is also a courageous boy, who returns to face his enemy. This is exactly what Vanja does when he returns alone to face Žučok. But the outcomes of the two episodes are entirely different. After his victory over the man-eater, Vanja plants his secret garden in the gully and returns there often, without fear. But his return to the forest is less successful. Although he claims to have overcome his fear of Žučok – and, indeed, his behaviour returns to normal during the rest of that day – in the evening when he goes to bed his nightmares return. What is the difference between the episode in the gully and the one in the forest that accounts for the diametrically different outcomes?

The episode in the gully echoes motifs in some of the other stories in the collection, especially in 'Prorok,' where Ženja rests by the side of his favourite cliff and remembers his childhood fear that the cliff was the home of a storybook dragon (*Tvory*, 66). As the years went by, the dragon faded, but the cliff never lost its fearful mysteriousness. Climbing the cliff, looking down at the forest, the river, and the village at his feet, Ženja would feel like a conquering general surveying captured territory and the scene of his glory. But that was in the past; in the narrative frame of the story, he does not, in fact, climb the cliff. He is nervous. He is troubled by a vague disturbance, which, we discover in the course of the story, is related to the conflict he experiences between his sexual drives and his religious scruples. Clearly, the visit to the cliff and the recollection of its childhood significance are meant to be contrasted with Ženja's current situation. In the past Ženja managed to overcome his fears and, indeed, to grow in the process. Like Vanja, however, he has now encountered fear and guilt that he cannot conquer.

The objects of Vanja's fears are the products of a child's imagination reformulating various cultural stereotypes. Vanja's visions of hell for example, derive from his grandmother's rather lurid descriptions of it. By including the determinants of a character's perceptions, Pidmohyl'nyj achieves a fortuitous confluence of method and purpose. Realistic psychology is both a means and an end in this story.

Another example of the same process can be seen in the second episode of the first half of the story, the description of Žučok's developing madness. The passage is short, but critical to the analysis of the story. As far as plot is concerned, the passage is unnecessary: It would have been sufficient to state that the dog had gone mad and had had to be killed. Hence, the details of the dog's behaviour are clearly meant to serve a particular purpose in the story. Like the grandmother's descriptions of hell, they are presented as a factor influencing Vanja's thoughts and actions. But, also as in the case of the grandmother's sermon, the text does not assert that such influence is at work; it simply presents the source of the influence, and makes no comment regarding its connection to subsequent events. The effect of the grandmother's descriptions of hell must be deduced from Vanja's behaviour. Similarly, the impact on him of witnessing the dog's progressive mental degeneration must be distilled from the events of the story.

Žučok's behaviour during the two days when he is tied down is described from Vanja's point of view. The immediate effect produced by this episode is fear:

Жучок простяг до його голову й затуманеними очима подивився. В цім мов би невидючім погляді, в очах червоних і нетямучих, у розтуленім роті, з котрого текла слина, Ваня побачив те, що зветься скаженіною. Ваня не знав і не розумів, що то воно є, але зразу

серцем відчув, що то сила уперта й руйнуюча, і йому зробилось
боязно. (*Tvory*, 32 / *Misto*, 276–7 / BUL, 61)

Žučok stretched his head towards [the boy] and looked at him with clouded
eyes. In that blank expression, in those red and uncomprehending eyes, in the
open and frothing mouth, Vanja saw that which was called madness. Although
he didn't know or understand what it was, in his heart he sensed instantly that
it was a stubborn and ruinous force. It frightened him.

The effect of this episode on Vanja is not made explicit in the text of the
story. None the less, a parallel can be seen between the dog's behaviour and
the description of the two boys as they are stoning the corpse:

Обличчя в їх стали довгасті і поблідли; иноді на їх проблискувало
шаленство, а в широкорозплющених очах світилось щось тупе й
дике. (*Tvory*, 35 / *Misto*, 278 / BUL, 63)

Their faces grew long and pale; occasionally a flash of madness was reflected
in them,[6] and something dull and wild gleamed in their wide-open eyes.

Vanja's behaviour in the forest is irrational and incomprehensible – just as
Žučok's was while he was tied down. Its key features are wildness and
madness. Vanja has only a dim notion of what rabid madness is, and,
understandably, defines it by the symptoms he observes. This may help to
explain why Vanja stones the dog's corpse in the forest. The dog's wild
behaviour frightens the child because it disturbs his naïve view of the world's
orderliness. This evil is more pernicious than that represented by the man-
eater because it disturbs established categories. It is so frightening that even
after it has been defeated (the dog is dead) Vanja attacks it in anger. But
what, then, of Vanja's own behaviour in the forest? If wildness and madness
in Žučok were so frightening, what is the significance of the experience of the
same qualities in Vanja? What happens to someone when they discover that
the evil they fear is inside them?

This question appears in various forms throughout Pidmohyl'nyj's first
collection of stories. In most of them, the evil force is sexual instinct, and it
provokes guilt. In a typically Nietzschean framework, Pidmohyl'nyj's stories
generally focus on the gradual adjustment of an individual psyche to the
discovery of its own guilt. Thus, in 'Vanja' the major focus is on the boy's
reaction to his experiences in the forest.

This is quite a different story from the one with which this presentation began. What has emerged is not a simple children's fantasy about a boy and his dog, but a serious allegory of alienation. Instead of a tale about unwarranted fears and the destructive power of imaginary guilt, we have a truly frightening account of the divergence between the individual and the environment in which he lives. That much is clear even before we attempt to determine what Vanja really encounters in the forest. There is good reason to pursue that question. A wealth of evidence, both from within the story and from other stories in the collection, suggests that the boys' visit to Žučok's corpse is a symbolic representation of the discovery of sexuality. But whether it is or not, the significance of what happens in the forest is clearly definable on the basis of the evidence from other stories that can be applied to it. What Vanja discovers in the forest is that there is something inside him that frightens him and that he does not understand. Whether it is sexuality or something else, it is fundamental to the human condition. In thematic terms, it is alienation reduced to a confrontation of the individual with him- or herself.

CHAPTER TWO

Ostap Šaptala
The Structure of Prose

Ostap Šaptala is Pidmohyl'nyj's first attempt to write a long prose work. The resulting *povist'*, or novella,[1] shows the author striving to overcome the psychological and aesthetic limitations of his earlier stories, to expand the technical limits of his works, and to balance their intellectual and artistic parameters. In other words, Pidmohyl'nyj is following a path familiar to many novelists, who often learn their craft by writing short stories, and then gradually advance to the longer forms. But in *Ostap Šaptala*, Pidmohyl'nyj takes a bridge too far from the front lines. In the years following the publication of the novella, the young writer returned to the short-story genre, further developing his skills as a writer and enjoying considerable critical success before trying his hand at the longer form once again, this time with much greater success in the novel *Misto*.

The first difficulty in constructing a long prose work is organizational. Among the stories in *Tvory: Tom 1* there is substantial evidence that the author paid very careful attention to the construction of individual works, (as for example, in 'Vanja' and 'Starec"), but the collection as a whole reflects no attempt on the author's part to connect the various stories beyond their association through thematic similarity. In the years 1920–1, when, presumably, Pidmohyl'nyj was working on *Ostap Šaptala*, he also produced a number of other works, among them 'V epidemičnomu baraci' and 'Povstanci.' The author himself designated the genre of the two works as, respectively, a sketch (*narys*) and sketches (*narysy*).

'Povstanci' is an assembly of five short narrative chapters, or sketches, each with its own title. The work is held together, very effectively, by three threads. First, each of the five chapters is about a band of partisans. (It may be the same band of partisans in all the chapters, but this is not made explicit.) The boys in the first chapter are off to join '*bat'ko* Zajčenko.' The *otaman* in the fifth chapter is named Kremnjuk. The unnamed, charismatic *otaman* in the second chapter is clearly not the same person as the reflective Kremnjuk. None of these characters correspond to the city commandant or the staff commander in the fourth chapter. Indeed, there are no recurring characters from one chapter to the next.

The second connecting thread is the fact that the sequence of the five chapters reflects a logical development, a gradual discovery of the character of partisans. The first chapter shows some boys setting off to join the partisans. In the second chapter the partisan commander welcomes a new recruit. The third chapter describes the night before the partisans go into battle. In the fourth chapter the partisans' resident journalist and propagandist suffers an ideological crisis when a fire breaks out in a city under partisan control, and it turns out that no one had bothered to organize a fire brigade. The final chapter offers a character portrait of the partisan commander, as he and his ensign experience the anarchic, destructive influence of the steppe.

Third, the five chapters in 'Povstanci' share a common thematic focus. The main subject of each chapter, and of the work as a whole, is the vain and ineffective struggle of reason, order, and good sense against the powerful, emotionally alluring force of anarchy and destructiveness. Reason is presented variously in the five chapters: as a child's bond with his parents; as a man's fear of battle; as the realization that victorious partisans, even if they are anarchists, must maintain some social infrastructure – such as a fire brigade. The force of anarchy and destructiveness is depicted with a single image in each of the five chapters. It is invariably characterized as emotional extremism born of a wild human instinct that is fuelled by contact with nature, particularly with the steppe. In the first chapter one of the boys literally falls to the ground and, like a modern, young Antaeus, 'drinks the earth's strength' (*Povstanci*, 6).[2] In the fifth chapter, *Otaman* Kremnjuk and his newly assigned ensign ride out into the steppe at night to renew their wavering ideological commitment to destruction. In the fourth chapter the journalist is transfixed by the fire:

Пишне кострище, що лизало хмари своїми язиками, зачудувало його було. А тепер, коли вогонь безсило плазував по землі, редакторська душа бгалася з жалю за минулою величчю палахкотіння.
(*Povstanci*, 19)

The luscious pyre, which licked the clouds with its tongues, had enchanted him. But now that the fire was weakly crawling along the ground, his journalist's soul twisted in sorrow at the lost grandeur of the flames.

The effect of the spectacle is to undermine the journalist's faith in his own ideological pronouncements.

The third chapter presents Oleksa Stel'max on guard duty at night beside the partisan headquarters. He is torn between two ideals. First, looking at the sky, he imagines himself a bright, golden star. But he associates stars with tears and sorrow and decides to maintain his link to the earth:

Вартовий водив очима по деревах, землі й вагонах.... Він не знав, чим саме хотів би бути.

Тоді він пустив ніч собі в серце, й воно защеміло від її тихого дотику. Воно стало велике, й тяжко було терпіти його великий бій.

'Ні, я не хочу бути зіркою, я не покину тебе, земле.... Хай житиму я, закутий тугою, хай гнітить мене воля твоя – я носитиму, земле, твої пута....' (*Povstanci*, 13)

The sentry scanned the trees, the earth, and the train cars ... He did not know which he might want to be.

Then he allowed the night to enter his heart, and it felt a sharp pain from the night's quiet touch. It became large, and it was hard to endure its heavy beating.

'No, I don't want to be a star. I will not abandon you, earth. Let me live shackled by longing, let your will oppress me – earth, I will carry your chains.'

Although this passage lends itself to a number of possible interpretations,[3] the presence of similar passages in the other chapters suggests that it is another manifestation of the dark, instinctive force of anarchy and destructiveness, that constitutes, in its confrontation with reason and order, the central unifying element of the work. What binds these diverse episodes together is the reader's recognition of that thematic link.

In 'V epidemičnomu baraci,' Pidmohyl'nyj adopts a different approach to structure. This story, subtitled '*Narys*' (Sketch), consists of a large number of brief, unnumbered sections.[4] The relationship of the sections to one another changes as the story develops. The first seven sections proceed chronologically, as follows: (1) The story opens at eight o'clock in the morning, as the doctor begins his rounds; (2) the orderly prepares the prescribed drugs; (3) Odarka, the nurse on duty, distributes the medications; (4) she gives an injection to the Red Army soldier; (5) everyone has lunch: (6) evening falls, the doctor returns, and Prisja and her friends take an evening boat ride on the river; (7) the following day, the Red Army soldier dies and is buried. Beginning with the eighth section, which describes Odarka's evening prayer ritual, Pidmohyl'nyj changes the organizational principle on which the story is built. The remaining sections are still sequential, in a general, chronological sense, but they are no longer linked by any specific causal connections. Odarka's prayers (sections 8, 17), Prisja's and Hanusja's singing (9) and mutual emotional support (16), the medical orderly's night fishing (10), the teacher's violin playing (15), and Prisja's affair with the stationmaster (11, 18) are presented as glimpses into the lives of particular individuals. Whereas the earlier sections had described these individuals in social interaction, the later sections show them in isolation.

Pidmohyl'nyj uses a number of techniques to minimize the disruption that this structural change entails. The entire story is narrated in the timeless context of present tense imperfective verbs. Thus, the sequential events of the first seven sections are the outline of a typical day. The story begins, 'До восьмої години ранку хворі кінчали сніданок, і починалась візитація' (By eight in the morning the patients would finish breakfast, and rounds would commence).[5] Consequently, the events of the second half of the story do not appear any less contiguous than those of the first half. Furthermore, a number of occurrences in the second part relate logically to one specific episode – Prisja's affair with the stationmaster. For example, the teacher's violin playing is an indirect result of his disenchantment with Prisja. (She has chosen the stationmaster over the teacher and all her other admirers.) The effect of Pidmohyl'nyj's choice of verbs, combined with his use of causal links, is to make the first half of the story seem less sequential, and the second half, more so. None the less, the unity of the second half of the story depends fundamentally on the thematic parallels among the various incidents depicted. The glue that binds the medical orderly's fishing, Odarka Kalynivna's praying, Josyp Martynovyč's selfless doctoring, the teacher's violin playing, and Prisja's romantic dreaming is irrational instinct. All the characters in this story seek some way to release their inner feelings, to address their desperate need for escape from a painful reality. The congruence of their needs is the structural backbone of the second half of the story.

The preceding analysis shows that Pidmohyl'nyj was consciously working out various solutions to the problem of structure in a longer prose work. In *Ostap Šaptala* he takes yet another path. The two stories just examined were constructed of essentially disjointed fragments that needed a tangible unifying element to hold them together. Even 'V epidemičnomu baraci,' which pretends to follow a causal sequence, is actually a series of character portraits, where the only material link among the characters is their shared workplace. The structure of *Ostap Šaptala* more closely resembles that of a traditional nineteenth-century realist novel, in that it follows a chronological and causal sequence of events in the life of a single character.

The novella consists of thirty very short, unnamed, and unnumbered chapters. The relationship among the chapters is sequential and causal. The first three chapters, for example, depict (1) Šaptala outside the church before the Easter service, (2) Šaptala walking home after the service, and (3) Šaptala eating Easter breakfast with his family. Occasionally a chapter breaks out of the sequence, but even in such cases, the departure is very slight. In the sixteenth chapter, for example, Pidmohyl'nyj presents Šaptala's friends Verbun and Halaj without Šaptala. But the function of the chapter in relation to the work as a whole is not as much thematic (although a thematic link does exists) as sequential. The chapter continues the story of the three-way friendship that was introduced in the fifth and sixth chapters. While Šaptala was in the village for his sister's funeral, his two friends in the city continued their friendship without him. The fifteenth chapter presents the pre-history of the friendship, describing the arrival of three boys at Mrs. Čužyns'ka's (literally, 'Mrs Foreign') boarding house. In the sixteenth chapter, this friendship grows in Šaptala's absence, a development that has consequences when he returns to the city. Similar departures from the established sequence occur in the twentieth and twenty-sixth chapters, where attention is once again focused on Verbun and Halaj in the absence of Šaptala.

The greater cohesion between chapters in *Ostap Šaptala*, relative to 'Povstanci' and 'V epidemičnomu baraci,' is matched by the greater linearity of its plot. Whereas the two stories followed events in the lives of a number of characters more or less in parallel, the novella focuses on the protagonist alone. Šaptala's relationship with Verbun and Halaj and the events in their lives (particularly Verbun's romantic relationship with Natalja) are provided as a standard against which readers can measure the protagonist. All the other characters are minor and appear only in dependent roles. Even Lasja, who is the catalyst for all the changes that Šaptala undergoes, is not developed or analysed independently. The linearity of the plot is further enhanced by its dramatic completeness. Whereas the action in 'Povstanci' and 'V epidemičnomu baraci' has no particular beginning or end, *Ostap Šaptala* follows a simple but unambiguous line of development. Ostap's sister dies, leaving him with a sense of guilt and emptiness. Rescuing Lasja and making sacrifices for her allows him to appease his own guilt and restore a purpose to his life. When she makes sexual advances towards him, Šaptala becomes confused and disgusted. Lasja leaves, and Ostap retreats back into inner solitude and monotony.

Although the general plot structure of *Ostap Šaptala* is linear and continuous, many of the individual chapters are still structured as sketches. The brevity of the chapters tends to limit them to the same narrative technique that Pidmohyl'nyj used in 'Povstanci' and 'V epidemičnomu baraci.' Rather than narrating an event, each chapter paints a portrait. A good example can be seen in the eighteenth chapter, in which Ostap rescues Lasja. In a dramatic work this chapter would likely end at a key moment, for example, when the protagonist pulls the woman onto shore or when he first sees her face, which reminds him of his sister. But Pidmohyl'nyj deliberately ends the chapter at an undramatic point:

Непритомніючи з захвату й утоми, схилив Шаптала голову на ліжко і заснув, посміхаючись.

[Chapter break]

Чепез кілька хвилин він прокинувся, обхоплений хвилюванням. Він обережно нахилився над жінкою: та ще лежала в забутті. (*Šaptala*,[6] 72 / *Nevelyčka drama*,[7] 240)

Losing consciousness from rapture and fatigue, Šaptala bowed his head onto the bed and fell asleep, smiling.

[Chapter break]

After a few minutes he awoke with a sense of apprehension. He carefully bent over the woman: she was still lying in forgetfulness.

Having the chapter break here focuses the reader's attention on the smile on Šaptala's sleeping face. It is a symbol of the inner peace that rescuing the woman has brought him. In terms of the plot, however, this chapter break impedes the dramatic flow of the action. It is an element of melodrama tied to the metaphorical narrative technique that is characteristic of Pidmohyl'nyj's early stories. Pidmohyl'nyj focuses the reader's attention on a symbolic detail that conveys the protagonist's emotional state, thereby evoking a similar emotional response in the reader. But like the melodramatic poses and closing irises of early silent movies, this emotional accenting is a device that implements structure based on the manipulation of emotions. In this story, Pidmohyl'nyj still conceives of structure largely in thematic terms.

The three works that we examined here exemplify different methods of structuring fiction. Although there are no formal criteria for analysing structure in a work of literature – at least none that are universally accepted – any theoretical model must account for the types of relations that can exist between individual constructive elements of a text. In *La Poétique de la prose* Tzvetan Todorov argues that there are three types of relations between structural elements (which he calls 'propositions'): temporal, logical, and spatial. The temporal and logical categories are self-evident and correspond to the chronological and causal sequences that we have identified in Pidmohyl'nyj's works, particularly in *Ostap Šaptala*. Todorov's spatial category, however, is ambiguous and ill conceived. Both its name and its definition clearly demonstrate the strain of Todorov's effort to force it into a harmonious model: 'A third relation is of a spatial type, insofar as the two propositions are juxtaposed because of a certain resemblance between them, thereby indicating a space proper to the text. Here we are dealing, evidently, with parallelism and its many subdivisions; this relation seems dominant in poetry.'[8] The metaphorical notion of a 'space proper to the text' belies the analytical function of Todorov's categories. The spatial category does not describe actual relations between blocks of text.[9] A theoretical model must account for many varieties of parallelism,[10] including, at a minimum, circumstantial and thematic juxtapositions.

Although literature has no rules for the structure of long prose, certain patterns and relationships can be apprehended and statistically or deductively verified. Todorov suggests as much when he asserts that relationships of parallelism are dominant in poetry. What he has in mind is something similar to Jakobson's definition of poetic function, but he expresses the idea in terms of genre. Actually, parallelism is usually considered characteristic of poetry, and when it occurs in prose, that prose is perceived to have a poetic flavour. Indeed, the disposition of structural relations in a work of prose can be seen as a discriminant of style or period. For example, the realist novel of the nineteenth century shows a strong attachment to temporal and causal relations rather than to parallelism. Balzac's *Père Goriot*, Dickens's *David Copperfield*, and Tolstoy's *Anna Karenina* rely heavily of these structural tools. The same is true of the novels of Ivan Nečuj-Levyc'kyj and Panas Myrnyj. But such works as Joyce's *Ulysses*, Virginia Woolf's *Mrs. Dalloway*, Robbe-Grillet's *Dans le labyrinthe*, Bulgakov's *Majster i Margarita*, Jurij Janovs'kyj's *Veršnyky*, and Majk Johansen's *Podorož učenoho doktora Leonarda [...]* modify the traditional balance of structural relations by injecting a strong and sometimes dominant parallelism into the structure of the text. Modernist fiction often modifies the structure of prose in a characteristically poetic manner.¹¹ Variations in the balance of structural relations can also be related to other characteristics of a novel, for example, its social and philosophical involvement. A descriptive work of social muckraking will have a different balance of relations than a contemplative intellectual study. Zola's *Germinal* is constructed differently from Proust's *Du Côté de chez Swann*. In short, structure is related to both the general literary climate and the specific intentions of an author.

The balance of structural relations in prose is linked to two other factors: length and aesthetic success. The structural needs of a short story are different from those of a novel, but the set of relations that holds short and long works together is the same. Longer works have a greater need for the various forms of parallelism to hold them together, even in the presence of a strong temporal sequence. What would remain of Dickens's *Great Expectations* if Pip learned life's lessons the first time he encountered them? How would Myrnyj span three centuries in the history of one village if he did not establish similarities as well as causal connections between the past and the present? As we saw in the analysis of 'Vanja' in the preceding chapter, plot parallels can play a very significant thematic role in a short story as well as in a longer work, but they are often fewer and less essential to the structural integrity of the work. This is one of the lessons that many authors must learn as they evolve from short-story writers into novelists. Another has to do with the relative effectiveness of the structural devices arrayed in any particular work. There is, of course, no 'correct' balance for any given work, but some works have a more effective balance than others.

Pidmohyl'nyj's longer works dating from 1920–1 represent important steps in his development from a short story writer into a novelist, but they are not entirely successful. After completing *Ostap Šaptala*, published in 1921, why did Pidmohyl'nyj not return to long prose until he wrote the novel *Misto*, published in 1928? Naturally, there could be any number of reasons why a writer would choose not to write novels while he was making a living as a teacher, bibliographer, or editor; while he was struggling with the numerous difficulties of survival in the newly conceived Soviet state; and while he was battling political hostility to his work from certain prominent literary figures and institutions. Moreover, no one else was writing novels in Ukraine during this period. Yet, the evidence contained in the works themselves indicates that there were technical, literary reasons as well.

'V epidemičnomu baraci' is the best of Pidmohyl'nyj's works from this period (an opinion held by the author himself),¹² whereas *Ostap Šaptala* is not a complete success. There are a number of reasons for the relative strengths and weaknesses of these works, the most significant of which is the problem of naïve psychology. All of Pidmohyl'nyj's early works are based on shallow, inadequate models of the functioning of the human psyche. This problem is least obtrusive in such works as 'V epidemičnomu baraci' and 'Vanja,' which do not call for profound psychological analysis, present the emotional motives of a character's behaviour extrinsically, and allow for the greatest subjective distance between the author and the characters he depicts. However, in works such as 'Važke pytannja,' 'Prorok,' or *Ostap Šaptala*, in which the psychology of the protagonist is the primary focus of the text, and the author identifies closely with the characters, the young writer's limited understanding of psychology is a major shortcoming.

Structure is another criterion on the basis of which the aesthetic success of these works can be evaluated. Even in his earliest short stories, Pidmohyl'nyj exhibited a good command of structure. But the structural balance of a long prose work is different from that of a short story. In particular, a traditional realist novel cannot be built on thematic parallels; 'objective' narration cannot be coupled with subjective structure. Where the structure of a work requires interpretive analysis, a strong temporal, causal plot sequence is potentially incompatible. Such is the case with *Ostap Šaptala* in which the linearity of the plot is at odds with the thematic and melodramatic organization of the episodes. The work is, in effect, a stretched-out short story. Before Pidmohyl'nyj sat down to write *Misto* he would need to devise a solution to this structural problem.

The progression from Pidmohyl'nyj's early stories to his later novels involved not only a bridging of the structural gulf between the short and the long genres, but also a gradual thematic evolution. Although they are thematically closer to the stories in *Tvory: Tom 1* than to *Misto*, the works from 1920–1 none the less reveal some important developments in Pidmohyl'nyj's understanding of his primary intellectual subject. The most important of these is the gradual enlargement of the role and the significance of reason.

Ostap Šaptala reflects elements of that change. In a general thematic sense, the novella continues to probe the questions that were addressed in stories such as 'Prorok,' 'Dobryj boh,' and 'Važke pytannja.' Here, as in many of the stories, a young man finds himself in the midst of a conflict between his values and his desires. In the novella, however, Pidmohyl'nyj introduces three significant innovations in the thematic structure: (1) desire is depicted as a general instinctive force, not just as the sexual awakening of an adolescent; (2) the system of values that collides with instinct is allowed to develop within the character rather than being imposed as a social constraint; and (3) an alternative, rational and pragmatic approach to the resolution of the central conflict is presented as a contrast to the failed resolution within the protagonist's world.

The conflict between restraint and desire is metaphorically identified in the first scene of the novella. Outside the church early Easter morning Šaptala lies down on the moist earth and feels the force of nature awakening with spring. Everything is branded with desire:

> Шаптала лежав не рухаючись і прислухався до того, що робилося в далеких глибинах землі. Почув, як звідтіль невпинно вириваються сили, розносяться вітром і накладають на все тавро жадоби. Він згадував, як жадібно випростували в день два дерева своє зазеленіле гилля, як напружались їхні стовбури, утворюючи молоде листя. Трава з якимсь одчаєм з'явилась на степах і кожна стеблина подібна була до широко-розтуленого рота галчати.
>
> Вдень дітвора гасала по вулицях і птахи кричали на небі; від почуття весни широкі посмішки лазили по обличчях людей, – в їхньому серці теж щось оживало і тавро жадоби не минало і їх. Бажання було написане в посмішках людей, в їхніх побільшених рухах, на їхніх чоботях, вкритих весняним болотом.
>
> Старий камінь край села теж бажав заслатися зеленим мохом. Так робив він впродовж сотень років, і мох захищав йому холодну душу від сонця.
>
> Жадоба й жага обнялись та в легкому танку, регочучи, пурхали над землею. А з їхнього реготу плодилось в повітрі безліч бажань, що ними труїлись навіть каміння.
>
> Земля ж готувалась задовольняти. Спокійно чорна повстала вона узгір'ями і розпадалась долинами, перетворюючись у велетенське лоно невидимої жінки. І все припадало до неї у млоснім напруженні та бажанні. (*Šaptala*, 3–4 / *Nevelyčka drama*, 206–7)

Šaptala lay motionless and listened to what was happening in the distant depths of the earth. He could hear forces escaping from there, spreading everywhere on the wind, and marking everything with the brand of passion. He remembered how passionately two trees had stretched out their green branches in the sunlight, how their trunks had grown taut in forming the young leaves. The grass appeared on the steppe with some kind of despair, and each blade resembled the wide-open mouth of a newly hatched crow.

During the day the children ran about the streets and the birds yelled in the sky. The feeling of spring made wide smiles crawl on people's faces; in their hearts as well something was being brought to life, and the brand of passion did not pass them by. Desire was written on people's smiles, in their exaggerated movements, on their boots, covered with spring mud.

An old rock near the village also desired to be covered with green moss. It had done so for hundreds of years, and the moss protected its cold soul from the sun.

Passion and yearning embraced in an effortless dance, laughing and fluttering above the earth. Their laughter spawned innumerable desires, with which even the rocks became poisoned.

And the earth was preparing to satisfy. Calmly the black land grew into mountains and dissolved into valleys, transforming itself into the giant womb of an invisible woman. And everything pressed close to her, languid with tension and desire.

This passage, reminiscent of D.H. Lawrence, clearly shows Pidmohyl'nyj combining the various elements of his definition of instinct into a thematic construct more complex than sexuality alone. Nature's reawakening in spring, the children running in the streets, and the smiles on the faces of the villagers combine with the mysterious power and latent sexuality of the earth to create a general force of primitive vitality. By way of contrast, Pidmohyl'nyj shows the interior of the church, also grey and moist like the night outside, but hushed, stifled, and static. The connection between the mortality in the church and the vitality outdoors is ironically captured in the setting itself. It is Easter, and the village is celebrating the resurrection of Christ from the dead. Even the church has acquired a feeling of energy and cannot offer Šaptala the sanctuary he seeks from life. For him, all that matters is that his sister is at home dying.

After his sister dies Ostap is despondent, but when he finds Lasja his life suddenly has new meaning. He devotes himself to her welfare and embraces his own vitality to help her:

Він ... був щасливий, чуючи в собі биття серця і шум легенів. Кожний прояв власного життя був йому цінним, бо його життя йому вже не належало. (*Šaptala*, 83 / *Nevelyčka drama*, 246)

He was happy, feeling his heart beating and his lungs breathing. Every sign of his own vitality was precious because his life no longer belonged to him.

Šaptala joins a team of stevedores hauling unusually heavy loads. Needless to say, this does not resolve the underlying problem of his guilt about his sister. The rational will cannot usurp instinct for its own purposes. By choosing to live for someone else, Ostap merely delays the eventual reckoning. It comes, finally, when he is confronted by Lasja's explicit sexual advances. Frightened and disturbed, he chases her away and shrinks into an emotionless, dispirited existence.

Accompanying the broader definition of instinctive vitality in this work is a more extensive examination of the repressive function that struggles against it. The novella begins, as we have seen, with what amounts to an erotic dream. In *Nevelyčka drama* Pidmohyl'nyj will take this opening gambit one step farther. Here, however, the pseudo-dream is interrupted deliberately by Šaptala, who feels alienated from life's yearning and commotion by the impending death of his sister: 'Думка про безглуздя її смерти спинила його серед світового руху' (The thought of the senselessness of her death stopped him in the midst of the world's motion; *Šaptala*, 5 / *Nevelyčka drama*, 207). After Oljusja's death, this temporary discomfort grows into a permanent condition. The chief nutrient sustaining this growth is guilt. Pidmohyl'nyj devotes special attention to the nature of Ostap's relationship to his sister, which comprises a curious mixture of frustration over the social and personal injustice of her sacrifice for him along with confused sexual feelings:

Що-раз глибше відчував Шаптала, що не кохання він мав від сестри, а віру; сестра піднесла його на височінь бога та все життя простояла перед ним навколюшках. Не дарма вона же не вірила в звичайного бога, бо не сила була їй поділяти на двох свою віру. Вона жила двадцять два роки й ніколи не кохала мужчини, – він це напевно знав, бо хіба ж здолала вона мати від нього таємницю. (*Šaptala*, 22–3 / *Nevelyčka drama*, 216)

Ever deeper grew the feeling that it was not affection he had from his sister, but faith. She had raised him to the heights of a god and spent her entire life before him on her knees. It was no accident that she did not believe in the regular god, because she could not possibly divide her faith between two. She lived for twenty-two years and had never loved a man – he knew this for a fact, for, after all, could she ever manage to keep a secret from him?

Guilt and fear of latent incest drive Šaptala to the brink of suicide. He hopes to expiate his guilt and repay his debt to his sister by dedicating his life to another. But when Lasja, in whom Ostap sees his sister resurrected, turns out to be more human than divine, Ostap again flees from perceived sin and withdraws into despair and passivity.

Because he equates vitality with sin, Šaptala is limited to a choice between sin or death. But this is not the only possible resolution to the underlying problem. Pidmohyl'nyj uses the secondary characters in the plot to illuminate other approaches to resolving the conflict between instinct and repression. Levko Verbun and Zin'ko Halaj are the control group against which the reading of the hero is to be calibrated. Something similar, but in an early, undeveloped form, can be seen in Omeljan Danylovyč, the engineer-musician who lives next door to the protagonist of 'Prorok.' Mature examples of the device can be found in the later works, *Misto*, *Nevelyčka drama*, and *Povist' bez nazvy*.

Levko, Ostap, and Zin'ko represent a full range of possibilities on the continuum of a rational individual's possible dispositions towards the instinctive, irrational world. It must be understood that this range of possibilities deliberately excludes non-rational approaches. In the novella, the non-rational approach is represented by Babusja Odarka, for whom the difficulties of daily existence are a practical problem that requires daily solutions. (The cat, Kovel'ko, views existence from a similar perspective.) Babusja Odarka's intellectual energy is devoted to mindless, usually political, chatter. Pidmohyl'nyj caricatures her intellectual world in the scene in which she reveals the secret she has overheard at the bazaar, that is that the name of the Ukrainian anarchist leader Nestor Maxno is actually an acronym for a monarchist slogan: 'Михаїл Алєксандрович Хазяїн Нашої Отчизни' ([Grand Duke] Mixail Aleksandrovič[13] is the protector of the fatherland). Pidmohyl'nyj gives the three young men a common school background to underscore their intellectual similarity. But in their relations with women, their responses to mundane frustrations, and their inclination to purely intellectual pursuits, they are strikingly different.

Levko Verbun is an early prototype of Jurij Slavenko in *Nevelyčka drama*. He is a paragon among rationalists. He lives quietly in his own intellectual world of abstract mathematics and pays little attention to what is going on around him. Indeed, when Zin'ko moves in to Levko's apartment and starts to hammer on his anvil, Levko is entirely undisturbed. 'Ти гадаєш я, багато уваги звертаю навколо?' (You think I pay much attention to what is going on around me?; *Šaptala*, 61 / *Nevelyčka drama*, 235), he asks. Indeed, he avoids people and ignores things, except when they pertain to his two passions, chess and Natalja. Chess is part of his rationalist credentials, but he plays the game to excess. When he is unable to find a willing and able partner he becomes angry, abusive, even violent. Without chess he is not himself. His other passion – more precisely, an intense biological need – is Natalja. When his relationship with her threatens to transcend the physical, Levko loses control:

'Вона не дійде добра,' прошепотів він: 'я скалічу її.... Ще слово – і знищу!'

Він почав ходити, хитаючись, не відводючи рук од голови. Наталя не розуміла, що йому потрібне лише її тіло, потрібне, як шматок хліба, і він ненавидить те тіло, як і хліб, що його ковтає. А вона силкувалась прикрити своє тіло якимись серпанками, непотрібними йому, яких він рвав, скаженіючи в що-часній борні з її недоладнім прагненням чистих пестощів. Вона хотіла мати до і після тіла: пестощі і дитину. (*Šaptala*, 80 / *Nevelyčka drama*, 244–45)

'She'll come to no good,' he muttered, 'I will hurt her ... One more word and I'll destroy her.'

He began to walk, swaying and holding his hands to his head. Natalja did not understand that he needed only her body, like a piece of bread, and that he hated it, that body, just as he hated the bread he gulped down. But she took pains to cover her body with veils of some sort, which he found useless, which he tore away, raging in his never-ending battle with her pointless longing for clean caresses. She wanted something before and after the body: caresses and a baby.

Levko's hatred of the physical is balanced by his extreme dedication to abstract intellectual problems. When his biological needs are satisfied and he is not playing chess, Levko is writing his philosophical treatise, entitled 'Transcendental Mathematics.' As he nears completion of this work he starts planning his next one, which will be entitled 'Problems of Variable Calculation.' The titles are, of course, ironic. They highlight the uncertainty of an ordered system, the spiritual side of material things. This irrational aspect of reason is also evident in the description of Verbun at work:

В ті менти, коли думка його досягала вищих ступнів напруження, обличчя його скупчувалось в одну цілість, робилось урочистим і віяло суворою красою жерця перед престолом бога. В ці менти провідна думка всевладно скоряла собі мозок; немов вона не була породженням його, а приходила відкілясь та оселялась в голові, як погірдлива господиня. Вона обхоплювала мозок своїми довгими пучками та ссала його снагу, щоб самій рости і міцнішати. Вона була, як висока струнка тополя з гнучким гиллям, посипаним сріблястим листям. (*Šaptala*, 25 / *Nevelyčka drama*, 217)

Ostap Šaptala

In these moments, when his thinking reached a higher level of tension, his face contracted into a single entity, became grand, and breathed the stern beauty of a pagan priest before the altar of his god. In these moments the almighty idea conquered the brain, as if it were not the brain's creation but arrived from somewhere else and settled in the mind, like a scornful housekeeper. She enveloped the brain with her long fingers and sucked its energy, in order that she herself might grow and strengthen. She was like a tall, straight poplar with limber branches sprinkled with silvery leaves.

The analogy to a priest performing worship and the simile involving nature once again emphasize the self-contradiction inherent in Levko's passionate devotion to logic, his irrational rationalism. This paradoxical formulation is characteristic of Pidmohyl'nyj. It recurs explicitly in Jurij Slavenko and Anatolij Paščenko in *Nevelyčka drama* and *Povist' bez nazvy*, respectively. In *Ostap Šaptala* Pidmohyl'nyj no longer sees the conflict between instinct and reason as a conflict between natural man and something alien to him. The scornful housekeeper is a product of the mind itself. A human being consists of a mind and a body, each with its own 'instinctive' demands. Unchecked reason is as irrational as unchecked passion. In the conflict between body and spirit an absolute victory by either side leads to undesirable results. Levko's passionate chess playing and dispassionate sex are a model of discord and disharmony.

Zinovij (Zin'ko) Halaj achieves a similar result with the opposite approach: Whereas Levko has empassioned reason, Zin'ko has rationalized passion. While Levko grudgingly allows himself food and sex to fulfil his bodily needs, Zin'ko welcomes all of life's pleasures, but only in his imagination. He is attracted to large crowds, he tells Ostap, by their colour and diversity; since he does not have friends, he can only watch the activity of others. He takes great joy in recollecting the image of a beautiful woman, but the woman remains a recollected mental image, not a reality. He is an admirer of the joys and beauty of nature, he spends leisure days lying naked in the sun on the banks of the river, but at night, under a starry sky, he dreams of climbing up into the 'Big Wagon' (the constellation Ursa Major, that is, the Big Dipper, or the Plough) and riding along the 'Teamster's Road' (the Milky Way). Although as a cobbler he might appear to be the symbol of the physical man, Halaj is, in fact, a disenchanted romantic. He explains his philosophy to Ostap while they are out on the town together, referring to himself in the third person:

'Зіновій Галай ... збагнув, що учитися треба лише доти, поки зрозумієш життя. А після – всяка наука зайва. Він облишив учитися. А як він ще дійшов, що всі засоби до життя однакові, то почав шевцювати, бо багацтва душі він постановив переховати про себе, а оточенню давати чоботи. Так він шевцює й досі, ні разу не пошкодувавши за вдіяним. Він зрозумів тоді, що життя чудове, коли скупчити його в собі самім, і отруйне, коли віддавати себе иншим; що чуття, коли їх виявити, в'януть, мов зірвані квітки, і живуть вічно барвисті, коли їх переховати в душі.' (*Šaptala*, 94 / *Nevelyčka drama*, 252)

'Zinovij Halaj ... realized that one should study only until one has comprehended life. After that, any learning is superfluous. He left his studies. And when he also deduced that all means of maintaining life were equal, he took up shoemaking, having he resolved that he would save the treasures of the soul for himself and give shoes to his surroundings. And so he is still a cobbler, never once having regretted what was done. He realized then that life was wonderful if you gathered it within yourself and poisonous if you give yourself to others. Feelings, if you reveal them, wither like cut flowers. But they blossom forever if you hide them in your soul.'

As a structural device and a thematic formulation, this measuring tape stretched between Verbun and Halaj, with Ostap somewhere in the middle, is an innovation in Pidmohyl'nyj's approach to his subject. Another important difference in the stories from 1920–1 as compared to those in his first collection, a difference that will become even more apparent in the stories from the subsequent period, 1922–5, is the growing specificity and topicality of his subjects. The protagonists of the stories in *Tvory: Tom 1* are mostly representatives of a large category of humanity – the young male. Vanja, Ženja, Viktor, and Petro have very little individuality. The problems that beset them are typical of their class, and the psychology of their responses is ordinary. It is melodramatic heightening rather than inherent complexity or originality that holds the reader's attention focused on their predicaments. In the stories written immediately after the appearance of *Tvory: Tom 1*, Pidmohyl'nyj attempts to deepen and individualize both his characters and the problems that beset them. To illustrate the resulting change we can juxtapose two very similar scenes from works written in the earlier and later periods. The first episode of 'Povstanci,' entitled 'Idut'' (They're Going), describes a situation similar to one depicted in 'Hajdamaka,' – that of young men leaving home to join the rebels. In 'Hajdamaka,' in the course of lengthy flashbacks that reveal the boys' homesickness, the narrator describes the feelings of the two main characters, Oles' and Vasyl', as they retreat from their city with the rebels:

Коли рідне місто, де були батьки, школа, знайомі, темніло вже ззаду невиразною плямою, над котрою манячили високі фабричні коміни, що, здавалось, зараз упадуть і віллються в загальну темряву, Василь похмуро сказав:
'Вже відступили.'
Олесь, котрому було боляче кидати рідні місця, батьків, яких він любив і котрі його любили, змахнув непрохану сльозину й радісно підтакнув:
'Авже ж відступили.' (*Tvory*, 92–3 / *Misto*, 259 / BUL, 43)

When their home town, with parents, school, and friends, was becoming just a dark spot topped off with tall factory chimneys that seemed ready to fall and blend into the general darkness behind them, Vasyl' said sombrely:
'We've retreated.'
Oles', for whom it was painful to leave home and the parents he loved and who loved him, wiped away an uninvited tear and cheerfully added:
'We've certainly retreated.'

The corresponding scene in the later story, 'Povstanci,' emphasizes emotions and forces less peculiar to children:

Вночі другого дня рушили. За селом Тарас із Остапом зупинились і чекали на Марка Чмуля. Той мав право спізнитись: у його була кохана.
Тарас притулився до ночі й застиг. Тиша його скорила і стала йому замість душі.
Остап заклав обійму в рушницю і клацнув. Він хвилювався. Тиша до нього не йшла, бо мав він маленьке серце.
'Найшов час,' мимрив Остап про Марка.
Він витяг обійму і став ладнати в ній набої.
Тиша тим часом стала Тарасові замість очей.
'Міг би вчора попрощатись,' бубонів Остап.
Синьою плямою підплив Марко і засміявся.
'Шлик є,' похвалився він: 'китиця срібна!'
Вони взяли рушниці на плечі й посунули назустріч шляхові.
Раптом Тарас одчув, що тиша покинула його й подалась назад до степу.

'Немає, хто б кохав,' похапцем заговорив він: 'немає і шлику ... немає срібної китиці ...'

Його сум грізною марою повис над Остапом. Він міцно стиснув рукою рушницю і промовив:

'Мовчи, мовчи!'

Маленький Андрійко наздогнав їх і влесливо забіг наперед.

'Тобі що?' здивувався Марко.

'З вами ...' винувато відповів хлопчик.

Марко похмурився.

'Додому,' суворо сказав, 'а то поясом.'

Андрійко несміливо зирнув на Тараса з Остапом. Ті мовчки кликали до себе тишу.

Тоді малий погірдливо струснув головою і миттю подався назад.

Остап глянув йому вслід і жахнувся степу: той збільшувався й поширювався, як потоп.

'Село ...' прошепотів він, показуючи рукою в той край, звідки вони йшли. Голос його захитався, як підрубане дерево.

Остап упустив рушницю, й сам упав обличчям до землі. Тільки-но почулося тремтіння його ридань, Тарас потонув у тиші.

Марко не зводив очей з того, що на повні груди пив силу землі.

'Ех ...' прошепотів він і здійняв шапку.

Та Остап ураз випростався й одійшов набік. Він нахилився до степу й гукнув:

'Я!...'

Сам же зробився кам'яним і сірим. Тільки кохання здолало б його ворухнути.

Вони знову пішли, лишаючи сліди на вогкій землі. Тепер їхні сліди червоніли перемогою.

Праворуч срібної криниці знову несподівано виринув Андрійко.

'Чи бачиш, пуцьвірінок,' з пошаною промовив Марко.

'Перестрінув таки,' додав Остап і лагідно забрязчав залізячкою на рушниці.

Тарас мовчав. Ніч оддавала йому своє прозоре тіло і стиха дихала сумом. Степ подавав йому міць нерухомости та спокій потужности.

Вони йшли далі, обережно ступаючи по землі, немов лізли по драбині на небо. (*Povstanci*, 5–7)

On the second night they left. Beyond the village Taras and Ostap stopped and waited for Marko Čmul'. He had a right to be late – he had a girlfriend.

Taras embraced the night and stiffened. The silence overcame him and replaced his soul.

Ostap Šaptala

Ostap loaded the magazine into the rifle with a clang. He was frightened. The silence did not come to him, because he had a small heart.

'Why in the last minute?' muttered Ostap about Marko.

He pulled out the magazine and toyed with the cartridges.

The silence meanwhile took the place of Taras's eyes.

'He could have said his goodbyes yesterday,' grumbled Ostap.

Like a blue spot Marko drifted up to them and laughed.

'I've got a Cossack hat,' he said, 'with a silver tassel.'

They slung their rifles over their shoulders and took off down the road.

Suddenly Taras realized that the silence had left him and had gone back to the steppe.

'No ... girlfriend for me,' he stuttered, 'and no hat ... or silver tassel.'

Taras's sadness hung over Ostap like a phantom. He tightened his grip on his rifle and yelled:

'Shut up! Shut up!'

Little Andrijko caught up and coquettishly ran ahead of them.

'What do you think you're doing?' asked Marko.

'I'm going with you,' answered the boy, guiltily.

Marko got angry.

'Home,' he said, sternly, 'or I'm getting my belt.'

Andrijko looked at Taras and Ostap shyly but they were quietly summoning the silence.

The little boy shook his head scornfully and ran away.

Ostap looked back after him and was alarmed by the steppe, which grew larger and wider, like a flood.

'The village ... ' he whispered, pointing in the direction from which they had come. His voice wobbled like a half-felled tree.

Ostap dropped his rifle and fell face down on the ground. As soon as Taras heard Ostap's trembling sobs, he sank into the silence.

Marko didn't take his eyes off the one who was drinking up the earth's strength in tearful mouthfuls.

'Eh ... ' he whispered, and took off his hat.

But suddenly Ostap got up and stepped off to the side. Leaning in the direction of the steppe he called out:

'I! ... '

He became stony and grey. Only love would have been able to shake him.

They took off again, leaving footprints in the moist soil. This time their footprints were red with victory.

To the right of the silver well Andrijko unexpectedly appeared once again.

'It's the greenhorn,' said Marko, respectfully.

'He has come out to see us off,' added Ostap and gently shot the bolt on his rifle.

Taras was silent. The night was giving him its transparent body and quietly breathing in the sadness. The steppe was offering him the strength of immobility and the serenity of power.

They went on, carefully choosing their steps, as if they were climbing a ladder to heaven.

A number of elements in this passage warrant attention. There is a difference between the motives and feelings of the boys in 'Hajdamaka' and the boys in 'Povstanci.' The boys in the latter story are not naïve. They are frightened but they understand what they are doing. In other words, they are not pursuing a child's quest for glory, but are following a reasonable, if not altogether rational, plan. In the passage just quoted, Pidmohyl'nyj differentiates the three boys on the basis of precisely this criterion. Taras has discussed his plans in advance with his father and has won his approval. He even says that he will return in time for the harvest, a comment that his father receives with scepticism. Marko seems to be more of a dreamer. His reference to his hat and tassel suggests an attachment to a romantic image of the rebel. The incident with Andrijko (apparently Marko's younger brother) reinforces that suggestion. The older brother's idealized vision has influenced the youngster. Ostap represents yet another aspect of the psychological portrait Pidmohyl'nyj is painting here. As his fumbling with his rifle and his impatience with Marko's delay make clear, he is more frightened by what he is doing than the other boys are. When he looks back and sees the village, he is overcome by fear and sadness. The emotional attachment to home and family is strong. But the boys are guided by a more powerful force, an instinct that Pidmohyl'nyj associates with the steppe and with darkness. Ostap symbolically absorbs this force from the earth itself. It overcomes his emotional attachments, as it does Taras's wavering belief in ideals of any sort whatsoever. This force is an extension and refinement of the dark forces that had frightened Pidmohyl'nyj's earlier protagonists.

In 'Povstanci' all the boys overcome their fear. This points to another important difference between the stories. Whereas in 'Hajdamaka' Vasyl' returns home when the opportunity presents itself and Oles' is sent home after being humiliated, in the first episode of 'Povstanci' the boys master their apprehension and join the rebels. Because the rest of the story does not focus on these boys, we do not know what happens to them afterwards. Judging by their victory over themselves in the passage just quoted, however, it is safe to assume that the reader is not meant to doubt the boys' subsequent courage.

This view is confirmed in the second episode by the rebel commander's interview of a young new volunteer, perhaps one of the three boys. The boy is shy and apparently nervous about meeting the commander, but the old soldier brings out his latent courage.

Success was not among the possible outcomes for a Pidmohyl'nyj hero in the earlier stories. This new option represents a change in the thematic structure of Pidmohyl'nyj's works. The world he had depicted in *Tvory: Tom 1* was very bleak. The endings of 'Prorok,' 'Dobryj boh,' 'Važke pytannja,' and 'Vanja' are characteristically desperate; those of 'V epidemičnomu baraci,' 'Povstanci,' and *Ostap Šaptala* are still bleak, but they lack desperation. Ostap may be eternally disenchanted, but he can sit in his apartment playing chess with Verbun and listening to Babusja Odarka's mindless chatter for many years to come.

The greater individualization of characters in the works from the later period is matched by a greater topicality in their settings and subjects. The stories in *Tvory: Tom 1* have little to tie them to a specific time and place. They depict timeless conflicts of young men everywhere. The references to socialism and to Marx in 'Na seli' and 'Did Jakym' and the events in 'Hajdamaka' clearly place those stories in revolutionary times, but these are only vague indicators, with little or no connection to the thematic structure of the stories. The stories from the second period of Pidmohyl'nyj's creativity show a growing attachment to a specific time and place and to a serious link between contemporary social and political issues and the essential philosophical theme of a story. In 'Povstanci,' for example, the chaos and social disorder of the revolutionary period have a significant connection to the theme. Although attributed specifically to the anarchists (who were an important political force, particularly in the steppes of southern Ukraine) the confusion and irresponsibility of ideologues and political leaders was part of the general social pattern in Ukraine and, indeed, throughout the former Russian Empire, in the years following the Revolution. On a thematic level, the confusion is a general metaphor for the condition of rational man in the natural world. Thus, Pidmohyl'nyj's philosophical subject is mirrored in the setting of his works.

An increasing emphasis on topicality is evident in a number of works from this period but nowhere more than in two stories that were unknown until recently. It was, no doubt, their very topicality that kept them hidden, since both stories paint an unflattering portrait of Communist Party activists. The story 'Komunist' (The Communist) was first published, under the pseudonym P. Val'čuk in the January 1923 issue of *Literaturno-naukovyj vistnyk*, which came out in Lviv under the editorial supervision of Dmytro Doncov. (Only through the research of Volodymyr Mel'nyk was it possible to confirm that the author was indeed Pidmohyl'nyj.) The story is about a young Jewish Communist named Ostrovs'kyj, who is captured, along with other Communists, by an unspecified enemy. To save himself from certain execution (the enemy Cossacks separate the Jews from the other prisoners and execute them), Ostrovs'kyj escapes from detention. With the help of the local Jewish community, particularly of Poale Zion members, whose secretary preaches Jewish solidarity to him, he acquires a false passport and new clothes. As he leaves the city on the train, however, Ostrovs'kyj thinks of the Poale Zion members as fools: 'Just wait till we re-take the city,' he thinks. 'I'll show that secretary the true path – he'll end up at the Cheka, not in Zion!'

'Komunist' is a politically sensitive story. It touches on a number of delicate questions. It presents a Bolshevik in a very disagreeable light and highlights the bad relations between Jews and non-Jews. The existence of this story helps explain the antipathy of communist officials to Pidmohyl'nyj in the early 1920s. But despite its title, the story has nothing to do with communism and the realities of revolutionary behaviour. Behaviour similar to that depicted in the story may certainly have occurred in reality during the revolutionary years, but the story neither makes accusations nor presents or advocates political ideas. The political affiliations of the characters in the story are not a central issue. The anti-Semitic Cossacks remain unidentified. The choice of Communists and Poale Zion is circumstantial, relevant only to the extent that these groups give the story a current, popular flavour. In fact, Pidmohyl'nyj may have chosen Poale Zion because it was a local organization founded in Katerynoslav. In the case of the protagonist, any affiliation other than Communist would seem unlikely and would be less resonant. In the final analysis, however, this is a story about the difference between instinctive and reasoned behaviour. Much is made in the story of the fact that Ostrovs'kyj does not 'look Jewish.' Because of that, he can choose, 'rationally,' whether or not to represent himself as a Jew, depending on circumstances. Other Jews in the story, those who 'look Jewish,' do not have that choice. Ostrovs'kyj is similarly flexible with respect to ideology. Unlike the anti-semitic Cossacks, who shoot the Jews for no reason at all, Ostrovs'kyj picks and chooses his enemies on the basis of expediency. The Cossacks are mindless brutes. Ostrovs'kyj is a machiavellian wretch.

A similar cluster of ideas can be found in the brief sketch 'Za den'.' In this story Pidmohyl'nyj contrasts two scenes. The first depicts the fanatical devotion of religious peasants, especially women, to the miraculous renewal of an icon in a particular village. The second depicts a village Communist council meeting at which the council's delegate to the national meeting is presenting an optimistic, upbeat report. The two scenes are ironically compared by a first-person narrator, who concludes both descriptions with the same words: 'Do not disturb the delusion.'

These topical subjects and settings give Pidmohyl'nyj's works of the second and later periods the flavour of popular, current fiction – an important quality for a writer trying to make a career. Whether in a capitalist North America or a socialist Ukraine, a writer's popularity and the readability of his works (rather than quality alone) are the best guarantors of a successful career. But for Pidmohyl'nyj, choosing to be topical was more than just a matter of speculation in the literary marketplace. At the deepest thematic level, Pidmohyl'nyj's works are about the gap between the way people perceive the world and the way it really is. He fundamentally disputes the idea that humans can understand the world. Their understanding is essentially and unalterably rational; the world is not. By locating his works in familiar settings and populating them with familiar figures, events, and ideas, but at the same time separating those trappings from the underlying theme, Pidmohyl'nyj reinforces the message of alienation. Furthermore, Pidmohyl'nyj is a realist, or at least he is becoming one. The gradual incorporation of topical allusiveness into his works brings him closer to the eventual goal – psychological realism in the novel. Unfortunately, it also puts him in a precarious situation. In an ideologically charged atmosphere, readers and government officials might mistake ironic topicality for political treason.

CHAPTER THREE

The Later Stories
Elements of Style

Literary style, whether conceived in terms of a period of literary history or as the idiosyncrasies of an individual writer, is a notoriously unstable notion. It is also a very problematical one. The famous disputes between literary historians of a previous generation[1] have demonstrated that periodization of the history of literature on the basis of a common style – as in Dmytro Čyževs'kyj's *A History of Ukrainian Literature*[2] – is invariably subjective and arbitrary. Similarly, definitions based on the assumption that style is a quality of the language of a text and that this quality is objectively identifiable and measurable have been shown to be unfounded and unworkable, most notably by Bennison Gray in his *Style: The Problem and Its Solution*.[3] Such objections notwithstanding, the fact that the term *style* retains its universal currency in discussions of literature indicates that it carries an implicit meaning in literary analysis.

In attempting to define this perceived meaning of style, Roland Barthes argues that the metaphor for the relationship of style to content in a literary text is not that of a fruit, with flesh and pit, but rather that of an onion, with innumerable layers of skin beneath which there is no heart or core, only more layers.[4] Another metaphor for the relationship between style and text, one that conveys the sense of the inseparability of style and text can be borrowed from nuclear physics, specifically from models of the behaviour of subatomic particles. The metaphor is based on the properties of quarks: Style relates to a text the way flavour, beauty, strangeness, or charm relate to a quark. Just as these attributes are inseparable from the particles that exhibit them, so style is inseparable from the text. Furthermore, the names of the properties have no relation to the nature of those properties. The point here is to confound the urge to attribute to style the properties of the metaphorical terms used to explain it.

Style in a work of literature does not consist of any particular combination of linguistic or other factors. It is not even a quality of the language of the text. Every reader sees in a text qualities that do not appear to be part of the essential nature of the text. For example, the proportion of Greek– to Latin–stem words in a novel by Charles Dickens is likely to be seen by most readers as an element of style (although not likely actually to be perceived). However, the imitations of various authorial styles in the 'Oxen of the Sun' episode of Joyce's *Ulysses* are seen not as an element of style but as a deliberate and purposeful, and therefore substantive rather than stylistic, construct. The features of Carlyle, Newman, Pater, Addison, Swift, Defoe, or Pepys that Joyce copies are elements of style, but the variations in style in Joyce's chapter are not. The number of lines and the rhyme scheme in one of Shakespeare's sonnets is not a matter of style; the relative proportion of active to passive verbs is. For most readers, the expression of personal views and feelings on the part of the authorial voice is an element of style in a novel, but not in a lyric poem. Style consists of the subjective perception of specific attributes of a text that are deemed to be extrinsic to the essential being of the text. All the features of style are objectively measurable, but their status as elements of style in a particular text depends on a particular reader's view of that text. In other words, every reader discerns style in literary (and non-literary) texts, but the components of that perceived style can differ from text to text and from reader to reader. What unifies the concept is the impact of these qualities on the reader's judgment, evaluation, and appreciation of the text. Style, like the work to which it refers, is understood as a totality.

From his earliest to his last works, Pidmohyl'nyj evolved as a writer on a number of different levels. He developed from a short-story writer into a novelist. He developed his thematic polarity from a conflict between instinct and repression to a conflict between spirit and matter. The sequence of his works also exhibits an evolution in style. Pidmohyl'nyj's stylistic evolution can be traced along a continuum from the home-grown impressionistic modernism, inspired by Vynnyčenko and Kocjubyns'kyj, evident in his early works, to the European psychological realism inspired by Maupassant and Balzac, present in his later works. The most significant of the stylistic elements involved are narrative technique, symbolism, the face of the hero, topicality, literary allusiveness, melodramatic pacing, and intellectualism. Two of these elements, topicality and melodramatic structure, have been discussed, at least partially, in the preceding chapters. Literary allusiveness and intellectualism will be discussed in subsequent chapters. This chapter focuses on narrative technique, symbolism, and the face of the hero.

Three factors are important in tracing the development of Pidmohyl'nyj's narrative technique: metaphor, authorial distance, and descriptiveness. These factors are closely related not only to one another, but also to other elements of style, structure, and theme, such as topicality and thematic evolution, and the boundaries between them are sometimes uncertain. Within the constraints of these occasionally indistinct borders, each factor can be observed evolving from its initial contours in the earliest stories to its mature form in the later novels.

The presence of metaphor and metaphoric description in Pidmohyl'nyj's works is tied to his literary ancestors and the current situation in Ukrainian literature, as well as to his philosophical subject. Late in the second decade of the twentieth century Ukrainian prose continued to be the weak sibling of Ukrainian poetry, as it had been for many generations. The major living prose writers in 1917, when Pidmohyl'nyj's earliest stories were being composed, were Ivan Nečuj-Levyc'kyj, Panas Myrnyj, Volodymyr Vynnyčenko, and, in Western Ukraine, Ol'ha Kobyljans'ka and Vasyl' Stefanyk. In addition, the works of Ivan Franko and Myxajlo Kocjubyns'kyj were still popular and influential. As this list of strange bedfellows indicates, the literary marketplace for prose was divided among competing tendencies, most notably between old-fashioned social and ethnographic realism (Nečuj and Myrnyj), still popular but decidedly outdated, and thematic (Vynnyčenko) and stylistic (Kocjubyns'kyj) innovation, collectively labelled 'modernism.'

The most distinctive quality of Ukrainian modernist prose is its poetic flavour, often referred to as 'impressionism.' The primary feature of this poetic quality, which developed in reaction to the perceived empirical and materialist focus of late realism, is subjective and laconic description, characterized by significant details rather than pictorial amplitude. This selective, metaphorical description is used in conjunction with subjective narrative technique and melodramatic composition. Together, these devices allow the narration to combine objectivity with subjectivity, the material with the abstract. Occasionally, the subject of narration becomes the metaphorized abstraction itself rather than the metaphorical object. Pidmohyl'nyj's early stories display some of these qualities, although to a limited degree. Over the course of his development as a writer he gradually moved away from metaphorical, impressionistic, and melodramatic techniques towards a more restrained, objective narration. That change can be illustrated by juxtaposing similar passages from early and later works.

In 'Starec',' one of his early stories, the city is anthropomorphized into a Baudelaireian living organism, as evidenced by the programmatic opening paragraph.[5] The objects that make up the city landscape are metaphorical markers of a cosmic disorder:

З божевільним ляцканням і гуркотом метальових маслаків літали трамваї, заглушуючи ті дивні слова, що ніч хотіла сказати пригніченій землі і сонливим деревам; з упертим нахабством блимали ліхтарі, гадаючи своїм промінням знайти і обсвітити вічно-величнє обличчя її. (*Tvory*, 11 / *Misto*, 290 / BUL, 75)

With an insane clanging and rumbling of their metallic bones, streetcars flew past, muffling the strange words that night wanted to speak to the trampled earth and to the dreamy trees; with stubborn insolence the street lights glimmered, thinking that their rays could find and illuminate night's eternal magnificent countenance.

Two years later, in *Ostap Šaptala*, Pidmohyl'nyj was still ascribing metaphorical value to objects. Preoccupied with the inevitability of his sister's death, Ostap visits the foundry, now shut down, where he used to work:

Він піднявся драбинкою на примосток і зверху дивився на залізний цвинтар. Щось привабливе таїлося в смерти колес та в звислих ланцюгах горішніх кранів. Насолода вічного спочинку вилискувала на вигибах криці і мерехтіла на мідяних частинах держальн та гаків. Всевладно панувала тиша над потужними працівниками, що в зойках і шаленстві тіпались були своїми тілами, бездоганно віддаючи свою силу і рух.... Тепер вони спочивали і радість нерухомости відчував кожний гвинтик цього знеможеного тіла. (*Ostap Šaptala*, 38 / *Nevelyčka drama*, 224)

He climbed the ladder to the walkway and looked down at the iron cemetery. Something attractive was concealed in the death of the wheels and the chains hanging from the overhead cranes. The pleasure of eternal rest glistened on the remains of steel and sparkled on the brass parts of the hoists and hooks. Almighty silence reigned over the powerful workers, that had strained their bodies with cries and fury, faultlessly giving their strength and motion ... Now they rested and the joy of stillness was felt by every bolt in this powerless body.

Although much of the metaphorical property of the narration remains unchanged (machines have feelings, abstractions perform functions), Pidmohyl'nyj has moderated the poetic flavour of the passage by associating it indirectly with the feelings of the protagonist, a man capable of such melancholy thoughts and, indeed, predisposed toward them by recent events. Furthermore, the essential metaphor of the closed foundry as an analogue to the ennui besetting Ostap is predicated on the fact that Ostap formerly worked at this factory and is justified in visiting it. In the previous passage, from 'Starec',' the association of Tymiš with the streetcars and street lights is incidental, making the device a challenge to realist canons.

When Nečuj-Levyc'kyj characterizes Mykola Džerja's father with a description of his work-worn hand, or when Balzac calls old Goriot a vermicelli maker, or when Flaubert describes in great detail Charles Bovary's hat, they are all engaging in a metaphorical transference of properties between things and people. But in each of these cases the relationship is direct: A man's clothes or furnishings characterize him because they are his, not because they share a metaphysical property with him. In realist fiction, metaphors are hidden beneath causality. Metaphorical prose in the modernist period, however, dispenses with causality as a precondition for a metaphorical connection. The transference of properties between people and things is premised on a universal similarity, an underlying monistic harmony. The relation between Marcel and the magic lantern or the madeleine, in À la recherche du temps perdu, and between Bloom and the potato in his pocket in *Ulysses*, are part of a metaphysical order, as are Tymiš's city and Ostap's foundry.

So, too, albeit to a lesser degree, is Serhij's airplane, in 'Vijs'kovyj litun' (Military Pilot). Serhij Dančenko is a disfigured, ugly man who has joined the ranks of the privileged few – he can fly. The essentially Nietzschean contrast between the earth-bound and the beautiful and free is a major concern in the story. The city to which the demobilized pilot returns is an image of decay:

А місто зустріло його суворо, і просто в обличчя йому війнув дух руїни. З усіх боків нахилились до нього пошарпані будинки, і вибиті шибки лягали йому тягарями на серце. І хоч п'ять років він тільки й бачив, що розпад і смерть, а не міг погодитися, що місто, де ступала його юнацька нога, так само гниє і розпадається....

Сергія тягло далі, вглиб міста. Байдуже розгортались перед ним вулиці, порослі травою, червоні прапори й чисте небо.

Замість буяння він спіткав тільки труп, і шумливе колись місто лежало купою стерва. (*Misto*, 372 / BUL, 158)

But the city greeted him sternly and the breath of ruin rushed full in his face. From all sides tattered buildings leaned toward him and broken windows lay heavy on his heart. Although for five years destruction and death were all he had seen, still he could not reconcile himself to the decay and devastation of the city his youthful legs had walked ...

Serhij was drawn on, into the heart of the city. Carelessly spread out before him were streets overgrown with grass, red flags, and a clear sky.

Instead of exuberance he found only a corpse, the once noisy city lay a rotting carcass.

An actual description of the plane does not occur in the story. Pidmohyl'nyj shows it only as it falls from the sky:

Мотор зітхнув, і то було останнє зітхання душі, що хотіла неба. Ущух пропелер, і велична тиша схолодила блакить. А за мить ревнули простори, сонце захиталось і земля розкрила свої обійми.
(*Misto*, 404 / BUL, 191)

The motor sighed and that was the last sigh of a soul that wanted heaven. The propeller faded, and the magnificent silence chilled the azure. After a moment the heavens roared, the sun wavered, and the earth opened its arms in embrace.

Dančenko's plane, unlike Ostap's foundry, is an indissoluble part of his personality. It forms an essential part of the structure of the story. Ostap and his foundry are paralleled in their chilly silence, but Serhij dies *because* the plane falls, even if it is by his own willful choice. Furthermore, the metaphorical descriptions of the plane and of flying are tied to the subjective views of the character. Dančenko himself sees flying as an escape, an exercise in freedom. Where the description of the city in 'Starec" was in the voice of the narrator, who allowed himself to express subjective judgments, the descriptions of flying in 'Vijs'kovyj litun' are the narrator's attempt to render the views of his protagonist. The implicit irony in this indirect narration is made explicit on two occasions in the story. When Serhij finally returns home from the airman's holiday, he finds a woman waiting for him. She is a poet who is enchanted by the poetic beauty of flying and she has come to give herself to Serhij. But when he lights the lamp and the woman sees his disfigurement she is horrified and disillusioned. By identifying the woman as a poet and by allowing her illusion to be broken, Pidmohyl'nyj ironically underscores the metaphoric quality of the illusion. Similarly, at Dančenko's funeral the oration by his fellow airman is appropriately bombastic, and thus doubly ironic. By allowing the airman to compare the expansion of human horizons by aviation to the building of communism, Pidmohyl'nyj puts both innovations on a par with religion. But what is even more important, he is deliberately distancing the views of the character from those of the author.

The last story Pidmohyl'nyj wrote before 'Vijs'kovyj litun' was 'Problema xliba' (The Problem of Bread). It is introduced by the following epigraph:

> Немає нічого хибнішого, як ототожнювати ідею твору з думками автора. На жаль, читач і критика слабують на цю недоречну хворобу. Тут я якнайрішучіше застерігаюся проти цього поширеного забобону. 'Гарний письменник користується не тільки з власних думок, але й із думок своїх добрих знайомих' (Ніцше). Хто має вуха слухати, хай чує. (*Misto*, 336 / BUL, 122)

> There is nothing more mistaken than to identify of the idea of a work with the thoughts of its author. Unfortunately, readers and critics suffer from this absurd disease. I hereby emphatically denounce this widespread superstition. 'A fine writer makes use of not only his own thoughts, but also the thoughts of his close acquaintances' (Nietzsche). Who has ears to hear, let him listen.

The quotation ascribed to Nietzsche in this epigraph is a free translation of aphorism number 180 in *Menschliches, Allzumenschliches*:

> *Collectivgeist*. Ein guter Schriftsteller hat nicht nur seinen eigenen Geist, sondern auch noch den Geist seiner Freunde.[6]

> *Collective mind*. A good writer possesses not only his own mind but also the mind of his friends.[7]

For Nietzsche, this aphorism is an expression of the universal intertextuality of literature as well as of the practical need of a writer to be able to capture the thoughts and feelings of another individual. For Pidmohyl'nyj the aphorism also carries meanings specific to his own circumstances. On the most practical level it serves as a political disclaimer. The story introduced by this epigraph is written in the form of a diary. Given the political climate of the time, a first-person narrative about a young man who is unable to find food could have been very dangerous for the author. But the disclaimer also has an important function in the story itself. The epigraph has the effect of distancing the first-person narration, establishing it as an objective specimen for examination. The synchrony of the diary form combined with the objective distancing of the frame creates the effect of a laboratory for psychological observation.

Between Reason and Irrationality

The epigraph to 'Problema xliba' and the irony observed in 'Vijs'kovyj litun' point to the gradual change in authorial distance that is evident in Pidmohyl'nyj's works. The stories in *Tvory: Tom 1* are narrated by a voice that presents a subjective, sympathetic view of the protagonists and the dilemmas they face. In the later stories, particularly 'Vijs'kovyj litun' and 'Tretja revoljucija,' the narrative voice is more distanced and adopts a more neutral position with regard to the events and characters in the story.

Narrative technique is one of the few areas of literary studies in which real technical progress has given rise to the development of useful analytic tools. Although there is no unified general model of narrative situation, the various tools that have been developed by different theorists are not mutually exclusive. Indeed, they are often complementary (if not similar or, in some cases, even identical). Thus, we can call upon two different critical approaches to fictional narration that are relevant to the 'measurement' of authorial distance: Gérard Genette's focalization[8] and Dorrit Cohn's consonance and dissonance polarity or harmony.[9] The term focalization refers to the perspective of the narrator's voice. Zero focalization describes a narrative situation traditionally called the omniscient narrator. Internal focalization, which can be fixed, variable, or multiple, describes a narrative situation in which the point of view, the information available to the narrator and reader, is limited by the point of view of a single character or a number of characters. External focalization, which is often used to create suspense and mystery, occurs when the perspective of a character or characters is deliberately excluded from the narrative perspective, for example, when the consciousness of the criminal in a story is kept from the reader. Dorrit Cohn's notions of consonance and dissonance also provide a framework for measuring the distance between authorial and figurative consciousness (the narrating consciousness and the consciousness of the characters, respectively),[10] but here the emphasis is on the degree of intellectual, ethical, and aesthetic sympathy between them. Dissonant narration is often used to convey a judgment, to separate the description of a psyche from an approval of it – in short, for irony. Consonant narration projects an identification of the authorial with the figural consciousness. Of course, these two categories are not absolute but relative; they are the endpoints of a continuum.

Measurements of the narrative situation need to be taken at particular points in a text and it is not uncommon to find wide variations within any given text. But on the whole, a text tends to display a certain profile, a general character in its narrative technique. Most of Pidmohyl'nyj's early stories rely on a partially focalized consonant narrator, with occasional passages of unfocalized dissonance. The narrator is usually more perceptive than the protagonist, but, on the whole, he sees things from the protagonist's point of view and presents the protagonist's ideas and feelings sympathetically. The description of Tymiš's frustration and pain when he first leaves the hospital without his leg, in 'Starec';' the report of Vanja's encounter with the man-eater; and the depiction of the jealous Viktor at Kusja's door, in 'Dobryj boh,' are all presented through the eyes of the characters themselves, without immediate authorial irony. But irony, in these early stories, is never far off. The stories are built on a melodramatic pacing of alternating sympathy and judgment.

In the early works irony is achieved by various means. Melodramatic structuring of the plot, as observed in *Ostap Šaptala*, is one method. Changes in focalization can also produce ironic effects. For example, 'Starec'' opens with the narrator's account of the meaninglessness of city life. Then follows a sympathetic portrait of Tymiš, who is clearly a victim and an example of the condition described in the opening paragraphs. In 'Dobryj boh' the narrative voice is usually consonant, but an occasional dissonant comment helps establish the pattern of alternating sympathy and judgment. In the second paragraph of the story, for instance, the narrator says that Viktor felt 'too good' (занадто гарно). Another gambit that helps support the melodramatic pacing of the narrative is the narrator's wide-eyed credulity. Although the narrator occasionally voices perceptive insights about a character's psychological state, at other times he fails to comment on obvious inconsistencies and willful self-delusions, as, for example, Viktor's religiosity. Something similar occurs in Vanja, when the narrator reports without comment the child's conclusions about a man-eater in the gully and a dog's ghost under his bed. Juxtaposing characters by means of shifts in focalization also promotes melodramatic pacing. This is the case in 'V epidemičnomu baraci' where the narrative is focalized through a variety of characters in order to reflect judgments in several directions.

Perhaps the best example of Pidmohyl'nyj's use of melodramatic pacing occurs in his only non-prose work of fiction. 'Smert'' is a short dramatic sketch that was published only once, in the first (1927), but not the second (1930), edition of the collection *Problema xliba*. It is mentioned in 1921 by Petro Jefremov,[11] and so must have been written in that year or earlier. The style and plot are characteristic of Pidmohyl'nyj's early works: A man is dying and he fears death. His wife attempts to comfort him, but he is inconsolable. Suddenly, he screams in pain and makes convulsive movements, then lies still. The room fills with light and a beautiful woman, the figure of death, enters and converses with the man. He is captivated by her and wishes he could be dying forever in order to remain in the embrace of death.

'Smert'' is built on a double irony. First, the dying man is confronted by an image of death very different from what he expected. Then, he chooses death for her sexual appeal, that is, her vitality. The entire sketch is an exercise in melodrama, conceived as a two-beat rhythmic dance. The perceptions of the reader (or viewer, if we take this to be a dramatic work) are preprogrammed with overwhelming, ponderous determinism.

Although melodramatic pacing and variable authorial distance never completely disappear from Pidmohyl'nyj's arsenal of literary devices, the frequency and density of their use are inversely proportional to his development as a writer. A measured step away from melodramatic irony toward an objective, descriptive narrative method is evident in stories such as 'Vijs'kovyj litun,' 'Ivan Bosyj,' and especially 'Tretja revoljucija' reveal. Technically, this abandonment of heavy-handed irony is achieved by a variety of means, among which are a movement away from dissonant narration and psycho-narration and a greater reliance on quoted dialogue and description, particularly objective (rather than metaphorical) description. The opening paragraph of 'Tretja revoljucija' provides an example:

Було коло першої години ночі. Ксана, схилившись на довге підвіконня, часом торкаючись чолом холодного скла, дивилася в сіру далечінь, де лунали такі дивні, страшні, а вже звиклі звуки. Бій ближчав. Прозоре стукотіння кулеметів, безладна тріскотнява рушниць, раптові вибухи шрапнелів, що недавно ще були мов марево невиразне, сунули і облягали місто. Несподівано знімались ракети й осяювали на мить небосхил. Потім важко били гармати.

Ксана дивилась на рівну вулицю, що простягалась туди, до стрілом напоєного мороку, і на будинки, що скам'яніли вздовж неї. Ксана думала: у тих будинках поховалися, прищулилися по льохах люди, залякані, тривожно чекаючи. І може, тільки хто цікавий, хоробрий, чи хороброго вдаючи, дивиться, слухає, як от вона, примарного бою.

Раптом десь зблизька розітнувся постріл. Ксана відсахнулась....

Ксану вабив бій. Ще й місяць чи буде тому, вона теж, мов стара пані грому, жахалася пострілів. І на селі, де жили вони, бої видавалися ще страшнішими. Тоді чоловік цілував її, а вона таки боялася....

Махно прийшов і розстріляв її чоловіка. Десь за селом, уночі. (*Tretja*,[12] 5–6 / *Misto*, 414–15 / BUL, 205–6)

It was close to one o'clock in the morning. Ksana, leaning on the long window sill, at times touching the cold window with her forehead, was looking into the grey distance where such strange, frightening, but by now familiar sounds echoed. The battle was moving closer. The transparent clatter of machine guns, the chaotic crackle of rifles, the sudden explosions of hand grenades, which, until recently, had been an obscure illusion, now neared and encircled the city. Flares shot up abruptly, momentarily illuminating the horizon. Then came the heavy fire of cannons.

Ksana looked at the straight street that stretched out there, into the bullet-fed obscurity, and at the buildings that had petrified along it. Ksana thought: in these buildings frightened people are hiding, hunkered down in their cellars, waiting nervously. And only perhaps someone curious, brave, or pretending to be brave, is looking at and listening to the ghostly battle, the way she was.

Suddenly, from somewhere nearby, a shot rang out. Ksana gasped ...

Ksana was drawn to the battle. It wasn't even a month ago that she, too, was frightened by the shots, like an old lady by thunder. And in the village, where they lived, the battles seemed even more frightening. Back then, her husband would kiss her, but she would still be afraid ...

Maxno came and had her husband shot. Somewhere outside the village, at night.

This passage shows a greater subtlety than did the earlier stories in the way it achieves irony. Ksana's obsessive fascination with battle after the execution of her husband does not become a subject of analysis or speculation by the narrator, or of metaphorical description. Irony is attained here through description and sequence. At first, Ksana's curiosity about the battle is presented through consonant descriptive narration, without comment. The narrative voice is focalized through Ksana, but its tone is restrained, as the choice of adjectives and the absence of metaphor show. Then Ksana is drawn away from the window by a shot nearby and, more importantly, by the information about her husband. The sudden narrative about-face parallels the melodramatic pacing of earlier stories, but here the melodrama is diminished. The ironic twist is purely intellectual. No specific judgment of Ksana is suggested aside from the one on which the plot is constructed: Ksana is fascinated by the man who killed her husband. Pidmohyl'nyj is gradually shifting from an impressionistic to an objective style. The chief function of the narrator is to show what happens, not to reflect a judgment of it.

Another element of Pidmohyl'nyj's style that can be seen evolving in the stories from the mid–1920s is the manner in which the hero is presented. Pidmohyl'nyj's early protagonists are victims of a cosmic order, and, as such, are depicted in a profound 'high' style. Later protagonists are no longer pawns in an Olympian chess match. They are ordinary people caught in existential problems, often of their own making. They are presented in a sympathetic but detached manner. In Northrop Frye's terms, they have moved up the scale from the ironic to the low mimetic mode.

This evolution is both stylistic and thematic. It involves the tools used to present the hero – that is, the narrative techniques just discussed, and the thematic parameters within which he is presented. In the stories from the mid-1920s, Pidmohyl'nyj introduces two new elements into the thematic composition of his hero: obsession and success.

In an interesting article that appeared in 1924, Myxajlo Dolengo (Klokov) argued that Pidmohyl'nyj's fundamental thematic preoccupation is 'the tragedy of futile exertion, of needless effort.' Characterizing Pidmohyl'nyj's thematic preoccupations as exclusively those of the intelligentsia (as opposed to the bourgeoisie or the proletariat), Dolengo outlined the basic structure of a typical Pidmohyl'nyj story:

1. A *Hero*, with a desperate antagonism to –
2. The *Environment*, which is completely oblivious to his presence (Representing this obliviousness there often, although not always, arises from this environment – a *heroine*).
3. *Strenuous exertion* by the hero in a supreme effort.
4. By way of an epilogue, an *attack on the emptiness*. The end reveals the tragic or tragi-comic needlessness of the hero's tragedy. Death and curtain.[13]

Although Dolengo's outline is tailored specifically to the stories in *Tvory: Tom 1*, his analysis is clearly applicable to the later stories as well. *Ostap Šaptala*, 'Povstanci,' 'Vijs'kovyj litun,' 'Tretja revoljucija,' and 'Ivan Bosyj' fit this general structure. Indeed, Pidmohyl'nyj's works all do.

Dolengo sees things from a Marxist perspective, evident in the condescension with which he describes the 'unnecessary tragedies' that Pidmohyl'nyj's heroes experience. For a Marxist, of course, an absolute faith in dialectical materialism makes all pessimism and existential uncertainty symptomatic of decadent intellectual theorizing. The 'tragedies' are unnecessary because they are completely preventable by conversion to the true faith (materialism). If this were the entire thrust of Dolengo's argument it would amount to little more than an interesting but tautological experiment. Indeed, his Marxist approach leads him to some very dubious assertions – for example, that the primary tension in 'Vanja' is in the juxtaposition of a child of the intelligentsia, Vanja, with a 'street kid,' Myt'ka, who tempts Vanja into actions not befitting a member of his class.[14] But Dolengo's argument is not based exclusively on Marxist principle: He suggests that the needlessness of the tragedies in Pidmohyl'nyj's stories is absolute. Any faith, whether it be Marxism, Christianity, or Buddhism, renders pessimism and cynicism unnecessary (and therefore evil, since by their intrinsic scepticism, these attitudes undermine the faith itself). Furthermore, pessimism and cynicism are also made unnecessary by an absolute lack of faith (pessimism is logically impossible in a world without values). It is on this level that Dolengo's argument is important, and it is on this level that its applicability to the Pidmohyl'nyj hero must be examined.

One characteristic that distinguishes Pidmohyl'nyj's later stories from those in *Tvory: Tom 1* is the nature of the 'tragedy' facing the protagonist. Although philosophically the difficulties confronting the protagonists in most of the early stories are instances of a universal situation – the individual's confrontation with his environment – in the text of the stories they are peculiar to the particular characters. For example, the sexual difficulties of the young heroes in 'Važke pytannja,' 'Prorok,' 'Na seli,' and 'Dobryj boh' are peculiar to inexperienced young men. In 'Hajdamaka' the disillusionment of Oles' is understood to be childish petulance even by the Red Army commander who takes pity on him. Vanja's nightmares are typical of a child's fears. And insofar as the hero of 'Starec'' is a cripple, his difficulties are seen to be peculiar to him. In the later stories, and in *Ostap Šaptala* Pidmohyl'nyj alters the nature of the hero's dilemma to allow for a universal thematic statement. Šaptala's struggle with mortality, Dančenko's battle against his own deformity, and Ksana's fascination with power are all experiences with which the reader can identify and sympathize. Furthermore, Pidmohyl'nyj depicts his later protagonists as obsessive people who struggle with their own psyches, and occasionally achieve partial victory. They are not mere puppets on a cosmic stage.

According to Dolengo's outline, the conflict in Pidmohyl'nyj's stories is between the hero and his environment. Again, we must make allowance for the critic's ideological bias. For Dolengo the 'environment' is a socioeconomic entity. In his analysis of 'Starec',' for example, he argues that Tymiš's difficulties arise from an incompatibility with the urban environment. Although this interpretation has some merit, it fails to explain the situation fully. Tymiš's conflict is not merely with the city, but with the world, in which he feels he has been denied a just and equitable place. Tymiš himself sees this injustice largely in financial and social terms, but the story as a whole does not endorse his perception. In most of the other stories in *Tvory: Tom 1*, this sociological definition of the parameters of the conflict is even less appropriate. Pidmohyl'nyj's heroes are in conflict with the environment in a metaphysical dimension. Conflict arises because humans are both physical and spiritual beings, whereas their environment is strictly physical.

The thematic conflict in Pidmohyl'nyj's stories is characteristically irresolvable. The dilemma of an individual in conflict with the environment has no philosophical answer. However, adjustment is possible. Man is capable of adapting – of learning to live in a world that seems hostile but is, in actuality, only indifferent. Among the stories in *Tvory: Tom 1*, that possibility never materialized; conflicts were not resolved. In 'Povstanci,' however, in the passage that describes the boys setting off to join the rebels, Pidmohyl'nyj offers a preview of the kind of solution he will present in some of his later stories. For the boys, success does not mean an intellectual balancing of the forces affecting their lives. They do not weigh the pros and cons of their decision. They do not evaluate the relative merits of home and family, on the one hand, and the social and political causes they are fighting for, on the other. Ostap drinks the strength of the steppe; Taras breathes the serenity of the silence. The victory is entirely one-sided. The boys have been absorbed into the fibres of a powerful, irrational force.

The force to which these boys are attracted and to which they eventually submit is not unique to this episode or even to this story. We have already seen it in Petro's soliloquy in 'Na seli,' in which he curses the sun because it beguiles the individual into abandoning his instinctive freedom, which is associated with night and the steppe.[15] It is the force that Šaptala feels within the earth as he lies on the ground outside the church before the Easter service. It is what pushes the dying man in 'Smert'' to rejoice at the sight of a beautiful woman. It is the force that drives the medical orderly to the river and Prisja into the arms of the stationmaster in 'V epidemičnomu baraci.' Indeed, this force is one of the most important recurring motifs in Pidmohyl'nyj's works. A miscellany published in Katerynoslav in 1921, *Vyr revoljuciji* (Vortex of the Revolution), contains an essay about Pidmohyl'nyj entitled 'Poet čariv noči' (Poet of the Magic of the Night). The phrase is particularly apt. For Jefremov it expresses Pidmohyl'nyj's 'realization of the subjective value of life and acceptance of it ... As if he were forgiving it all of its wrongs, its evil, its brutality and mercilessness, even harsh slavery, all on account of the beauty and magic of the night from the free steppes.'[16]

Jefremov has captured an essential feature of the early Pidmohyl'nyj. In his later works, however, Pidmohyl'nyj expands the 'magic of the night' into a larger force, the force of the material, non-reasoning world. It consists of the irrational, instinct, randomness, spirituality, mysticism, creativity, sickness, cruelty, violence, the fantastic, the metaphysical, the creative, the mysterious, the subconscious. This force is generally associated with the night, the steppe, and silence. It is commonly contrasted with sunlight, the city, and institutionalized human interaction. In the stories in *Tvory: Tom 1*, it often appears as sexual drive, in conflict with religion and public morality.

In 'Povstanci' the magic of the night appears as a central thematic element. In the first episode the boys overcome their rational and sentimental fears through physical contact with the talismans of night's magic. In subsequent episodes the magic of the night appears as the primary motivating force of the rebels. In the second episode, 'U štabi' (At Headquarters), the leader of the rebels, the *otaman*, is shown interacting with his soldiers. The *otaman* is friendly towards his men, who like and respect him. Their behaviour bears no resemblance to normal hierarchical military discipline. The model for this military organization is clearly the traditional, stereotypical image of the Zaporozhian Sich. One of the officers, a captain, is telling the *otaman* that the enemy unit, which numbers 150 men, has four machine guns. According to villagers in that area, the captain reports, the enemy unit is already scared to death of us. 'Bat'ku dozvol'' (Permit it, *otaman*), he pleads. When the *otaman* seems to hesitate, the captain's face darkens and his hand moves instinctively towards his sword. The crowd of rebels begins to grumble, soldiers call out, arguing among themselves: 'Of course he'll let us,' 'You don't find four machine guns just walking down the street.'

The *otaman* allows – or, rather, orders – his men to capture the machine guns. But the episode makes clear that his leadership is precarious. This group of soldiers, an anarchist band, is not really under the *otaman*'s command at all. They are a law unto themselves or, more specifically, they serve the magic of the night. A dark, irrational force is evident in the crowd's confrontation with their leader, particularly in the confrontation between the *otaman* and the drunk Omel'ko. The *otaman*'s gesture of yielding a seat to Omel'ko is a sign of his friendly, paternal attitude towards his men, a quality further evidenced in his interview with the young volunteer. None the less, the gesture is also part of a rational, calculated policy – namely, one of appeasement, which in the absence of any alternative, is good policy. In short, the *otaman* cannot command the wild forces of the steppe.

The motif of confrontation between rational leadership and the wild, explosive forces of the steppe recurs throughout 'Povstanci.' In the fifth episode, *Otaman* Kremnjuk calls Ensign Loboda out on the carpet. Loboda has openly displayed dissatisfaction with the rebel artillery's indiscriminate shelling of the city, which was unnecessary and avoidable:

Отаман посміхнувся й поклав руку на плече хорунжому.

   'Друже мій, ви прибули позавчора до повстанського табору з посвідкою від ес-ерів...'

'Ес-деків,' прикро заввважив хорунжий.

'Чи ес-деків, але вас іще треба виховувати. Так! Треба переробити вашу душу з партійної на повстанську та, замість соціялістичних мрій, вкласти вам у душу повстанську правду.' (*Povstanci*, 20)

The *otaman* smiled and put his hand on the ensign's shoulder.
  'My friend, you came to this rebel camp the day before yesterday from the S-Rs ... '
  'S-Ds,' the ensign noted with annoyance.
  'Or from the S-Ds, but you still need to learn. Yes! Your soul needs to be remade from that of a party member to that of a rebel. We need to replace your socialist dreams with rebel truth.'

With paternal solicitude, Kremnjuk tells Loboda about his own conversion from an idealistic, bourgeois social reformer into a rebel. It was only a year ago that he first rode out at night into the steppe, which frightened him. In wild ecstasy he galloped across it until his horse fell from exhaustion, and then he crawled on hands and knees, unable to escape its embrace. From that moment on, the force of the steppe, the magic of the night, had become a political program for the *otaman*:

І від того часу я не покинув степу. Я забув про кривду народню, коли відчув, як мучиться він, зораний безглуздям та засіяний містами. (*Povstanci*, 22)

Since then, I have never abandoned the steppe. I forgot about the injustices endured by the people when I felt how it suffers, ploughed with stupidity, sown with cities.

Like a common weed, Loboda bends to the influence of the flintlike Kremnjuk. At night, they mount up and set off into the steppe. When they reach a sown field, Kremnjuk deliberately charges through it, despite the ensign's protestations about trampling the grain. The *otaman* wants vengeance against those who torture the steppe, who restrict its expanse and freedom. By the time their exhausted horses stop, the ensign, too, has heard the song of the steppe. With spiritual solemnity, Kremnjuk proclaims: 'О, степе! Величній, неосяжний степе! Слава, слава тобі!' (O, steppe! Mighty, infinite steppe! Glory, glory to thee!). The magic of the night and Kremnjuk's passionate commitment to his political program have infected Loboda. When the *otaman* calls for the destruction of cities and villages in the name of the steppe, 'Хай гине все во ім'я його' (Let everything die in its name), Loboda intones.

The explicit combination of metaphysical forces and politics helps to explain the peculiarities of the structure Dolengo outlines. The conflict between hero and environment must be understood not as a social conflict, but as tension between two forces, a battle of ideas, a conflict between values that are uniquely human and values that are characteristically natural. On one side of the scales are reason, morality, sentiment, and civilization. On the other side are power, instinct, and sensuality. This vaguely Nietzschean dichotomy represents an irresolvable conflict from which, as Dolengo asserts, the protagonist attempts to escape. Escape is impossible, however, because both forces exist within the protagonist. The struggle itself is the obsession that typifies Pidmohyl'nyj's heroes in his later stories. What Dolengo calls the epilogue, the attack against emptiness, is the protagonist's response to the realization that the struggle is hopeless.

Superimposing this structure on the political formulas in 'Povstanci' reveals a number of paradoxes. For instance, in identifying the rebels with the irrational force Pidmohyl'nyj was not endorsing anarchism. Indeed, the critics who condemned him for his 'sympathetic' portrait of an anarchist band betrayed a careless reading of the story. The rebel city commander who is so proud of his ability to establish order in the city within three days has, in fact, failed to provide for the basic safety and well-being of its citizens: a building burns down because he did not organize a fire brigade. Similarly, no justification is offered for the indiscriminate bombardment of the city by rebel artillery. Loboda's conversion to Kremnjuk's point of view is a victory for the *otaman* and for the magic of the night, but not necessarily for the author or the reader. Unlike the earlier stories, those from Pidmohyl'nyj's second period do not end in a stalemate between the two forces. From the protagonist's perspective, victory is possible, the conflict can be resolved. In the thematic structure, however, this victory is still nothing more than an attack on the emptiness, an act of self-delusion.

Self-delusion and obsession are important motifs in two of Pidmohyl'nyj's best-known stories, 'Tretja Revoljucija' and 'Ivan Bosyj.' 'Tretja Revoljucija' is a story about the experiences of the Opanasovyč family after their city is taken by Maxno's forces. The family comprises Hryhorij, an official of the postal service; his wife, Marta Danylivna; her elderly brother, Andrij Petrovyč, apparently a widower; Andrij Petrovyč's daughter, Ksana, whose husband was recently killed by Maxno's rebels; and Marta and Hryhorij's younger son, Kol'ka, a tenth-grader. In the course of the story, their older son, Al'oša, visits his mother at home. He is a Bolshevik spy in Maxno's camp, and his political education comes from his uncle, Andrij Petrovyč, an old socialist who had been sent to Siberia under the tsar.

As the story opens, Ksana is staring out the window, hoping to catch a glimpse of the battle. Her father urges her to join the rest of the family, who are waiting out the danger in the basement. The colour wheel of imperial politics takes another turn – the Whites lose, the Blacks win – and Maxno's forces enter the city. Each member of the family reacts in his or her own way. When she learns that Maxno has won, Marta Danylivna cries out in terror, but when three soldiers enter her home in the night, she greets them with forced graciousness, seating them on her finest chairs and later inviting them to come again. When she relates their visit to Ksana, who was asleep at the time, she convinces herself that the situation is not so bad:

'Знаєш, вони такі прості.... Зовсім не такі страшні як казали.... Прості хлопці. Взяли гроші – так усі ж беруть. Погрозились убити – – так це всі так. А не грабували.' (*Tretja*, 13 / *Misto*, 419 / BUL, 211)

'You know, they're just regular boys ... Not at all as frightening as people had said ... Just regular boys. They took money – well, they all do that. They threatened to kill us – they all do that, too. But they didn't rob us.'

When the official shakedown comes a few days later and her home is indeed robbed, Marta Danylivna's illusions will dissipate. So will her husband's, but for now he has retreated into the illusion of routine and tranquillity at the post office. They both want to believe that their lives will not change drastically, that the revolution will not alter the values they hold as eternal verities. They both know, too, that they are deceiving themselves.

Andrij Petrovyč is another willing victim of his own illusions. He is obsessed with political action and has lost touch with reality. When Al'oša comes home, uncle and nephew discuss politics together, as they did of old. Their conversation focuses on the divergence between ideals and tactics, between theory and practice. The old socialist praises the bolsheviks for their vigorous implementation of theoretical principles. In the course of the discussion, he holds forth on the opposition of wisdom and passion:

'Золота старість, а хто хотів би її мати? Хіба всю мудрість не варто віддати за однісінький шматок невеличкого, поганенького пориву? Мудрість шкідлива, коли не служити пориву.... Це зрозуміло, і це трагедія! Щоб жити, треба знати, а знання вбиває. Людськість хитається між дикунством і культурою. А їх треба поєднати, не протиставити! Мудрість, де не бренить тонкий відгомін голодного вию й поклику на самицю – є мудрість смерти....' (*Tretja*, 20 / *Misto*, 423 / BUL, 214–15)

'Golden old age, who wants it? Isn't it worth trading all wisdom for a single smidgen of passion? Wisdom is harmful, when it's not in the service of passion. This is understandable, but it is also a tragedy. To live, you need knowledge, yet knowledge kills. Humanity vacillates between savagery and culture. But the two should be united, not kept apart as opposites. Wisdom without the ringing of the thin quiver of hunger's howl and of the instinct for the female is the wisdom of death.'

In Andrij Petrovyč's opinion, the Bolsheviks have combined these extremes successfully. Social justice is finally coupled with the magic of the night. His praise for party tactics does not, however, extend to party members:

'Дитино моя,' мовив він, 'я хотів сказати, що є схема для людей і схема для душі. Так от не давай, щоб схема душу опанувала! Бо це провадить до неприємного царства папуг і малп....' (*Tretja*, 21 / *Misto*, 424 / BUL, 215)

'My son,' he said, 'I meant to say that there is a scheme for people and a scheme for the soul. Don't let the scheme overcome your soul. That leads to an unpleasant kingdom of parrots and monkeys ... '

Andrij Petrovyč is comfortable casting himself as a symbol of venerable wisdom in an age of vigorous action, but he is also happy to chop down trees along the city streets for firewood. When the shakedown is over, he is content because he has lost only a hat and his favourite glass. He reads the various newspapers and wonders at the monotonous sameness of all the political platforms and at the number of people who lose their lives because of them.

Al'oša, the Bolshevik, is as complacent as his uncle. He defends his party's practical measures against his uncle's charge of savagery, but admits that, as a spy in Maxno's camp he has witnessed the execution of seventeen fellow Bolsheviks. He laughs condescendingly at his uncle's armchair philosophizing and offers an elaborate but unconvincing rationalization for his own role as a spy.

When Maxno's forces take the city, only Kol'ka and Ksana are not disappointed. Kol'ka has an adolescent's interest in battles and in the larger-than-life figures, like Maxno, who participate in them. Moreover, his stature in the family has risen dramatically since the disturbances began. Whether as a lookout at the window or as an escort for the women when they leave the house, his services are taken seriously. Kol'ka wants nothing more than to be taken seriously, to show his helpless elders that his practical skills are necessary for survival in the current situation. He does not distinguish between savagery and civilization. In his world, success is its own reward. But when he discovers Ksana in the pantry after the shakedown, he can only call his uncle for help.

It is no accident that Ksana, like her cousin, Kol'ka (Mykola, Nikolai), is referred to by a children's diminutive form of her name. Oksana (Ksana) has, since her husband's murder, reverted to a child-like state. The trauma of her husband's death has also apparently released a repressed sexuality. Her childhood sexual fantasies return in dreams featuring the powerful, bloodthirsty savage Maxno, who gently and tenderly embraces her:

Їй здавалося вже, що вона бачила була переможника в своїх юнацьких снах, коли вперше прокидалося тремтіння її грудей. Все життя її, що було, схилилося перед заповідним, що має бути. Серед блідого дня, в схолоднілих промінняx осени розцвітала її остання любов.

То не була жага. Коли прийде вечір цього дня, вона гладитиме його закинуте назад волосся й дивитиметься вглиб його могутніх очей. Він лежатиме їй на радісних колінах і тихо розповість у тьмяних присмерках дивну історію свого життя. Він розкриє в її обіймах таємниці своєї сили і ті сховані джерела, що живлять його волю. Вона відчуватиме його серце, напоєне хвилями чужої крови, що він мусів пролити, щоб бути. І смертельна рука його спочине на її плечі, оповита великою ніжністю, що створила вона в жаху і болю. (*Tretja*, 42 / *Misto*, 436 / BUL, 228)

It seemed to her that she had seen the conqueror in her youthful dreams, when the first tremors were awakening in her breast. All her past life was fading before the promised future. On a pale day, in the cool rays of an autumn sun, her final love was blossoming.

It was not lust. That evening she would stroke his thrown-back hair and look deeply into his powerful eyes. He will lie on her joyful knees and in the dim twilight he will tell her the strange story of his life. In her arms he will uncover the secrets of his strength and the hidden sources that nourish his will. She will feel his heart, nurtured by waves of the blood of his victims, which he had to spill in order to exist. And on her shoulder he will rest his deadly hand, wrapped in a great tenderness created in terror and pain.

Pidmohyl'nyj's use of Freudian psychology in this passage offers another objectification of the magic of the night. In the characters of Maxno and Ksana, the instinctive force appears as a combination of peasant anarchism and sexual libido. But in both cases, the characters perform their roles uneasily or self-consciously. Like the *otaman* in 'Povstanci,' Maxno has two sides to his character. On one hand, he is the notoriously savage leader of a bloodthirsty band of anarchists. At a victory celebration he shoots a prostitute because he does not like the way she smiles at him. But the next day he is remorseful, and worries about the savagery of his army. He writes sentimental poetry in which he apostrophizes the steppe and the night, lamenting his lost youth.[17] As commander, he administers justice, distributes money, and establishes order. The magic of the night is balanced in his character by rational and sentimental concerns and by the tactical advice of his ideological adviser, Volin, 'the Lenin of the anarchists.'

Ksana is in some ways a much simpler character. She appears in only a few scenes and the reader is not given much of an opportunity to judge her before her encounter with Maxno. To the extent that her fascination with violence and her attraction to Maxno are pathological results of the psychological trauma caused by the murder of her husband, her character is simply a case study along Freudian lines. But Pidmohyl'nyj does not allow the reader to pity Ksana. By associating her with Kol'ka and by discrediting those who pity her – her father and her aunt, for example – as muddled dreamers, Pidmohyl'nyj suggests to the reader that Ksana is a strong, confident woman who does not need the reader's pity. On this level, Ksana is another example of Pidmohyl'nyj's use of obsession as an integral feature of personality. Ksana cannot resist the self-destructive impulse of her obsession. In the thematic structure of the story, the actual cause or stimulus of the obsession is irrelevant. Obsession as a thematic element is a reaction to disillusionment and alienation. When her mundane, ordered, bourgeois life is shattered by the murder of her husband, Ksana chooses to follow the opposite force, the chaotic and sensual magic of the night, which is personified by Maxno's army and, in her mind, by Maxno himself. But her idea of the nature of this force is mistaken: The magic of the night does not inhabit prettified sentimental illusions. It is not a mixture of civilized sinfulness, thoughtless brutality, and intellectual dishonesty, as in the depiction of Maxno, but a wild and violent power that leaves Ksana on the pantry floor, a monstrous mound of raped flesh.

The title character of 'Ivan Bosyj' is another of Pidmohyl'nyj's obsessed protagonists. Ivan Bosyj, as he calls himself (the surname means 'barefoot'), is a twentieth-century Old Testament prophet, a descendant of Jevhenij

Pereponenko in 'Prorok' and a precursor of Anatolij Petrovyč Paščenko in *Povist' bez nazvy*. He chastises the people for their sinfulness. They have forgotten God and installed the Antichrist. The current drought in the land is God's punishment for these sins. Ivan Bosyj calls on the people to repent:

> Схаменіться, люде, прозріть свої злочини й покайтеся! Проженіть Сатану із свого серця й дітей Антихриста зпоміж себе. Освятіть мечі і станьте на захист Бога. Затопіть свої гріхи у крові тих, хто олукавив вас, і нею принесіть вечірню жертву Богові. Тоді впаде дощ на ваші землі й ласка Божа вам у серця. (*Povstanci*, 27 / BUL, 132)

> Come to your senses, people. See your sins and repent. Chase Satan from your hearts and the children of the Antichrist from among you. Bless your swords and rise in defence of God. Drown your sins in the blood of those who have deceived you and, by their blood, bring an evening sacrifice to God. Then the rain will fall on your lands and God's grace will come into your hearts.

After Bosyj's dramatic appearance in the village the incidence of rebel activity rises dramatically. Trains are derailed and looted, government and party officials are assassinated. The army is sent in to quell the rebellion, and a party committee meeting is called to decide what to do about Bosyj. The chief of police is given the committee's instructions. 'This is interesting,' he says, 'I've never fought against saints before.' One day, while out in the countryside on other business, he and another policeman encounter Bosyj, who makes one of his usual speeches.

> Їхні погляди, врешті зустрілись, і здивований начміліції перестав сміятися. Він побачив, що тут має бути якась дивна боротьба, зовсім не схожа на ті, що їх йому доводилось досі мати. Їхні погляди схрестились, як шпади, й вони напружено дивились один-одному в вічі. За хвилину начміліції почув, що в'януть його очі і бгається його душа. Він затремтів, ніби падаючи, перед ним потьмарніло, й він сам ніби потопав у сухих хвилях, що падали йому на голову, як розпечений пісок. Тоді, скрививши обличчя, він з'єднав усі сили й наставив револьвер на груди пророка.
> Когутик клацнув, а пострілу не було. (*Povstanci*, 33 / BUL, 137)

> At last their eyes met, and the astonished chief of police stopped laughing. He saw that this was to be a strange battle, not like any he had fought before. Their gazes crossed like sabres, and they stared at each other tensely. After a

moment the chief of police felt his eyes wilting and his spirit bending. He trembled, as if he were about to fall, and his vision dimmed. He seemed to be sinking in dry waves that were falling on his head like sun-baked sand. His face contorted, he summoned all his energy and put his revolver to the prophet's chest.

The hammer struck, but there was no shot.

The second policeman runs off, terrified by the miracle. Bosyj, with otherworldly serenity, curses the chief and slowly walks away. The chief recovers after a moment, jumps off his horse, and runs after Bosyj. When he gets to within a few steps of him, he takes his rifle off his back, aims, and shoots.

'Ivan Bosyj' differs from many other Pidmohyl'nyj stories in that it is not the obsessed character who experiences psychological conflict. Bosyj exists in the story only as a catalyst, a symbol of the magic of the night. It is the chief of police who must confront his own illusions. In the encounter with Bosyj, the chief feels the power of a superior force. When his pistol fails, so does the chief's faith in his own daylight world. A moment later, the chief recovers his composure and kills Bosyj with brutal contempt, but his faith in himself has been shaken. The second shot he fires into the prophet's body is guided by the very that force whose symbol he has just killed. In Dolengo's scheme, the story of the police chief is a parallel to that of Bosyj. They are both heroes. In this parallel subplot, the chief's second shot is the futile attack on the emptiness that Dolengo's scheme predicts.

'Ivan Bosyj' is the only story besides 'Vanja' in which Pidmohyl'nyj makes the fantastic explicit. Although it might be possible to explain the failure of the pistol and the spontaneous opening of the lock on the church door naturally, this is not done in the story itself. Ironically, and as in the work of such masters of the *conte fantastique* as Guy de Maupassant, Pidmohyl'nyj's use of the fantastic goes hand in hand with a degree of realism that would be appropriate in historical fiction. 'Ivan Bosyj,' for example, is built around the facts of the famine in Ukraine in 1921–22. The drought and the concurrent peasant uprisings are historical facts.[18] Realistic elements such as these have an independent significance both as subjects and as themes, but in the thematic structure of the story, their role is symbolic. They are part of the constellation of forces mythologized by Bosyj. In other words, they are deliberately given a dual status, as both material actuality and spiritual manifestation. This combination makes them symbols of the psychic tension of the Pidmohyl'nyj hero.

The famine of 1921–22, a precursor of the genocide that followed a decade later, also appears in another of Pidmohyl'nyj's stories, 'Syn' (The Son), which, in one edition is subtitled 'A Story from the Time of the Famine.'[19] In this story Pidmohyl'nyj describes a son's heroic efforts to save his mother from starvation. He succeeds in enrolling her on a list of those eligible for American relief supplies, but she dies before the supplies arrive. The son, Vasjurenko, who is also starving, pretends his mother is still alive in order to get her food ration. Hunger and trauma have affected his mind, however, and he drifts in and out of madness. After he misses a food pick-up, his rich sister, who refused Vasjurenko's pleas to help their mother, comes to see what has happened. When she finds him alone, lying motionless on the floor, she accuses him of cannibalizing their mother and runs out of the house to get help:

Ввесь двір наливався народом. Баби штовхались, щоб стати попереду. Переказували, що хтось бачив, як Васюренко білував матір і вночі варив з неї юшку. Догадувались, що й малий Савчин син, що пропав, пішов теж Васюренкові на печеню.
Голова сільради постукав ціпком у двері.
'Виходь.'
Васюренко вийшов і спинився на порозі, держачись за двері. Всі ойкнули – він повстав ніби з домовини, сухий, згорблений, якийсь покручений, мов корч.
'Признавайсь, ти з'їв матір?' гукнув голова.
'Ні,' відповів Васюренко, 'вона сама померла, а я викинув її у льох.'
'Бреше, бреше,' загомоніли навкруги.
Голова сільради звелів оглянути льох. Там справді лежало тіло.
'Ти нащо так зробив? Ти знаєш, як строго тепер нащот мертвяків? Щоб зарази не було! Тобі ліньки було поховати!'
Баби були невдоволені. Казали, що Васюренко вже добре матір об'їв, а сьогодні вночі докінчив би, так оце перебили.
'Щоб ти мені льох закидав! Щоб мені тут зарази не було. Чуєш?'
Васюренко похитав головою.
'Ні,' промовив він, 'несила вже мені.'
Голова сільради ударив його ціпком.
'От, злодюга! То це я мушу робити?'
Натовп розходився. Стара Кандзюбиха казала, що це місце треба посвятити. (*Misto*, 370 / BUL, 155–56)

The yard was filling up with people. The old women were pushing and shoving to get up front. They were saying that someone had seen Vasjurenko skinning his mother and cooking up a broth from her corpse. They decided that Sava's boy, who was missing, had probably become Vasjurenko's roast.

The chairman of the village council knocked on the door with his staff.

'Come on out.'

Vasjurenko came out and stopped on the doorstep, supporting himself on the door. The crowd gasped. He seemed to have risen from a coffin, thin, bent, and somehow twisted, like a shrub.

'Did you eat your mother?' yelled the chairman.

'No,' answered Vasjurenko, 'she died on her own, and I threw her into the cellar.'

'He's lying,' murmured the crowd.

The chairman ordered that the cellar be searched. The body was, indeed, there.

'Why did you do that? You know how strictly burial laws are enforced now. To prevent the spread of disease. And you were too lazy to bury her.'

The old ladies were disappointed. They said Vasjurenko had eaten most of her already and would have finished her off tonight, but for this interruption.

'You fill in that cellar, you hear! I'd better not have any disease spreading from here.'

Vasjurenko shook his head.

'No,' he said, 'I don't have the strength.'

The chairman hit him with his staff.

'What a thief! So now I have to do it?'

The crowd was dispersing. Old Kandzjubyxa was saying that this place had to be blessed.

This passage illustrates, once again, how realistic detail acquires both stylistic and thematic significance in Pidmohyl'nyj's works. The depiction of conditions in the village is, of course, an independent element. Social realism is not Pidmohyl'nyj's chief priority as a writer, but his works are replete with images that detail social and political conditions in Ukraine in the 1920s. The story opens with Vasjurenko returning by train from the city, where he has tried to buy food. Returning on the same train is his wealthy brother-in-law, Kornijčuk. Whereas Vasjurenko has managed to exchange all his possessions for a single loaf of bread, Kornijčuk sits on sacks of grain, eating heartily. The suggestion that food can be found in the city away from the starving villages amounts to an indictment of the current regime. Moreover, the famine is further impoverishing the poor while Kornijčuk and others like him buy up the property of starving peasants for pennies. Other important elements of social realism in the story are found in the depictions of the impact of the railway, the workings of the American relief program, and the general backwardness of the village.

In the passage just quoted Pidmohyl'nyj displays the various forces at work in the village. In a different context the scene could be taken for comedy. Two very different worlds are presented. The chairman of the village council is a reasonable and compassionate, if rather selfish, man. Kandzjubyxa, by contrast, is a small-minded, superstitious old woman. As individuals, they represent extremes on a black-and-white matrix of village society. The majority of the villagers are, of course, somewhere in between, and Pidmohyl'nyj depicts them in shades of grey. The two principles of human motivation, reason and instinct, are not mutually exclusive. Kornijčuk sits on his stacks of grain, unwilling to help his starving brother-in-law because he is greedy. But the advice he gives Vasjurenko about prospects in the province of Poltava is, if not well-intentioned, at least reasonable. His equally greedy wife refuses to share a loaf of bread with her starving mother, but when she suspects her brother of cannibalism, she is sincerely outraged. Stepan Bezrukavyj has the good sense to find a way to exchange his possessions for enough grain to feed himself and his family, but, when he is robbed on his way home with it, he falls into utter despair.

The central figure in the drama of mixed motives is Vasjurenko. He is a man of honour. He will not steal for food or beg beyond the point of self-respect. He starves himself to keep his old, sickly mother alive. But hunger for food, like the hunger for sex in Pidmohyl'nyj's earlier stories, is an irresistible force.[20] As Vasjurenko's mind dims from starvation, his dogmatic principles cannot withstand the natural imperatives of his body. He succumbs to dishonesty. He keeps his mother's death a secret so that he may continue to receive her portion of the relief supplies, which are issued only to children and the infirm. But in Pidmohyl'nyj's world, this moral compromise is nothing more than an attack on the emptiness. Vasjurenko tolerated hunger to maintain his honour, but when he could hold out no longer, traded honour for life. In the end, he is left with neither. In an earlier story entitled 'Sobaka' (The Dog), a young student experiences hunger for want of money and discovers a fundamental dichotomy between his stomach and his intellect. There is no choice, however, only a dichotomy.

Stories such as 'Syn' and 'Ivan Bosyj,' and, especially 'Tretja Revoljucija' and 'Povstanci,' have an important theme in common. In all of them, the city and the village are in conflict. They are presented as natural antagonists. For the village, the city is a disease that must be defeated and expunged from the social organism. In 'Tretja Revoljucija,' the narrator describes the general shakedown of the city by Maxno's soldiers as follows:

The Later Stories

Цей день записано на скрижалях міста, що знало чотирнадцять влад перед тим і багато по тому. Кам'яне й гордовите, оселя культури і зверхности, воно навколішках приймало ганьбу від буйного села, що залило його вулиці. Село вийшло з своїх мазанок і стріх, поклало руку на той незрозумілий механізм, звідки йшли усі накази, куди возилось податки, де жили дідичі, лунала чужа мова і зникав викоханий у степах хліб. Село прийшло один раз могутнє, і місто стенулося з палкого подиху степів, здавалось уже підвладних назавсігди. А от сталася третя революція – похід села на місто. (*Tretja*, 44–45 / *Misto*, 438 / BUL, 229)

> This day was etched in the city's memory, despite the fact that the city had known fourteen occupations before this one and would know many after it. Proud and unshakeable within its stone walls, this seat of culture and superiority received on its knees the shame inflicted on it by the wild village, which had poured out onto its streets. The village had emerged from its mud huts and thatched roofs and had put its hand on that incomprehensible mechanism from which came all orders, to which taxes were sent, where the fat landowners lived, where a foreign language was spoken, and where the steppe's lovingly cultivated grain disappeared. This time, the village was strong and the city trembled under the torrid breath of the steppe, which had seemed to be conquered forever. But a third revolution had come – the attack of the village on the city.

The theme of village and city is very important in Pidmohyl'nyj's works. As we shall see in chapter 5, it has particular relevance in his first novel, *Misto*, and many critical discussions of that work focus on this subject. It is no less important in the earlier works. Indeed, from the earliest stories to his last work, *Povist' bez nazvy*, the contrast between village and city is rarely absent from Pidmohyl'nyj's works.

One key to the significance of the juxtaposition of village and city is the similarity of this theme to the conflict between the magic of the night and the logic of the day. In such scenes as that of *Otaman* Kremnjuk and Loboda galloping through the steppe and threatening destruction to all cities ('Povstanci'), that of Ivan Bosyj condemning the new Tower of Babylon (*Povstanci*, 27 / BUL, 132), or that of Maxno's anarchist army pillaging the city and raping its inhabitants, the village is closely associated with the magic of the night. The association of the village with irrational forces can be interpreted as a political statement, and it is hardly surprising that many did interpret it that way.[21] Even today, readings of Pidmohyl'nyj's stories often insist on a political and sociological perspective. Volodymyr Mel'nyk, for example, sees in Pidmohyl'nyj's stories a reflection of the national and economic problems facing Ukrainian villages as a result of a hostile government policy.[22] Indeed, given the divergence between the actual social conditions in Ukraine and the regime's ideological insistence on harmony between the city and the village, any writer who depicted reality was likely to be accused of politically subversive motives. And when the writer's subject matter included such delicate issues as that of Nestor Maxno, an accusation of treason was virtually assured.

To the extent that Pidmohyl'nyj did not bend his pen to the shape demanded by the prevailing ideology, he can be considered an enemy of the regime. But a thematic interpretation of his works shows that whether it be the conflict he depicts between city and village or any of the other subjects for which he was accused of disloyalty, Pidmohyl'nyj's recurrent themes are part of a consistent pattern of ideas that has no direct political significance. While he was certainly not an active supporter of the new regime, the anti-Soviet quality of his writing lies in the eye of the beholder.

During the third period of his creativity, urban landscapes occur more frequently in Pidmohyl'nyj's stories than they did in *Tvory: Tom 1*. The city serves as a setting in 'Tretja Revoljucija,' 'Vijs'kovyj litun,' 'Problema xliba,' 'Istorija pani Jivhy,' and 'Sobaka.' Even more significant than the frequency of urban settings is the greater number of urban characters in these later works. In Pidmohyl'nyj's first collection, the only urban character is Tymiš in 'Starec," and even in that case, there is little to distinguish him from a villager. The protagonists of 'Dobryj boh,' 'Važke pytannja,' 'Prorok,' and 'Na seli' may occasionally visit the city, some may even live there for a time, but they are never more than transplanted villagers. By contrast, the family of Hryhorij Opanasovyč, in 'Tretja revoljucija,' is distinctly bourgeois. Their behaviour, values, and interests are clearly related to their urban status. Hryhorij's loyalty to his job at the postal service, Marta Danylivna's attachment to her furniture, and Andrij Petrovyč's sentimental theorizing about socialism are all qualities that would be alien to village characters. The same is true of the protagonists of the other stories set in urban environments.

Jivha Narčevs'ka, the protagonist of 'Istorija pani Jivhy,' may be a villager transplanted to the city, but her suggestions to her son, André, about distributing the land to the peasants make it clear that she has lost her ties to the soil. Her attitudes are now based on abstract principles of justice acquired through her reading of socialist literature, not on instinctive feelings of good will. She has no more understanding of the peasants now than she did before the revolution of 1905, when they killed her husband. Her son is different: He has a native ability and a natural inclination for estate management. Pidmohyl'nyj compares André with Ser'oha, the maid's son, whom Jivha tries to teach. The difference between them and Jivha lies in their motivation. For better or worse, André and Ser'oha act out of instinct. By contrast, Jivha Narčevs'ka is a textbook example of bad faith: She is guided by an acquired abstract notion. The city is mannered and intellectual, whereas the village is straightforward and physical.

A similar juxtaposition of the physical and the intellectual is at the thematic centre of 'Sobaka' (The Dog), a story Pidmohyl'nyj wrote in 1920. The date is significant because the story, about a young man who has run out of money and can no longer buy food, shows that Pidmohyl'nyj was drawn to the theme of hunger before it emerged as a major social issue a year later with the famine. To Pidmohyl'nyj, offered an opportunity to describe a confrontation between the physical and intellectual sides of human nature, between material and spiritual reality. Tymerhej, the protagonist of the story, is a student at the university. His daily life is governed by two mutually exclusive forces: 'Кант і борщ. Ніцше і ковбаса' (Kant and borsch. Nietzsche and sausage; *Misto*, 330 / BUL, 116). Since the story is written in a comic mode, Pidmohyl'nyj allows himself direct exposition in the form of indirect narration:

Тимергей ліг на Кнайбенкове ліжко й застиг. Почав думати й пригадувати все. Пригадав, що до цього часу він тільки й робив, що будував високу й грубу стіну з книжок. Пригадав, як з кожною книжкою, вкладеною в стіну, щораз менше бачив він життя. Воно було десь там, ніби далеко від нього, одмежоване паперовою цеглою. Іноді тільки доносився гомін життя й намагався потурбувати його своїми барвами, але Тимергей не піддавався: він жив у своїй фортеці як хотів.

Не стало грошей. Раптом розлетілася стіна, життя накинулось на Тимергея, почало шарпати його, зводити з людьми, що з ними він не мав нічого спільного, та примушувало писати в канцеляріях безглузді картки.

Коли ж йому стало до моторошності ясно, що він ненавидить картки і товстого діловода, що робив йому розпорядження, він кинув усе: канцелярію, картки, навіть лекції й улюблений паперовий мур.

Так, так, під три чорти все! (*Misto*, 329 / BUL, 115)

Tymerhej lay down on Knajbenko's bed and began thinking and remembering everything. He remembered that until now he had done nothing more than build a high and thick wall of books. He remembered how with each book he put into the wall he saw less and less of life. It was somewhere out there, far away, on the other side of the paper wall. Sometimes just the echo of life would get through to him, trying to disturb him with its colours, but Tymerhej did not surrender. He lived on in his fortress as he pleased.

The money ran out. Suddenly, the wall crumbled and life pounced on Tymerhej. It began to tear at him, running him up against people with whom he had nothing in common, forcing him to fill out ridiculous forms in the offices of some bureaucracy.

When it became frighteningly clear to him that he despised the forms and the fat bureaucrat who gave him instructions, he gave up everything: the office, the forms, even the lectures and the paper wall.

Yes, yes, to hell with everything.

In this story Pidmohyl'nyj is still concentrating on the magic of the night, on the physical side of human existence. What Tymerhej isolates with his paper wall is defined explicitly as life. Kant and Nietzsche – the intellectual side of the opposition – are packed off in an imaginary comic dialogue with Descartes:

Пообідавши, заплющую очі та кличу до себе Декарта. Питаю його:
'Декарте! Ти голодував коли?'
'Ні,' каже.
'Біжи ж мерщій та нищи свої праці. Потім не поїж тиждень і створи нові. Тоді матимеш ти певний ґрунт. Тоді ти, на приклад, не скажеш:
'Cogito, ergo sum ... ' А закричиш: 'Ой, їсточки ... ergo sum!''
'Пам'ятай, що право на існування має лише те, що можна спожити.'
'Іди ж, Декарте.' (*Misto*, 331 / BUL, 116–17)

After dinner I close my eyes and call Descartes and ask him:
'Descartes! Did you ever go hungry?'
'No,' he says.
'Go, immediately, and destroy all of your works. Then don't eat for a week and write new ones. Then you'll stand on a firm foundation. Then, for example, you will not say 'Cogito, ergo sum ... ' but rather you'll yell, 'Give me food ... ergo sum!''
'Remember, only that which is edible has a right to exist.'
'Go now, Descartes.'

The Later Stories

At first glance 'Sobaka' may seem far removed from the city-versus-village theme, but, on closer consideration, an important connection becomes apparent. Tymerhej is a quintessentially urban man. His paper wall is the municipal boundary. The conflict he experiences is not between city and village *per se*; rather it is the urban variant of a conflict whose rural equivalent we have already seen in other stories. The two sets of thematic polarities, urban versus rural and intellectual versus physical, are parallel expressions of a single underlying idea. What is important about 'Sobaka' is that it shows Pidmohyl'nyj exploring different manifestations of his central theme. In most of the stories we have examined thus far the protagonists welcome the power of the magic of the night. With Tymerhej, Pidmohyl'nyj makes a preliminary, comic attempt to examine a character who willfully struggles against it.

Another such character is Serhij Dančenko, the hero of 'Vijs'kovyj litun.' Dančenko is one of Pidmohyl'nyj's more complex creations. The son of a family who had been wealthy landowners before the Revolution, Dančenko is returning to his native city after five years of active military service in the Soviet Air Force. In the 1920s, airplanes were a very new development, and Pidmohyl'nyj's choice of pilots as representatives of a new age was particularly apt. Such are Dančenko and his fellow pilots, whose squadron is being stationed in the city. The epigraph that introduces the story, the last four lines of Franko's *Mojsej* (Moses), describes the nation of Israel in its historic role of trail-blazer. Dančenko and the other flyers are also champions of a new age, but they are also men who live in an illusory past:

З неяснимострахом пішов Данченко у місто. Він давно вже носив його в своїй душі. П'ять років безупинної мандрівки з фронту на фронт, голод, безсонні ночі взимку коло вогнища, коли все всередині бралося кригою і застигало, тисячі таких ночей і одноманітних днів – викохали йому теплий малюнок рідного міста. Там, звідки вернувся, він не мав нічого свого, і цей малюнок переховував, як єдине багацтво. Він любив тепер місто більше, ніж тоді, коли жив тут. Ночі холоду й дні спраги виткали йому чудове мереживо спогадів, може й неправдивих зовсім, але теплих і втішних. (*Misto*, 372 / BUL, 157–58)

Dančenko felt a vague fear as he entered the city. He had been carrying that fear in his soul for a long time now. Five years of ceaseless wandering from front to front, hunger, sleepless nights in the winter by a fire when everything inside turns to motionless ice – thousands of such nights and monotonous days had bred in him a warm image of his native city. Back there, where he was coming from, he had nothing of his own and he held on to that image as his only treasure. He liked the city more now than he had when he lived here. Cold nights and thirsty days had woven a beautiful tapestry of recollections, and though they may not have been altogether true, they were warm and comforting.

Amid the waste and destruction of the city, Haločka, Dančenko's cousin, is a breath of springtime. Her beauty and vitality rekindle for him the illusion he longs for, which the city itself proves inadequate to sustain. Dančenko is all the more attracted to her because her beauty contrasts so sharply with his own deformity. A hunchback from birth, he is short and has overly long arms, a flat nose, thin lips, narrow eyes, and sparse hair. His deformity has isolated him from people:

Він думав про себе, і йому було шкода свого життя. Він чудно жив – якось між іншим. Уродився калікою – його віддали нянькам, він батьків навіть бачив нечасто. Жив на самоті, родичі цурались його, хлопці, з якими він хотів гуляти, глузували й тікали від нього. Так і виріс з думкою, що на цьому світі для нього немає нічого. На той світ він не покладав теж надій, і врешті байдужість опанувала його. Тільки деколи мріяв, але й мрії були невиразні, – він навіть добре не знав, про що треба мріяти. Книжок читав багато, захоплювався буддизмом і довго міркував поїхати до Індії. Але так і не поїхав, зробивсь літуном підчас війни, полюбив літунство й уже не кидав його. Так двадцять вісім років прожив, чи то дурнем великим, чи великим мудрецем.

'Треба спочити,' гадав Сергій; 'обридла вже блуканина.'

І наймиліше було йому те, що спочиватиме він тут, коло рідних. Разом обідатимуть, ввечері розмовлятимуть, і Галочка буде сміятися своїм чистим сміхом. (*Misto*, 375 / BUL, 161)

When he thought about his life he felt sorry for himself. His life was strange. Born a cripple, he was turned over to nursemaids – he didn't often see his parents. He lived in isolation: his parents shunned him, the boys he wanted to play with made fun of him and ran away. He grew up thinking that there was nothing in this world for him. He didn't put much faith in the next world either, and eventually he was overcome by apathy. Sometimes he would still dream, but the dreams were indistinct – he didn't really know what he should dream about. He read a great deal, became fascinated with Buddhism, and even thought of going to India for a time. But he didn't go. He became a flyer during the war and came to enjoy flying and wasn't going to give it up now. Twenty-eight years he had lived this way, either a great fool or a very wise man.

'I need to settle down,' Serhij thought. 'I've had enough wandering.'

The best part was that he would settle here, by his family. They would take meals together, spend the evening in conversation, and Haločka's clear laughter would ring through the house.

The hope and idealism that spring from suffering and deprivation may be noble sentiments, but they are not healthy ones. Beauty and good intentions cannot alter human nature, they can only mask it. Human nature, moreover, is neither cruel nor evil; it is merely instinctive. Serhij Dančenko has spent his life investing his emotional energies in a series of symbols, which, because they were only symbols, dreams that did not and could not partake of reality, invariably failed him. So it was with Buddhism and with his image of the city, and so it will be with Haločka and with the café that the pilots' squadron has established.

In the course of the story, Serhij discovers that the feeling he has for Haločka is not just an abstract affection but also a physical drive. Sexual obsession gradually replaces his platonic idealism. As he becomes conscious of this change in his feelings, he becomes increasingly withdrawn and frightened. When Haločka decides to send her sick mother to an institution rather than care for her at home, Serhij realizes that she, too, is guided by interests and instincts that outweigh her sense of duty to her mother. Finally he confronts his own image in the poet who comes to give herself to him because he is a flyer, a symbol of the new age, but who runs away when she sees his deformity. Her last words to him stick in his mind: Pilots like him should not descend to the ground. The next day he takes up one of the squadron's planes and dies in a crash when it runs out of fuel.

In 'Vijs'kovyj litun' Pidmohyl'nyj presents several obsessed characters who struggle with reality. Serhij cannot come to terms with the dissolution of his ideals into instinctive sensuality. Haločka, too, is shocked to discover that the happiness for which she sacrificed her sense of duty to her mother is only temporary, as her flyer-boyfriend is reassigned to another city. Nor can Haločka's mother accept the world as it is. Hopelessly absorbed in political speculation, she pursues a naïve revenge against the Communist government that has destroyed both her husband and Serhij's father. On the other side of the political divide, Vasyl', Serhij's only friend in the flyers' squadron, is a cynic and an opportunist. He meets all his enemies head-on, but he cannot vanquish his self-disgust. Always seeking escape in battle, Vasyl' joins the Cheka, the secret police, even though he is aware of its real function.

Between Reason and Irrationality

The obsessive characters in 'Vijs'kovyj litun' can be seen as a series of lenses and mirrors used to focus or reflect a single thematic motif. Vasyl' and the aunt are mirror images of each other, and both are variants of the essential conflict embodied in Serhij. Haločka is both the object of Serhij's obsession and a victim of her own parallel delusion. The device of parallel and contrasting images is particularly appropriate to the underlying theme. Pidmohyl'nyj presents thematic material in an objective, almost pictorial manner, as if in an experimental laboratory, because any other technique, such as intervention through an authoritative narrator, would undermine the implicit assertion of cosmic indifference.

The experiment under observation in 'Problema xliba' is the now familiar tug of war between spirit and matter. The unnamed diarist in the story is a hungry young student living in the city. Here, as in 'Syn' and 'Sobaka,' hunger is shown to affect both the body and the mind. When the protagonist fails in his attempt at speculation (trading urban goods for rural food), he is driven to extremes. Eventually, he kills an old peasant who catches him stealing food. After that, he returns to the city to become a gigolo to a fat old woman who is a very successful speculator. In his first diary entry the student asserts:

Я не потребую багато – аби підтримати життя. Я люблю читати, гуляти ввечері, міркувати й не вбачаю достатніх підстав на те, щоб відмовитися від цього через шлунок. (*Misto*, 337 / BUL, 123)

I don't need much – just enough to sustain life. I like to read, to go out in the evenings, and to think, and I don't consider my stomach sufficient cause to renounce all of this.

By the end of the story the student has become a different person – his spirit has contracted, and his mind is focused on his own person. Ironically – and this irony is the reason for the disclaimer in the epigraph (quoted earlier in this chapter, on page 75) – he now considers himself liberated from physical needs:

Я споглядаю сам себе. Там на базарі, де моя подруга продає пиріжки, – сварка, лайка, заздрість, брехня, – а я виростаю з цього, як холодна хризантема на угноєній землі.... Так де-не-де на ланах життя постаємо ми, самотні, пишно-холодні квітки, і вдивляємось у самих себе як у безодню світла і тіні.

Уже вечір. І в мені сутеніє, скрізь запалюються живі вогні, мов світляки серед лісу. То – спогади. (*Misto*, 344–45 / BUL, 130)

The Later Stories

> I contemplate myself. Out there, in the market where my consort sells dumplings, there are arguments, name-calling, jealousy, and lies. I grow out of this like a cold chrysanthemum out of the fertilized soil ... Yes, here and there on the fields of life we rise, solitary, coldly beautiful flowers; and we look into ourselves as into an emptiness of light and shadow.
>
> It's evening. There's twilight within me, too, and little flames light up, everywhere, like lightning bugs in a forest. These are memories.

The magic of the night has overcome the student, despite his resistance. He has retreated into the falseness and artificiality of the past. Confronted with the incompatibility between his own moral principles and the laws of material existence, he has chosen to sacrifice his principles in order to survive. Whereas at the beginning of the story he sympathized with a prostitute who complained that her trade was falling off because women were giving themselves for free, at the end he wonders why feminists complain about the 'kept' status of women.

As Dolengo's scheme correctly states, most of the protagonists in Pidmohyl'nyj's stories are in the process of discovering a disharmony within themselves. The thematic structure of the stories focuses on the drama of the discovery. Once the discovery is made, the story is over. The protagonist either dies or simply remains suspended in an undefined existence, but there is no resolution of the fundamental conflict. The synchronic thematic structure seems to be a feature of the short story genre. Thematic structure in the novel, by contrast, is diachronic: Characters change in response to the forces that affect them, and thereby evolve through a thematic process rather than discovering a static conflict. This may explain Pidmohyl'nyj's genre designation for 'Tretja revoljucija,' which was subtitled 'narysy' in its original publication in *Červonyj šljax*. Fundamentally, it resembles that of 'V epidemičnomu baraci' more than that of *Ostap Šaptala* or one of the novels.[23]

In 'Problema xliba' Pidmohyl'nyj's thematic interest has advanced to a higher plane, and he comes close to a thematic breakthrough. The story ends when the dimensions of the conflict become evident. Although its thematic structure is still synchronic, the possibility of a continuation is implicit in the story. Most of Pidmohyl'nyj's stories end with the victory of the magic of the night, but in 'Problema xliba' that victory is not complete. In the course of his struggle with hunger, the student has found a way to adapt to the magic of the night rather than to surrender to it. Pidmohyl'nyj has made a first step in the direction of the novel.

CHAPTER FOUR

Misto
The European Connection

Pidmohyl'nyj's *Misto* is arguably the finest novel in Ukrainian literature. It is an interesting, readable story about familiar characters in an ordinary, contemporary setting, yet it is also a profound intellectual and psychological study that deals with issues at the forefront of contemporary philosophy. The novel was popular in its own time; it went into a second printing; many newspapers and magazines published reviews of it, as well as book and essays about the author; and it was discussed at official and unofficial meetings.[1] Today, outside Ukraine, where the novel has been available in the 1955 edition, prepared by Hryhorij Kostjuk,[2] it is a staple item in Ukrainian literature courses and among readers of Ukrainian literature in general. In Ukraine, the novel was republished in 1989, that is, in the first wave of forgotten and previously banned works that appeared under glasnost. For all its popularity, however, *Misto* is a complex work whose intellectual depth can easily escape the casual reader.

Misto was a turning point in Pidmohyl'nyj's career and in his development as a writer. Before it, he had been, essentially, a short story writer with a style still burdened by traditional metaphorical imagery and with a deep but narrowly defined intellectual subject. The author of *Misto* emerges as a mature and confident writer with a lean and consistent style and a broader, more dynamic philosophical perspective. The contrasts between Pidmohyl'nyj's early and later works are mirrored in the development of Ukrainian literature in general, which changed noticeably around 1926–7. What had been a voluminous stream of breathless, naïve, neoromantic lyrical poetry and short prose became, in the second half of the decade, a deep ocean of various genres, subjects, approaches, and styles. From a passionate cry in the desert by the visionary few of an oppressed nation, Ukrainian literature changed into the echo of a mature and diverse society. For the first time in history, Ukrainian literature was, within the limits then allowed by the government, a viable and vital cultural product that both reflected and shaped Ukrainian society; it was even becoming something of a market phenomenon, where demand influenced supply. Pidmohyl'nyj reached artistic maturity at flood-tide in the affairs of Ukrainian culture. Ironically, however, his personal literary development was in large measure the result of his continuing attraction to foreign, particularly French, models.

Pidmohyl'nyj's ties to French literature date back to his first years as a writer. In his review of *Tvory: Tom 1*, Petro Jefremov, who presumably had personal knowledge of Pidmohyl'nyj's reading habits, mentions (but deliberately sidesteps) the 'as yet incompletely manifested influence of certain western European (e.g., Anatole France and Knut Hamsun) and Polish (Przybyszewski) writers.'[3] Jefremov's suggestion is confirmed elsewhere. In November 1921 it was announced that Pidmohyl'nyj had completed a translation of Anatole France's *Thaïs*.[4] The translation did not appear until several years later, but the fact remains that the twenty-year-old writer was already translating French novels. Indeed, Pidmohyl'nyj's was renowned for his Fluency in French. In his memoirs about writers from the 1920s, Jurij Smolyč recounts how he, Vasyl' Vražlyvyj, and Pidmohyl'nyj jointly hired a French tutor in order to practise the language. The venture was short-lived: It soon became clear that Pidmohyl'nyj's French was better than the tutor's.[5] He had learned the language, according to Mel'nyk,[6] from a tutor his father hired for him and his sister when they were children. The volume and the quality of his translations from French give ample evidence that he knew the language well and was widely read in French and European literature. This impression is borne out by his letters to his wife from the Solovecki Islands prison camp and by his acquaintances' personal reminiscences of him – he was invariably described as an erudite intellectual.

Although numerous connections to French prose are evident in Pidmohyl'nyj's early stories,[7] the overall influence of French literature on his early works is, as Jefremov suggests, partial and uncertain. In other words, the elements of structure, style, and theme that constitute these links in the early stories are too general to support a convincing attribution of influence. Guy de Maupassant is a master of structure in the short story, but not every well-constructed short story written in the twentieth century reflects his influence. In the novel *Misto*, however, the influence of French literature is clear and convincing.

Misto

In the years between 'Tretja revoljucija' (1925) and *Misto* (1928) Pidmohyl'nyj was active as an editor and literary professional but he wrote no original works. During this period, however, he was diligently translating. As Mahdalyna Laslo-Kucjuk observes in her *Šukannja formy*,[8] in 1927 alone, Pidmohyl'nyj published seven volumes of translated French prose: Balzac's *Le Père Goriot*; Mérimée's *Colomba*; Voltaire's *Candide*; Maupassant's *Bel-Ami* and, separately, his *Sur l'eau* along with *Fort comme la mort*; Anatole France's *Thaïs*; and a collection of stories by Pierre Hamp (pseudonym of Pierre Bourillon). Also in 1927, two of Georges Duhamel's *Lettres au Patagon* appeared in Pidmohyl'nyj's translation in *Žyttja j revoljucija*. Although some of these translations may have been completed earlier (*Thaïs*, for example), it is none the less evident that Pidmohyl'nyj took time out from his own writing to study and translate some popular works of French prose. Later in his career Pidmohyl'nyj would take up translating once again, assuming editorial responsibility for multivolume editions of Anatole France, Guy de Maupassant, and Honoré de Balzac. The choice of authors is significant. What Pidmohyl'nyj focused on in French literature was realist fiction.

Among the works that Pidmohyl'nyj translated in 1925-7, two in particular are key to an understanding of *Misto*: Balzac's *Le Père Goriot* and Maupassant's *Bel-Ami*. The influence of these works, particularly of *Bel-Ami*, on *Misto* can be seen in plot, structure, style, and theme, but the net effect of this influence is greater than the sum of its parts. Maupassant, Balzac, and the traditions of nineteenth-century French prose gave Pidmohyl'nyj's writing a flavour entirely different from that of his contemporary Ukrainian novelists. At a time when fashion dictated either radical experimentation or plodding ideological sermonizing, Pidmohyl'nyj reinvigorated and modernized traditional forms by introducing into Ukrainian literature something it had been missing in the decades before the Revolution: psychological realism with an intellectual subtext. Like his professional colleague Mykola Zerov, Pidmohyl'nyj looked to Europe not for its newest and most fashionable cultural offerings, but for its historical and traditional strengths. Unlike Zerov, however, Pidmohyl'nyj was no ivory-tower élitist. Although he made no appeal to the masses as such, he was clearly seeking a wide general audience.

The most obvious parallels between Pidmohyl'nyj's *Misto* and Maupassant's *Bel-Ami*[9] are on the level of plot. Both are *Bildungsromane* in which a young man from the provinces with some military experience comes to the city and makes very rapid progress in his career and in a succession of amorous conquests. In addition to this overall parallelism in plot, the two novels contain related situations and episodes. Stepan Radčenko and Georges Duroy are both writers, the former a belletrist, the latter a journalist; in this as well as other respects they are both autobiographical projections. Stepan and Georges are physically active men, whose demeanour and aggressiveness attract women and occasionally intimidate men. Both are shown callously pushing their way through pedestrian traffic on a city street, attuned to the sexual attractiveness of the women they encounter. Both are also depicted, although at different points in their careers, blowing kisses out of windows to the slumbering expanse of a city. Clothing is important to both protagonists. Georges does not have a formal suit to wear when he is invited by his mentor, Forestier, to dinner. Stepan has only his army jacket and trousers with just one pocket. Both he and Georges, like Balzac's Eugène de Rastignac and Lucien de Rubempré before them, measure their success by the quality and fashion of their clothes.

Many episodes link the two characters. As writers and as lovers, they often find themselves in similar situations. Their first pieces of writing are based explicitly on their military experience: Duroy writes a politically sensitive article about his experiences in French colonial Algeria; Radčenko writes a story about a razor that passes through a succession of hands during the conflicts of 1917–20. They experience a similar joy on the day they first see their works in print.[10] On occasion, a blank sheet of paper becomes a frightening test of their abilities. Their careers as writers extend, in both cases, to the editorship of a periodical. Both writers change their names in order to project a less pedestrian image: Georges Duroy becomes Du Roi de Cantel: Stepan (stress on the second syllable) becomes Stefan (stress on the first syllable), because, he says, 'He was a king, or something' (Kostjuk, 95 / *Misto*, 87 / BUL, 397).[11] In addition, both men are given pet names by their lovers: Clotilde de Marelle and her daughter call Duroy 'Bel-Ami' (beautiful friend), while Zos'ka calls Radčenko '*božestvenyj*' (divine one). Indeed, Georges and Stepan have similar experiences with women. They both find themselves in need of a place to conduct their trysts, and both discover that their relationships with women are depleting their meagre financial resources. They take their women to the Folies Bergère or the movie theatre and to seedy restaurants. For both men, starting and ending relationships with women are problems related directly to sexual appetite and satiety, respectively.

Links also exist between secondary characters in the two novels. Georges Duroy's amorous career is an ascent through the social classes. He begins with a prostitute, Rachel, and quickly moves on to Clotilde de Marelle, a middle-class wife. After Forestier dies, Georges marries his widow, Madeleine, an exceptionally intelligent and free-spirited woman. Next, he seduces Madame Walter, his employer's attractive but stout wife. Finally, having manoeuvred his own wife, Madeleine, into a divorce, Georges elopes with Suzanne Walter, his boss's daughter. The parents are blackmailed into allowing the young couple to marry and into promoting Georges to the position of editor-in-chief.

Radčenko's amorous conquests also represent a progression of sorts, although a different one from Duroy's. His first love is Nadijka, a girl from his own village. Although both are naïve and inexperienced in matters of the heart, their feelings are mutual and sincere. Next, he has an affair with his forty-two-year-old landlady, Tamara Vasylivna Hnida (Musin'ka), a counterpart of sorts to Duroy's Mme Walter. Forced into a loveless marriage by her father, Musin'ka releases years of repressed feelings on her young boarder. After he tires of her, Radčenko moves away and finds Zos'ka Holubovs'ka, a romantic young dreamer who, like Clotilde de Marelle, is 'capricious, eccentric, highly imaginative, and proud and independent in her own way.'[12] At a party to which Zos'ka invites him, Stepan meets Rita, a sophisticated and urbane ballet dancer. The novel concludes with the prospect of a summer romance between them. In the final pages of the novel, just before his second meeting with Rita, Stepan meets the last of his women in the novel, a Dostoevskian prostitute. Unlike Maupassant's Rachel and Georges, however, this prostitute and Stepan have no physical contact. As the novel unfolds, Radčenko's encounters with women reflect an ever-diminishing level of sincerity, a growing distinction between love and sex. Ironically, in the climactic moments of Stepan's confusion and alienation, when he realizes he is looking for love, he turns to a woman who gladly provides only sex.

There are also similarities between the supporting male characters in the two novels, for example, between Norbert de Varenne and Vyhors'kyj. Although Vyhors'kyj is a far more important character in *Misto* than de Varenne is in *Bel-Ami*, they have similar functions in the development of the novels' thematic undercurrents. Both are poets with a philosophical view of the world; both are pessimists and sceptics. Norbert de Varenne makes a long speech to Duroy, as the two men return home from a party given by their employer, on the uselessness of all endeavour in face of the inevitability of death. In *Misto*, Vyhors'kyj takes such pessimism one step farther, speculating on the inevitable demise of the universe through entropy:

'Всесвіт загине через розпорошення тепляної енергії,' сказав він. 'Вона рівно розподілиться. Все урівноважиться й зітреться. Все спиниться. Це буде чудове видовисько, якого ніхто не побачить.'
(Kostjuk, 179 / *Misto*, 157 / BUL, 451)

'The universe will end because of the dissipation of thermal energy,' he said.
'It will spread out evenly. Everything will be equalized and wiped out.
Everything will cease. This will be a beautiful sight which no one will see.'

Links exist, too, between Duroy's parents in Normandy and the Latinist Andrij Venedovyč and his toothless wife. To a less significant degree, Borys Zadorožnij bears some resemblance to Charles Forestier, while Maksym Hnidyj embodies some of the traits of Georges Duroy that are not part of Radčenko.

The settings of the two novels are also similar. The fact that Pidmohyl'nyj's novel is set in Kiev and entitled *Misto* (The City) is in itself a sign of western European literary influence. Although Kiev was not the capital of the Soviet Ukrainian republic at the time that Pidmohyl'nyj was writing the novel, it was still the largest and most important city in Ukraine – in short, Kiev is easily cast as a Ukrainian Paris. In both novels the urban setting comprises a mixture of cultural creativity, financial machination, and social high life, combined with intellectual cynicism, bourgeois boorishness, and decadence of all kinds. In Maupassant's Paris and Pidmohyl'nyj's Kiev, political and social disenchantment over events of the recent past is starting to give way to self-interest, ambition, and speculation.

These connections between the plots and settings of the two novels – and the diligent reader could no doubt catalogue many more – offer ample evidence to support the proposition that Pidmohyl'nyj deliberately borrowed the general outline of a plot. And along with it, he also borrowed a number of techniques for structuring a novel.

In earlier works Pidmohyl'nyj had shown great skill in constructing short fiction but some uncertainty in longer forms. The plot outline Pidmohyl'nyj borrowed from Maupassant effectively solved this problem. The *Bildungsroman* as a genre generally follows a firm chronological and causal structure. The protagonist initially appears in a state of immaturity. A sequence of experiences influences and alters his character until, in the end, he achieves a state of maturity. This simple pattern is used to mould material into the genre, but it can also be used to explicate elements of the resulting work. For example, identifying *Misto* as a *Bildungsroman* helps explain the ambiguous ending of the novel. The protagonist must be judged in light of the maturity he has achieved relative to his condition at the beginning of the novel.

By adopting a ready-made plot, Pidmohyl'nyj has overcome the difficulties he experienced in *Ostap Šaptala*. The thematic parallelism of 'Povstanci' is replaced with a much looser sequence of events, which share only a very superficial parallelism. Stepan's career and maturity advance with the help of five women, but the similarities between successive affairs are few. Indeed, the reader perceives the differences in Stepan's relationships with women as a significant element in the causal sequence of the novel. Stepan is learning. This progressive maturation offers a sturdy, effective framework for the novel.

Individual sections of *Misto* also show Pidmohyl'nyj employing a new approach to structure. The chapter divisions here have an entirely different logic from those of *Ostap Šaptala*. In the earlier novella the individual episodes were arranged in a linear, chronological sequence, but, as in many of the short stories, their internal logic was thematic and melodramatic. In *Misto*, however, structure at both levels is based on inherent logic and the parallelism of the plot itself. Although no formal links can be established, this approach to structure is comparable to that found in nineteenth-century novels.

The novel is divided into two sections of fourteen chapters each. *Bel-Ami* is also in two sections, but they are uneven in length. The two sections of Pidmohyl'nyj's novel cover identical periods of time, from early fall to midsummer, essentially a full year each. Both sections are defined by a residence: Part one ends when Radčenko moves out of the Hnidyj home; part two ends when he moves out of his apartment on L'vivs'ka street. At the end of part one Stepan burns his old clothes as a gesture of his complete transition to urban life. At the end of part two he reaffirms his urban status once again, this time after a failed attempt to return to the village. In part one Stepan was reaching towards success as a writer of stories about razors. In part two he is reaching towards even greater success as a writer of novels about people.

The individual chapters follow an analogous if less rigid pattern. Chapter one brings the protagonist to Kiev. Chapter two recounts his first day in the city. Each of these two opening chapters ends with a references to the chimney and moon visible through Stepan's window. Further chapters are not so meticulously ordered, but are still structured by developments in the plot. Relations with Musin'ka, first attempts at writing, the university – these are some of the subjects of individual chapters, many of which begin with morning and end with evening. Continuity between chapters is episodic. Chapters follow one another in chronological order and each chapter is a complete unit. There are no melodramatic or symbolic bridges connecting the chapters, and individual chapters are not interpretive microcosms of the work as a whole.

Pidmohyl'nyj's use of plot-based structure in *Misto* must be seen in the context of his remarks on the value of plot in the preface to his 1927 collection, *Problema xliba*. The preface takes the form of a comic letter to his close friend, Jevhen Plužnyk, and is dated 1926, at Gurzuf, a resort town on the Crimean Black Sea coast. With feigned erudition and seriousness, Pidmohyl'nyj, agreeing with advice his friend has offered, chastises himself for his own lack of seriousness as a writer. After a brief disquisition on the general tendency of man to complete himself with his opposite quality (following the Platonic model), Pidmohyl'nyj meekly acknowledges the need to counteract his own frivolous nature:

> І цей мій обов'язок доповнити себе серйозністю в письменстві має виявитись насамперед в одкиданні сюжету. Ох, цей хвальний сюжет і не менше славетна фабула! Чи не в катастрофічному прагненні сучасного читача до легкотравності і забавності бере свої коріння ця непевна пара? Його рація, і читач може бути певен, що його вимоги задовольнять – він споживач, він купує.¹³

> And this obligation to complete myself with seriousness in writing is to manifest itself first and foremost in the rejection of plot. Oh, that praise-worthy plot and the no-less-famous fabula! Is it not in the catastrophic desire of the contemporary reader for something easily digestible and entertaining that this dubious pair take root? The reader is right, and he can be certain that his wishes shall be met: He is the consumer, he is buying.

Pidmohyl'nyj goes on to qualify these remarks with an equally tongue-in-cheek discussion of the danger that literary fashion might turn all literature into mindless adventure stories and thrillers. By way of warning he offers the examples of Oleksa Slisarenko and Mykola Xvyl'ovyj, who, it appears, have completed themselves in their opposites by becoming popular writers of works that rely on exotic and unusual plots. But I, continues Pidmohyl'nyj, cannot fall into this trap because I am incapable of writing works of plot or fabula, for the simple reason that I don't know how.

The entire preface is a literary joke whose allusive twists and turns are not easy to follow across the distance of so many years. But the joke is also a deliberate answer to various literary critics and an indirect demonstration of precisely that which Pidmohyl'nyj is humorously denying. On the face of it, the preface appears to be a serious defence of intellectual fiction against the dictates of current ideology and the literary market, both of which favoured low-brow writing. In the political atmosphere following the Literary Discussion of 1925, this is a moderate but unmistakable jab at the advocates of mass culture. But the piece also casts serious doubt on the readability of popular literature. When the king of adventure stories is a former symbolist-cum-futurist poet, and the pinnacle of exotic plots is found in the work of a devoted communist ideologist, then self-completion through opposites seems to be a levelling force that works against literature. Finally, the fact that the preface is an effective parody of pretentious literary discussions demonstrates Pidmohyl'nyj's real concern with questions of audience and market in literature. Ironically, this comic dismissal of plot is a sure indication that the question has been given serious thought. The result of this thinking is a major victory for plot over theme. In *Misto* Pidmohyl'nyj abandons structure based on thematic parallelism and symbols and replaces it with traditional plot-based organization.

Two other structural features distinguish *Misto* from *Ostap Šaptala*. In thematic structure the earlier novella closely follows Dolengo's schematic outline of Pidmohyl'nyj's stories – in fact, Dolengo himself uses it as an example.[14] The key element of that scheme is thematic stability. Ostap faces a conflict that is intensified by the events of the story. He takes dramatic steps to resolve the problem, reifying Lasja as the emblem of virtue (an element that constitutes the attack on emptiness in Dolengo's scheme). When that fails, the situation returns to what it had been before, with Ostap still facing a conflict but now, in despair, resigned to it. On the structural level, the protagonist may learn, change, and develop, but the basic relationship between man and his environment is unchanged. On a thematic level, the story presents one simple philosophical thesis – alienation.

Pidmohyl'nyj's stories, as well as Maupassant's, conform to this type of stable thematic construction. Both writers, however, build their novels on thematic dynamism. The novels do not exemplify a thesis; they dramatize a thematic argument. A set of thematic ideas is presented and then undergoes a transformation over the course of the work. In *Bel-Ami*, for example, the greed, selfishness, and injustice with which the novel begins are, by its conclusion, transformed into elements of an existential condition. As we shall see, Pidmohyl'nyj's novels, follow the same pattern. To the degree that *Ostap Šaptala* does not, it reflects a closer tie to the short stories.

The second difference between Pidmohyl'nyj's novella and his novel lies in the attention given to social setting. Like Maupassant, Pidmohyl'nyj builds most of his short stories on character types. The short genre seldom allows for full character development. Social setting and interaction do not fit into anything less than a novel. Maupassant's works offer a good example. Even his longest *nouvelles* – 'Le Horla,' 'Yvette,' 'L'Héritage,' 'Boule de suif,' and 'Le Docteur Héraclius Gloss' – focus on isolated individuals. All his novels, by contrast, have a broad social setting. Although the difference in Pidmohyl'nyj's works is not as sharp, it is no less real. While Ostap Šaptala and Stepan Radčenko are in many ways similar characters, Stepan interacts with a larger society whereas Ostap is confined to a community of seven: his parents, his two friends, his landlady, his sister Olena, and Lasja.

Between Reason and Irrationality

Despite these and other differences, there are also certain parallels between *Ostap Šaptala* and Pidmohyl'nyj's novels, particularly *Misto*. When Pidmohyl'nyj set out to write his first novel, he adopted many of the ideas and techniques that he had noted in the French novels he translated, but he did not abandon the themes that characterized his earlier stories. Ostap Šaptala and Stepan Radčenko were cast in the same mould. They are both young men from the village who have migrated to the city. Both are scientists and intellectuals of a sort: Šaptala, an engineer with an interest in philosophy; Radčenko, a student of agriculture and economics who becomes a writer. They are physically alike: both are tall, muscular, well-built men. They share a problem common to most of Pidmohyl'nyj's young male heroes: They have difficulty establishing and maintaining normal relationships with women. Their perception of their own identity – like their attitude towards women, which is not unrelated – is highly problematical. Characteristically, they are men caught between opposing forces: science and humanism, tradition and modernity, city and village, sexuality and intelligence, instinct and reason.

The links between Pidmohyl'nyj's first novel and his earlier works constitute an important guide for interpreting *Misto*.[15] Continuity among the works of a given author is one of the more reliable yardsticks in the literary scholar's toolbox. Influences from external sources merge with this continuity to create a deeper and richer channel of literary creativity. *Misto* lies at the intersection of the line of internal continuity and the line of influence from Maupassant, specifically from *Bel-Ami*.

In addition to structural parallels in plot, setting, and characterization, *Misto* and *Bel-Ami* share several stylistic devices, the most important of which is the objective method. Like Maupassant, Pidmohyl'nyj approaches his subject in a way that involves presenting the world as it appears to the protagonist. In his preface to *Pierre et Jean* Maupassant makes a programmatic statement about writing that echoes the views of his literary mentor, Gustave Flaubert.

> Il s'agit de regarder tout ce qu'on veut exprimer assez longtemps et avec assez d'attention pour en découvrir un aspect qui n'ait été vu et dit par personne. Il y a, dans tout, de l'inexploré, parce que nous sommes habitués à ne nous servir de nos yeux qu'avec le souvenir de ce qu'on a pensé avant nous sur ce que nous contemplons. La moindre chose contient un peu d'inconnu. Trouvons le....
>
> Quelle que soit la chose qu'on veut dire, il n'y a qu'un mot pour l'exprimer, qu'un verbe pour l'animer et qu'un adjectif pour la qualifier. Il faut donc chercher, jusqu'à ce qu'on les ait découverts, ce mot, ce verbe et cet adjectif, et ne jamais se contenter de l'à peu près, ne jamais avoir recours

à des supercheries, même heureuses, à des clowneries de langage pour éviter la difficulté.[16]

It is a matter of looking at anything you want to express long enough and closely enough to discover in it some aspect that nobody has yet seen or described. In everything there is an unexplored element because we are prone by habit to use our eyes only in combination with the memory of what others before us have thought about the thing we are looking at. The most insignificant thing contains some little unknown element. We must find it ...

Whatever we want to convey, there is only one word to express it, one verb to animate it, one adjective to qualify it. We must therefore go on seeking that word, verb or adjective until we have discovered it, and never be satisfied with approximations, never fall back on tricks, even inspired ones, or tomfoolery of language to dodge the difficulty.[17]

Two essential ideas are embedded in the text. The first is purely aesthetic. Language is an instrument, not a goal. The artist uses this instrument to achieve his goal, which is the representation of familiar things in a new perspective. Vision is the cornerstone of the technique. Visual perception is the writer's most important tool. As realists, as sceptics, and as anti-romantics, Flaubert and Maupassant both argue in favour of observation and against deliberately 'artful' uses of language. Alongside this aesthetic principle is a philosophical one. The represented image must be new because the reader is not likely to see the world around him except through stereotypes and outmoded ideologies. The writer's duty is to challenge intellectual inertia and to reveal the world as it actually is.

The descriptive passages in *Misto* are few and brief, and they are always part of Stepan's consciousness. His first impressions of Kiev offer a good example. He steps off the boat and stops to get his bearings:

Степан скрутив з махорки цигарку й закурив. Він мав звичку спльовувати після цього, але тут ковтнув слинку з гірким махорчиним пилом. Все навкруги було дивне і чуже. Він бачив тир, де стріляли з духових рушниць, ятки з морозеним, пивом та квасом, перекупок з булками, насінням, хлопчаків з ірисками, дівчат з кошиками абрикос і морелів. Проз нього пропливали сотні облич, веселих, серйозних і заклопотаних, десь голосила обікрадена жінка, кричали, граючись, пацани. Так звичайно тут єсть, так було, коли його нога ступала ще м'якою курявою села, так буде й надалі. І всьому цьому він був чужий. (Kostjuk, 16 / *Misto*, 21–2 / BUL, 313)

Between Reason and Irrationality

Stepan rolled a cigarette from his cheap tobacco and smoked it. He had a habit of spitting after this, but here he swallowed the bitter tobacco- and dust-flavoured saliva. Everything around him was strange and unusual. He saw the shooting gallery where they were firing air guns, the stalls with ice cream, beer, and kvas, the huckstresses with rolls and seeds, the boys with irises, the girls with baskets of apricots and morellos. Hundreds of faces floated past him, some happy, some serious, and some troubled. Somewhere a woman was yelling because she had been robbed. Children were playing and making a racket. This is how it usually is here, and how it was when his foot was still treading the soft dust of the village, and how it would continue to be. And to all of this he was a stranger.

As this passage demonstrates, Pidmohyl'nyj's objective method does not merely catalogue visual images. Stepan's first impression of Kiev is conditioned as much by his foul tobacco as by the street scene before him. The variety and multiplicity of people and activities are a new experience for the young man from the village. The passage concludes with a generalization that reflects Stepan's unformulated and unarticulated thoughts at that moment. The voice, however, is unmistakably the narrator's.

Like Maupassant's, Pidmohyl'nyj's objective technique is built on a careful blend of photographic realism and the impressions of the protagonist. Pidmohyl'nyj's Kiev, for example, is unusually vivid. In naming actual streets and neighbourhoods, Pidmohyl'nyj uses the same device that Balzac, Maupassant, Dickens, and Dostoevsky used to bring Paris, London, and St Petersburg to life. In Ukrainian literature, this was a new technique. The list of Radčenko's addresses – first on Nyžnij val in the Podil area, then on L'vivs'ka street in a modest northwest section of the city, and, finally, a 'genuine' room, as the broker calls it, in the Lypky district – is a measure of his success. His promenades along Xreščatyk or down Andrijivs'kyj uzviz conjure very real images in the minds of readers who are familiar with the city.[18]

Such verisimilitude is also applied in the temporal dimension. Stepan, unlike so many heroes in Soviet Ukrainian fiction, has an identifiable past. As some contemporary Soviet critics noted,[19] Radčenko was for a time a supporter of the independent Ukrainian state. Later he joined the Bolsheviks and, after the hostilities ended, he became an active Party worker in his village. He has come to the city to study so that he may return to the village better armed to continue the struggle against inefficiency and ignorance. This was no doubt a common biography in the 1920s. Common or not, however, it gives the character a depth he would not otherwise have had. The same is true in the case of Musin'ka. Historical realism is further evident in the caricature of Mykola Zerov, represented by the eminent critic Svitozars'kyj; in Stepan's taking a position as a teacher in the Ukrainization program; and in the frequent references to NEP (Lenin's New Economic Policy) and the NEP-men (the businessmen from before the Revolution whose skills and experience were needed to stimulate the economy).

Geographical and historical realism exists in a multitude of details throughout the novel, from the acronyms of various public institutions to the names of popular French perfumes. Not all of these, however, are actual. Stepan's native village, for example, is called Tereveni. Even if such a village existed – indeed, it may have – Pidmohyl'nyj is not thinking of a real place: the place-name translates roughly as 'Joke-ville.' The number under which Stepan is registered by the admissions committee of the Institute is spelled out: one hundred twenty-three. It seems less arbitrary when converted to numerals: 123.

As the latter examples show, *Misto* has an ironic undercurrent. This irony surfaces in a variety of forms, from humorous or sarcastic comments by the narrator to significant coincidences or juxtapositions in the plot. Pidmohyl'nyj allows his narrator considerably more freedom than Maupassant did. For example, as Stepan Radčenko reaches for a match to light his cigarette, the narrator explains that his trousers have only one pocket because the niggardly tailor thought that, for some people, one pocket was enough. 'Nature,' the narrator continues, 'by following the tailor's idea, could save an eye or an ear on many a person, as the myths about Cyclopses suggest' (Kostjuk, 18 / *Misto*, 23 / BUL, 314). Elsewhere, the narrator explains that, in spite of forecasts by the weather bureau, spring was delayed 'for reasons beyond the control of science' (Kostjuk, 107 / *Misto*, 97 / BUL, 389).

The narrator in *Misto* makes many such remarks in the margins, as it were, of his story. The result is a narrating personality who is humorous, worldly, and sceptical. Although the narrator's comments occasionally make light of Stepan's naïve hopes or personal foibles, the ironic distance created by them is only in part a distance between narrator and protagonist. It is also between the world of the story and a larger, disembodied universe of ideas, in which reader, narrator, and protagonist are all on an equal footing. Pidmohyl'nyj's irony does not victimize the hero, as, for example, Flaubert's does. Instead, it is used to encourage a reading of the story from a larger perspective. Perhaps the most interesting example of this technique occurs in the first few pages of the novel. As the boat carrying Stepan, Levko, and Nadijka approaches Kiev, the passengers see other boats in the river:

'Дивіться, дивіться!' скрикнула дівчина, задивившись на незвичайні трикутні вітрила. На палубі яхти було троє хлопців і дівчина в серпанку. Вона здавалася русалкою з давніх казок, їй не можна було навіть заздрити. (Kostjuk, 15 / *Misto*, 20–1 / BUL, 312)

'Look, look!' yelled the girl, captivated by the unusual triangular sails. On the deck of the yacht were three boys and a girl in a veil. She seemed a water nymph from old fables. She was even beyond envy.

The four people on the unusual yacht might be any young sailing enthusiasts in Kiev, but a description of the crowd of people on the city beach helps to clarify their identity: 'Вода й сонце приймали всіх, хто покинув допіру пера й терези – кожного юнака, як Кия, і кожну юнку, як Либедь' (The water and the sun welcomed everyone who had just abandoned pens and balance scales – every young lad, as if he were Kyj, every young lass, as if she were Lybid'; Kostjuk, 15 / *Misto*, 21 / BUL, 312). According to legend, Kyj, Lybid', Šček, and Xoryv are the four siblings who founded the city of Kiev. The appearance of these mythological figures on a sailboat near Kiev in the 1920s seems to contradict the fundamental principles of realist prose. But their identity is almost invisible and their presence is not disruptive to the calm surface of Pidmohyl'nyj's novel.

The presence of the legendary founders of Kiev points to another stylistic device in Pidmohyl'nyj's arsenal – symbols. In addition to their function as signposts in a larger ironic universe, the legendary founders of the city also embody an important correlation to Stepan and his village friends who are flocking to the city. In the political agenda of the early years of the Soviet state, the fusion of village and city was to be the foundation for a new social order. Stepan is very taken with this idea and sees himself as a trail-blazer in a great human experiment. The subtle symbolism of the legendary figures in the yacht undermines this heroic self-esteem by relegating it to a world of legendary beings.

Other symbols are scattered throughout the novel. Perhaps the most important is the one specifically designated as a literary symbol, namely, the razor that appears in Radčenko's first story. Nadijka herself is a symbol. Among the novel's other symbols (some of which are more than that) are Stepan's clothes, the lottery Stepan and Zos'ka play, the bingo that Musin'ka plays, the glass of milk Musin'ka offers Stepan, his exercise regimen, the Ukrainian language, and the city itself.

Pidmohyl'nyj uses relatively fewer symbols in *Misto* than he did in his earlier stories, for at least three reasons: First, *Misto* is technically more mature than Pidmohyl'nyj's earlier works and thus naturally less dependent on technical devices. The more polished the writing, the fewer the devices needed to accomplish any specific task. Those that do remain are woven seamlessly into the fabric of the writing – this is part of the stylistic lesson Pidmohyl'nyj has learned from the French realists. The second reason for the relative paucity of symbols lies, ironically, in the already very highly symbolic perspective of the protagonist. Radčenko sees the world in symbolic terms – the coupling of city and village, the importance of clothing, the fashionable sound of a name. Because the narrator relies on the symbolic values developed by the protagonist, he does not need to add his own. The third reason anticipates an examination of the thematic structure of the novel: There are fewer symbols in *Misto* than in Pidmohyl'nyj's earlier works because here the logical categories and epistemological systems that support symbolic associations are no longer the thematic anchor. What had appeared as a vague metaphysical force in the earlier stories is now materialized in the psychology of characters.

The reduced importance of technical devices is also apparent in the diminished frequency of repetitive structures. Of course, Pidmohyl'nyj does not abandon the device altogether. Radčenko's five women are meant to be compared with one another and to be viewed collectively as a progression. The three village men – Stepan, Levko, and Borys – are also meant to be compared. The primary juxtaposition is between Radčenko and Vyhors'kyj. There are a number of similarities between the two characters. Both are writers, although one is a poet and the other a prose writer. Both change their names. Radčenko makes a small change in his given name, while Vyhors'kyj becomes 'Lans'kyj.' Considering the roots of the latter two names – *hora* (mountain) and 'lan' (cultivated field), respectively – Vyhors'kyj's name change suggests a shift between opposites, a psychological dualism. Such dualism is characteristic of both Radčenko and Vyhos'kyj and is a central thematic element in the novel. Vyhors'kyj is the person who helps Radčenko establish himself as a writer. Radčenko takes over his that is, Lans'kyj's position as a language instructor in the Ukrainization program.

As Mahdalyna Laslo-Kucjuk observes, Vyhors'kyj is Radčenko's double.[20] More specifically, he is his alter ego. Whereas Radčenko is a somewhat naïve optimist trying to find his place in both literature and society, Vyhors'kyj is a worldly pessimist running away from the city. His escape to the countryside to follow in the footsteps of the eighteenth-century philosopher Hryhorij Skovoroda is an ironic self-deception. Skovoroda's dictum 'understand yourself' is a prescription for moral and social responsibility, yet that is precisely what Vyhors'kyj is running away from. Radčenko, by contrast, is in search of mankind. While his early stories focus on things, his progress as a writer is in the direction of writing a 'novel [*povist'*] about people.'

Parallels in plot, along with symbolic images, are major players in the line-up for Pidmohyl'nyj's implementation of the objective method. The star on this team, however, is indirect narration – specifically, third-person, consonant, focalized narration. As the passages about the niggardly tailor or the uncooperative weather demonstrate, Pidmohyl'nyj allows his narrator a wider range of independent comments than Maupassant does. This freedom extends to another area of comparison with Maupassant – the use of pathetic fallacy.

In contrast to his French counterpart, Pidmohyl'nyj limits the degree to which descriptive passages mirror the lives of the characters. However, the Balzacian device, so evident in *Bel-Ami*, of allowing a room or a place to mirror its inhabitants, does occur in *Misto*. Andrij Venedovyč, the retired Latinist, has a mind filled to overflowing with trivia about classical Roman civilization, and especially about his beloved Seneca. His apartment mirrors the crowded order of his mind:

Кімната його являла дивний збіг найрізноманітніших речей, що ніби рушивши з різних покоїв, зсунулись сюди від жаху й тут закам'яніли. А як їм абсолютно бракувало місця, то стояли вони чудною юрбою по-під стінами й просто серед хати. Широке двох-спальне ліжко визирало краєм з-під куцої ширми, впираючись головами в шафу на книжки, де замість колишнього скла сумно темнів брунатний картон. Поруч шафи, одбираючи їй змогу вільно відчинятись, стояв великий горорізьблений буфет, прихилившись верхушкою до стіни, що без неї він втратив би рівновагу. Далі під вікном праворуч тулилась повна нот етажерка, хоч піяно в хаті не було. Косяком до вікна, трохи заслоняючи його своїм краєм, пишалась струнка дзеркальна шафа на одежу – єдина річ, що зберегла свою незайманість і чистоту. Симетрично до грандіозного ліжка навпроти височів потертий турецький диван, а на його широкій спинці, що кінчалась угорі довгастою дерев'яною площинкою, самотньо підносив до стелі свій рупор грамофон, оточений з боків рівними купками платівок. (Kostjuk, 33–4 / *Misto*, 35–6 / BUL, 327)

His room presented a strange collection of the most diverse things, which, it seemed, had moved here from various rooms in terror and had petrified. And since there was absolutely not enough room for all of them, they stood in an odd crowd along the walls and simply in the middle of the floor. The edge of a wide double bed peeked out from under a short screen. Its head abutted a bookcase, in which sad brown cardboard had replaced the glass panels. A large sideboard with high relief wood carving stood next to the bookcase and prevented it from opening properly. The top of the sideboard leaned against the wall, without which it would lose its balance. Farther along the wall, under the window, were shelves full of sheet music, although there was no piano in the house. At an angle to the window, partially obscuring it with its edge, stood a tall mirrored wardrobe – the only thing that retained its original, clean appearance. Symmetrically across from the bed a worn Turkish divan rose high above the floor. On its wide back, which was topped off with a long wooden surface, a gramophone, flanked by two even stacks of records, raised its lonely horn towards the ceiling.

Less elaborate but no less effective associations between characters and their living spaces are made in the following descriptions: Borys's room before Stepan moves into it, the same room after Stepan has lived there for half a year, Svitozars'kyj's apartment, and the apartment on Andrijivs'kyj uzviz where Borys and Nadijka live. On a larger scale, Kiev itself is presented as a physical mirror of the diversity of its inhabitants.

In Maupassant's works, the association between environment and character sometimes extends to specific actions and situations, beyond a general reflection of a character's personality. In *Misto*, however, nature does not mirror the protagonist's moods. Generally, Pidmohyl'nyj simply avoids the pathetic fallacy. In some cases, however, he deliberately reverses it. Ricocheting off the fact that the cultural life of a city flourishes in the winter months, Pidmohyl'nyj creates a deliberate oxymoron, the autumn springtime of the city:

Останні літні дні використовували решту прав. Кінець вересня ранки стали хмарні, а в полудень виринало сонце, сповнюючи повітря весняними міражами й стримуючи на час опадання листу. Але вночі його зривали й розвіювали по вулицях вітри, завдаючи клопоту двірникам. По цих жовтих застілках осени місто вступало в смугу свого буяння, прокидаючись після літньої сплячки.... Починалось властиве життя міста, весна його творчости, такої замкненої в мурах і разом такої безмежної. (Kostjuk, 88–9 / *Misto*, 81 / BUL, 373)

Summer's last days were running out. Towards the end of September, mornings became cloudy, but the sun came out in the afternoons, filling the air with spring mirages and halting for a time the falling of the leaves. But the night winds tore the leaves off and scattered them on the streets, creating headaches for the caretakers. On autumn's yellow tablecloths the city entered into the period of its flowering, waking from its summer lethargy ... The city's real life was beginning, the springtime of its creativity, so totally walled in and yet so infinite.

In a similar vein, the autumn rain is depicted as posing obstacles to sex:

> Природа замкнула свої вигідні притулки, але жоден дощ не спроможний був залити жаги, що бере людське серце не тільки від віку, а й від часу незалежно, противно серцям інших тварин, яким призначено пору любовного настрою. (Kostjuk, 143–4 / *Misto*, 127 / BUL, 420)

> Nature closed its convenient trysting places, but no rain could drown the desire that captures the human heart with regard neither for age nor for season, unlike the hearts of other animals, which have a fixed time for amorous moods.

These deliberate disharmonies between humans and nature, like Maupassant's deliberate harmonies, are rooted in the novel's thematic centre. For Pidmohyl'nyj, a human being is not merely another creature in the natural order. Humans hold a special position in that order – but not one that is necessarily a blessing.

Pidmohyl'nyj's blend of narrative devices also reflects his view of man's place in the universe. Events, descriptions, and ideas are presented from the protagonist's point of view. For Pidmohyl'nyj, as for Maupassant, all knowledge derives from experience. The narrator is not in a privileged position. From the very first sentence of the novel, he does not know what will appear around the bend.

> Здавалось, далі пливти нема куди. Спереду Дніпро мов спинився в несподіваній затоці, оточений праворуч, ліворуч і просто зеленожовтими передосінніми берегами. Але пароплав раптом звернув, і довга, спокійна смуга річки протяглася далі до ледве помітних пагорків на обрії. (Kostjuk, 11 / *Misto*, 17 / BUL, 308)

> It seemed you couldn't go any farther. Ahead, the Dnieper appeared to stop in an unexpected cove, surrounded on the right, on the left, and straight ahead by the faded green banks of approaching autumn. But the steamboat suddenly turned and the long smooth streak of the river stretched out to the barely visible hills on the horizon.

Pidmohyl'nyj's narrator, then, is a fusion of conflicting inclinations. On the one hand, he is the humorous, worldly, and sceptical ironist discussed earlier, while on the other, he is an objective and unintrusive reflector of Radčenko's experiences. The blend of these two features is a hallmark of Pidmohyl'nyj's narrative technique. This blend is evident in the following passage, in which Stepan still new to the city and uncomfortable with its strange ways, finds himself window shopping:

Дальший зупинок зробив він коло вітрини кондитерської, де в поетичному порядкові, на білому мереживному папері, в розмальованих коробочках, фаянсових тарелях та вазах розташувалось солодке, невимовно смачне їстиво. Він пожирав похмурими очима всю цю навалу бісквітних і мікадних тортів, ромових бабок, заливних горіхів, купи шоколаду, шари кольористих тягучок і тістечок різної форми та змісту, не знаючи їм назви, але добре розуміючи, що назви ці – не пампушки, не пундики і не пірники. В своїй єдиній кишені він намацав двадцять копійок, але до крамниці зайти не зважився і купив пару тістечок на вулиці в милої дівчини, що мала приємність їх продавати й ніколи не їсти. Взявши до рук ці слизькуваті вироби цукерної індустрії, він нагло ковтнув їх, суворо сам до себе промовивши:
 'Цить! Я теж хочу поласувати.'
 Це було йому мов перше причастя, що полишає по собі у вірного тугу від спожитої крови й надії на вічне життя. (Kostjuk, 75–6 / *Misto*, 70–1 / BUL, 362–3)

He next stopped by the window of a bakery, where, in a poetic arrangement on white doilies, in delicately painted boxes, on china plates and vases, were displayed sweet and unspeakably delicious foods. He devoured with his sad eyes this heap of wafer and almond tortes, rum babas, glazed nuts, mounds of chocolate, layers of colourful candies and pastries of various form and content, without knowing their names, but understanding full well that they were not doughnuts, muffins, or cupcakes. He fingered the twenty kopeks in his only pocket but he did not dare enter the store and bought himself a couple of pastries on the street from a lovely girl who had the honour to sell them and never to eat them. Taking these slippery products of the sugar industry into his hands, he suddenly gulped them down, telling himself sternly:
 'Quiet! I, too, want to savour them.'
 To him it was like a First Communion, which leaves in the faithful a sadness for the blood consumed and a hope for eternal life.

Between Reason and Irrationality

In this passage the narrator quietly moves through three different perspectives. On one level the passage presents a catalogue of what Stepan sees through the window. The various pastries, chocolates, and candies are precisely what one would expect to see in a bakery window. The china plates and paper doilies add realistic detail. There is even a small history lesson in this display. The NEP was a success if a country that had experienced a famine five years earlier could fill its bakery windows with such delicacies. But this particular catalogue of sweets is also peculiar to Radčenko: What he notices are the exotic and expensive items. The narrator specifically notes that Stepan did not know the names of the objects he was admiring but understood that they were not the conventional sweets with which he was familiar. On this level the narrator subtly reflects Stepan's feeling of inadequacy, his conviction that city life is so much better and richer than village drudgery. The rhythm and associational logic of the passage further suggest a self-deluding falseness in Stepan's reaction. The protagonist's envious gaze at the bakery sweets is 'bad faith,' in Sartre's sense of the term. Stepan does not in fact know that the pastries he buys from the girl on the street are inferior; he is conditioned to think so by his stereotypical view of the city.

This last impression is confirmed in the third narrative perspective evident in the passage. The final sentence, about First Communion comes directly from the persona of the narrator. There is nothing in Radčenko's experience or imagination to prompt such a simile. It is a purely authorial comment and is even made to seem gratuitous – just another one of the cynical storyteller's little jokes. But the comment reflects the dualism of Stepan's reaction to the bakery and the city. By presenting Stepan's admonition to himself as a direct quotation, Pidmohyl'nyj already suggests the presence of a psychological dualism. This dualism is then echoed in the narrator's reference to the contradictory feelings that Communion inspires: sadness at the idea of Christ's dying for the sins of humankind and happiness in the hope of salvation. But this dualism itself falls within a larger division, since only believers are likely to embrace such a view. Overall, then, the apparently gratuitous comment by the narrator has the effect of underscoring the symptoms of existential bad faith in Stepan's attitude as well as the relativism of all judgments.

The ease with which the narrator moves from one perspective to another in this passage and throughout the novel attests to Pidmohyl'nyj's skill as a writer. It also reflects a fundamental relativism at the centre of the novel. In contrast to the links between Pidmohyl'nyj and Maupassant on the level of technique or in the areas of plot, setting, and character, the relationship between *Misto* and *Bel-Ami* on the thematic level is not merely a matter of similarity or influence. Pidmohyl'nyj's novel is, in a sense, a reaction to

Maupassant's, and its thematic substance consists of an intellectual interaction, a dialogue with its literary predecessor.

Misto and *Bel-Ami* share three significant thematic concerns. The most important is surely the role of sexuality in human affairs. In Maupassant the issue boils down to a Schopenhauerian view of women as a natural procreative trap. The perception of sexuality as an evil force necessarily relegates this view to a world without Freudian psychology.

Maupassant was not a philosopher. It would be fruitless to search for a complete and detailed philosophical system in his works, and a certain level of inconsistency and ambiguity should be expected. Within these limits, however, he is a disciple of the philosophy of Arthur Schopenhauer.[21] The link to Schopenhauer is confirmed by Maupassant's story about the philosopher's frightening smile and his dentures. The description of Schopenhauer's philosophy in this story makes clear its proximity to Maupassant's own ideas:

> Qu'on proteste et qu'on se fâche, qu'on s'indigne ou qu'on s'exalte, Schopenhauer a marqué l'humanité du sceau de son dédain et de son désenchantement.
>
> Jouisseur désabusé, il a renversé les croyances, les espoirs, les poésies, les chimères, détruit les aspirations, ravagé la confiance des âmes, tué l'amour, abattu le culte idéal de la femme, crevé les illusions des coeurs, accompli la plus gigantesque besogne de sceptique qui ait jamais été faite. Il a tout traversé de sa moquerie, et tout vidé. Et aujourd'hui même, ceux qui l'exècrent semblent porter, malgré eux, en leurs esprits, des parcelles de sa pensée.[22]

> One may protest and lose one's temper, one may be indignant or loftily disdainful, but Schopenhauer has stamped humanity with the seal of his contempt and disenchantment.
>
> A disillusioned hedonist, he has overturned beliefs, hopes, poetry, and idle fancies, destroyed the aspirations and laid waste the trust of souls, killed love, abolished the idealized worship of woman, exploded the illusions of the heart, accomplished the most gigantic labour of scepticism that has ever been achieved. His mocking spirit has traversed all things, and drained them all dry. And, even today, those who execrate him bear in their spirits, despite themselves, fragments of his mind.[23]

The attempt to abolish the idealized romantic view of women is the primary link between Maupassant and Schopenhauer. Maupassant's misogynous – and only partially ironic – chronique, entitled 'La Lysistrata moderne,'[24] which appeared in *Le Gaulois* on 30 December 1880 makes this evident. Yet Maupassant's link to Schopenhauer extends beyond misogyny. As Micheline Besnard-Coursodon demonstrates,[25] the view of the function of women that Maupassant borrowed from Schopenhauer is only the most vivid example of his notion of cosmic entrapment and the invincible power of a mindless fate.

Maupassant's novels, even more than his short stories, demonstrate the extent to which his own thinking paralleled Schopenhauer's pessimism. The plots themselves emphasize the idea of the individual's inescapable subservience to fate. Jeanne, the protagonist of *Une Vie*, helplessly endures a continuous stream of cruel shocks and undeserved difficulties. Christiane Andermatt, in *Mont-Oriol*, endures similar humiliations, but here Maupassant shows that fate treats equally those who passively accept it and those who actively struggle against it. In *Pierre et Jean* the author concentrates on fate's ironic backlash against those who struggle against it. Like a figure from classical Greek tragedy, Pierre seeks to know that which will destroy his life. In *Fort comme la mort* and *Notre coeur* Maupassant returns to the basic Schopenhauerian theme of men caught in the 'trap' of female sexuality, but the women in these works do not accept their assigned role.

Pidmohyl'nyj casts the problem of human sexuality into a larger arena. For him the issue is not to evaluate the morality of sex, but rather to reconcile it with human intellect. His perspective on the subject is reflected in the epigraphs to the novel:

Шість прикмет має людина: трьома подібна вона на тварину, а трьома на янгола: як тварина – людина їсть і п'є; як тварина – вона множиться і як тварина – викидає; як янгол – вона має розум, як янгол – ходить просто і як янгол – священною мовою розмовляє.

Талмуд. Трактат Авот

Як можна бути вільним, Евкріте, коли маєш тіло?

А. Франс, *Таїс*

Man has six qualities: in three he resembles an animal and in the other three he resembles an angel. Like an animal man eats and drinks, like an animal he procreates, and like an animal he expels waste; like an angel he has reason, like an angel he walks upright, and like an angel he speaks in a blessed language.

Talmud. Avot (Aboth) tractate[26]

Tell me, Eucrites, how can one be free when he has a body?[27]

A. France, *Thaïs*

It is characteristic of Pidmohyl'nyj's view of sexuality that Radčenko's relationships with women, unlike those of Maupassant's Duroy, do not have a direct impact on his career. Duroy is dependent on women in all aspects of his career: They write his stories, suggest political manoeuvres, provide financial information, and serve as negotiating chips in blackmailing employers. This also explains the difference in the professions of the two heroes. Radčenko is a creative writer rather than a mere journalist because Pidmohyl'nyj needs to contrast his profession and his instincts. Duroy's instincts and ambition lead to the same goals. As a writer he has no aesthetic principles; his goal is to manipulate the public in order to attain personal wealth and power. He treats his writing and his sexuality as means to the same end. Radčenko's passion for women, by contrast, often interferes with his professional obligations. Nevertheless, in depicting the relations between men and women Pidmohyl'nyj uses some of Maupassant's motifs. Stepan's reaction to the pregnant Nadijka, for example, is reminiscent of Maupassant's young men who recoil from the sight of a pregnant woman. On the whole, however, although some of the associated thematic issues are similar, women play different roles in the works of the two authors.

Stepan's relationships with women in *Misto* reflect Pidmohyl'nyj's evolution away from the naïve sexual psychology that dominated his early stories. Radčenko does not find sexuality ugly and frightening, as many of Pidmohyl'nyj's earlier heroes did. The sexuality of characters such as Ostap Šaptala or Viktor Xobrovs'kyj was based on a strictly Freudian model, in which sexuality is an instinctive force against which a battery of repressive mechanisms is arrayed within the individual's unconscious. Stepan's sexuality is also an instinctive force, but the challenges to it come from the rational, conscious side of the psyche. The confusion Stepan experiences in his relationships with women is a result of the collision of unconscious instinct with the expectations of the conscious psyche. The model at work here is closer to existential formulas than to Freudian theories.

The sequence of women in Stepan's life follows certain linear progressions. We have already noted the diminishing degree of sincerity. Also significant is the increasing urbanity of each new partner. Nadijka is a villager in fact as well as in Stepan's imagination. Musin'ka's father and her husband are both urban merchants, but their lifestyle still resembles that of the village (they keep cows, which Musin'ka milks herself). Zos'ka, the daughter of a minor bureaucrat, is twenty-two and naïve, but nevertheless far more urbane than Musin'ka, at least in Stepan's estimation. Stepan meets her at the symphony. She enjoys French perfume and likes to exchange greetings in French. Stepan even associates her size with urbanity:

Через малий зріст жіноче тіло своїх притяжних властивостей не втрачає. Навпаки, в сухості його обрисів він зачував витончені, містом породжені чари, бо в сільських умовах це тіло не могло б існувати. Саме міськість і вабила його в ній, бо стати справжнім городянином було першим завданням його сходу. (Kostjuk, 140 / *Misto*, 123–4 / BUL, 416–7)

A woman's body does not lose its attractiveness when it is small. On the contrary, in the diminutiveness of its characteristics he discerned the effect of refined, urbane charms, since this body could not exist under rural conditions. It was precisely her urbanity that attracted him, because becoming a true city-dweller was the first step of his ascent.

Rita, who is visiting her parents in Kiev, is a mature and confident flirt. Although her behaviour appears to be carefree and aggressive, it is in fact entirely deliberate and calculated. She combines vitality with passivity. She dances with grace and sensuality, but at other times she is distant and inert:

Вона складена була з двох тонів, без жодних переходів між ними – чорного: волосся, очі, сукня й лаковані черевики, та смуглого: обличчя, тіло рук і плеча та панчохи, і це просте поєднання надавало її постаті гордого чару; жодних кучерів чи гребінців у рівній зачісці, жодних прикрас чи гаптування у рівній сукні, що від стану трохи ширшала й немов підрізана була внизу, як і пасмо над чолом. Все чорне мінилось на ній від жвавих очей, а смугле застигло, життя було в убранні, а в тілі сон. (Kostjuk, 238 / *Misto*, 206 / BUL, 501)

She was assembled in two tones, without any transitions between them; black: hair, eyes, dress, and patent shoes; and tan: face, the skin of her hands and shoulders, and stockings. This simple combination gave her figure a proud charm. There were no curls or combs in her smooth hair; there were no decorations or embroidery on her smooth dress, which widened slightly from the waist and seemed to be cut straight across at the bottom, like the fringe of hair on her forehead. Everything black glistened on her, because of her vibrant eyes, while the tan was still; life was in the clothing, while the flesh slept.

The growing urbanity of Stepan's women is tied to the diminishing degree of illusion in these relationships. Nadijka is largely a figment of Stepan's youthful idealism. As the narrator observes: 'Саме ім'я її було надією, і він повторював його як символ перемоги' (Her name itself was hope, and he repeated it as a symbol of victory; Kostjuk, 31 / *Misto*, 34 / BUL, 325. The word *Nadija* means 'hope'). Ironically, Stepan's relationship with Nadijka is built on despair. She is the safety net that protects him from failure in his new life. Indeed, it is after his unsuccessful visit to the critic Svitozars'kyj that Stepan, soured by his failure, rapes her. Like the heroes of Pidmohyl'nyj's earliest stories, he then promptly excuses himself and blames her for the incident. Towards the end of the novel, in a moment of despair, lonely and dispirited, Stepan again turns to Nadijka, only to discover that the past cannot be recaptured.

Musin'ka helps Stepan dissolve his illusions about himself. After raping Nadijka, Stepan convinces himself that he, too, has a right to enjoy the pleasures of life. But when Musin'ka first comes to him at night, he instinctively pushes her away. Later, like Julien Sorel, the protagonist of Stendhal's *Le Rouge et le noir*, he convinces himself that he will be measured by this conquest:

Володіння цією пишною, вищою за нього, дозрілішою за нього жінкою могло б зміцнити йому дух, впевнити волю, як буває по перемозі, що самому героєві показує його вартість. (Kostjuk, 87 / *Misto*, 80 / BUL, 372)

Possession of this lush woman, who was above his reach and more mature than he, could strengthen his spirit, temper his will, as sometimes happens after a victory that shows the hero himself what he is worth.

Of course, manliness does not come from sexual conquests, particularly when it is the woman who makes the advances. Furthermore, Stepan soon forgets the lesson he has learned and confuses sexual gratification and love. Pidmohyl'nyj completes the picture with Musin'ka's autobiographical narrative, a masterpiece of Freudian character engineering. She, too, lives in the hope of recapturing an illusory past through her secret liaison with Stepan.

In his relationship with Zos'ka the nature of Stepan's illusions, as well as those of his partner, change. There is little thought of love on Stepan's part, only urban favours. Zos'ka, by contrast, is an impulsive dreamer. But unlike Musin'ka, Zos'ka finds her dreams in pure fantasy or in romantic literature. During her first date with Stepan she tells him she would like to go on a boat ride. Stepan is willing to oblige until she explains that she wants a boat ride on the street. 'Where's the water?' asks Stepan. 'Make some!' answers the starry-eyed girl. At other times she wants to fly in an airplane, fire a canon, become a musician, a professor (of any subject), a sailor, or a shepherd. Her desires are always unrealistic. For Zos'ka, the real, material world is merely a source of disappointment. When she finally allows herself to think of love and to entertain realistic hopes, the resulting disappointment is completely overwhelming.

Pidmohyl'nyj uses a shared symbol to link the fantasies of Zos'ka and Musin'ka. Stepan first meets Zos'ka at a charity lottery booth at the symphony. Out of sheer boredom and loneliness, Stepan buys a lottery ticket, and soon becomes the object of general attention as he buys one losing ticket after another. He is rescued by Zos'ka, who interrupts him, buys a single ticket, and wins. Dreamers, it turns out, always win at games of chance.[28] Later, Maksym Hnidyj takes Stepan to a bingo parlour where he shows him Musin'ka, now hopelessly devoted to the game. 'She always wins,' explains her son (Kostjuk, 165 / *Misto*, 145 / BUL, 438). The connection between gambling and illusions is thematically significant for Pidmohyl'nyj. It will recur in his last work, *Povist' bez nazvy*.

Rita and the prostitute complete the succession of Stepan's disillusioning pairings. At the party where he meets Rita, Stepan, overwhelmed by her sensuality and an excess of liquor, falls into melancholy meditation:

Невже тут знову почнеться оте кохання, ота нудна тяганина між чоловіком та жінкою? Любов – це довге алгебрійне завдання, де після всіх зусиль, розкривши дужки, дістаєш ноль. (Kostjuk, 240 / *Misto*, 208 / BUL, 503)

Not again, this love?! This boring tug of war between a man and a woman! Love is a long algebraic equation where after all the effort has been exerted, after all the parentheses have been opened, you are left with zero.

Thus, when Stepan learns that Rita is in Kiev for only a brief visit, he is overjoyed. Sensual gratification without emotional or social commitment will at last be possible. Indeed, the kind of human contact Stepan seeks is not only possible, but even easy, in a room full of intoxicated party-goers. The discovery of Zos'ka's suicide, however, unravels this new-found confidence. Afterwards, Stepan visits the prostitute, who explains to him: 'Жінка продається, а людина ні' (The woman is for sale, the person is not; Kostjuk, 264 / *Misto*, 228 / BUL, 523). Love and sex, the spiritual and the material, are not equivalent, and it is dangerous to confuse them.

Stepan's progression through a series of relationships with women is, thus, very different from Duroy's. Maupassant's protagonist is advancing his career;

Stepan is learning a philosophical lesson. Maupassant uses the series of women in *Bel-Ami* to highlight the view that sexual appetite is a remnant of the animal nature of human beings. Pidmohyl'nyj begins where Maupassant leaves off. Human animal nature is only half the equation; man's other foot is in the stars. The ability to distinguish these two natures is the key to inner harmony.

The second major thematic link between *Misto* and Maupassant is embodied in the character of Vyhors'kyj, whose philosophy of pessimism has many parallels to Maupassant's Schopenhauerian views. Indeed, Mahdalyna Laslo-Kucjuk goes so far as to assert that 'the model for the character of Vyhors'kyj was none other than Maupassant.'[29] Although this assertion may be unverifiable, there is no doubt that Vyhors'kyj's views are similar to those expressed by Maupassant. Moreover, the identification of the character with Maupassant is an important thematic insight.

Unlike Norbert de Varenne in *Bel-Ami*, Vyhors'kyj cannot be taken as the author's spokesman in *Misto*. The prediction that the universe will dissipate because of thermal entropy is not meant to be taken seriously. Furthermore, Vyhors'kyj's behaviour also undermines the credibility of his views. When he argues that progress is an illusion and that happiness is impossible, he guzzling beer in his favourite pub at Stepan's expense. When Stepan answers that such pessimism seems unnatural, Vyhors'kyj answers with a phrase that echoes Maupassant and attacks Nietzsche: 'Після того, як **над**природнє заперечено, **не**природнє лишилося нашою єдиною втіхою' (Once the **super**- [above-] natural has been negated, the **un**-natural remains as our only joy; Kostjuk, 191 / *Misto*, 167 / BUL, 461). This sentiment parallels Maupassant's admiration for those individuals – Madeleine Forestier, for example – who resist the appeals of instinct even at the cost of losing direct contact with nature. Vyhors'kyj's combination of pessimism and hedonism may well be an allusion to Duroy or Maupassant. It is certainly an indication of bad faith.

In a world in which all people are divided between nature and intellect, Stepan chooses nature while Vyhors'kyj chooses intellect. Nevertheless, Vyhors'kyj considers intellect an exercise in futility. For him, progress, science, and idealism are all illusions. What he values most is pure abstraction. He even has a scheme for a relative ranking of the arts according to the degree of abstractness of the medium they employ. The highest art, he argues, is the non-existent art of smells. Theatre is the lowest form of art since its medium is anything but abstract. The final irony of Vyhors'kyj's position, and the quality that most clearly distinguishes him from Stepan, is his preference for things over people: 'Мені здається навіть, що до людини не можна так прилюбитись, як до мертвої речі' (It seems to me that you can never like a person as much as you can like a thing; Kostjuk, 177 / *Misto*, 155 / BUL, 449). Stepan's great ambition to write a story about people puts him on the opposite side of this central thematic issue.

Vyhors'kyj is a disillusioned idealist who pretends to be completely at home with cynicism. He is an intellectual hedonist who argues that everything is meaningless, yet at the same time he is the mentor who helps Stepan establish himself as a writer, and a poet who escapes from himself and from the city in order to seek inspiration. He writes under a pseudonym, he tells Stepan, in part because 'Це надто велика відповідальність – підписуватись власним ім'ям. Це немов зобов'язання жити і думати так, як пишеш' (It is too big a responsibility to sign one's own name. It's like an obligation to live and think the way you write; Kostjuk, 115 / *Misto*, 104 / BUL, 396). Vyhors'kyj escapes the difficulty of intellectual consistency and unity by plunging into the psychological dualism of existential bad faith.

Although it is not one of Maupassant's primary concerns, bad faith is a significant element in *Bel-Ami*. Duroy looks at himself through the eyes of others. The *comme* that Philippe Bonnefis[30] sees in Maupassant is, among other things, a symptom of bad faith, which is most clearly reflected in the mirror on the landing of the stairs leading up to Forestier's apartment. On a number of occasions in the novel, Duroy is surprised at his own appearance in this mirror.

> Tout à coup il aperçut, dans la grande glace du second étage, un monsieur pressé qui venait en gambadant à sa rencontre et il s'arrêta net, honteux comme s'il venait d'être surpris en faute.
>
> Puis il se regarda longuement, émerveillé d'être vraiment aussi joli garçon; puis il se sourit avec complaisance; puis, prenant congé de son image, il se salua très bas, avec cérémonie, comme on salue les grands personnages. (*B-A*,[31] 270–1)

> Suddenly, in the large mirror on the second-floor landing, he saw a man hurrying and skipping towards him and he stopped short, feeling as ashamed as if he had been caught doing something wrong.
>
> Then he took a long look at himself, amazed at being such a really handsome young man. He smiled, well pleased with what he saw; then he took leave of his reflection with a very low, ceremonious bow, the kind of bow you reserve for people of high degree. (*Friend*,[32] 58)

Duroy's bad faith is also evident in the attention he gives to clothes, in his agitation before the duel, in his public reading of his first newspaper article, in his ennobling name change, in the way he reacts to being called Forestier, and especially in his curiosity about Madeleine's faithfulness to her former husband.

Vyhors'kyj and Duroy are not the only ones who see themselves as objects. Stepan Radčenko is a master of the *comme il faut*. Except where they pertain to sex, his decisions are shaped by fashion and convention.[33] Stepan has come to the city to get an education that will prepare him for further, more productive work in the village. He is happy to expound his noble sentiments about the coupling of village and city at his university entrance examination. But contemporaries would immediately recognize these sentiments as popular political slogans. Stepan even reads about them in the newspaper while waiting for his interview. His self-appointed halo sustains a conspicuous dent when a friend turns this social-improvement program into a sexual pun: 'Так і у вас змичка?' (You two are coupling too?; Kostjuk, 46 / *Misto*, 46 / BUL, 337). Stepan's lack of sincerity is further evidenced by the ease with which he abandons these plans. Despite such setbacks, however, Radčenko is intent on recasting his life in a city mould. On the morning of his first day in the city, he adopts an exercise program out of a sense of social propriety rather than a concern for physical fitness:

> Йому конче хотілось розпочати день **нормально**, по-міському, так нібивін уже зовсім у нових обставинах освоївся. Важливо ж відразу поставити себе в норму, бо норма й розпорядок – перша запорука досягнень. (Kostjuk, 22 / *Misto*, 26 / BUL, 317)
>
> He decidedly wanted to start his day **normally**, as they do in the city, as if he were completely at home in his new surroundings. It's important to set yourself a standard, because standards and schedules are the best guarantors of achievement.

Another sign of his urgent desire to identify himself with the city occurs when his landlady offers him a glass of milk: he feels compelled to refuse it even though he would gladly drink it. He interprets the offer of milk as a reference to his rural past.

Stepan is vain. In the course of exercising, for example, he 'lovingly feels his biceps.' But his attention to his wardrobe goes beyond vanity. While still a poor student, he stops to examine the display in the window of a clothing store:

Хлопець усвідомлював ту мить чудесну вагу одежі, що давно перестала вже бути способом прикривати тіло, прибравши ширшого й благороднішого завдання – прикрашати та поліпшувати його. Він може створив би щось геніяльне, коли б одягти його ту мить в англійську сорочку. (Kostjuk, 76 / *Misto*, 71 / BUL, 363)

In that moment the boy realized the wonderful importance of clothing, which had long since stopped being merely a means for covering the body but had acquired a larger, more noble function – to enhance and improve it. Perhaps he would create a work of genius if he were dressed in an English shirt.

Inspired by the clothes in the window, Stepan embarks on a series of fantasies of glorious possibilities for himself:

Він робився народнім комісаром, що їздив у його уяві автом і виголошував промови, які хвилювали його до самого шпіку; приймав чужоземні делегації, вів перемовини, запроваджував дивні закони, що змінили лице землі, і по смерті скромно відкривав собі пам'ятники; то раптом ставав надзвичайним письменником, що кожен рядок його котився по світі віщим дзвоном, бентежачи людські серця, а власне серце найперше; то занедбавши великі діла, надавав своєму обличчю чарівної краси, прибирався в найвиборніші костюми й скоряв жіночі серця поспіль, розбивав подружжя й тікав з коханками за всі можливі кордони, крім межі уяви; то кульбачив повстанського коня, добував із льохів сховані одрізани й на чолі ватаги безумців облягав місто, одмикав кулями ті крамниці, вантажив вози тих костюмів, тих ласощів та тістечок і клав під себе пахучу жінку, як полонянку. (Kostjuk, 77 / *Misto*, 72 / BUL, 364)

He would become a people's commissar, who, he imagined, rode in a car and gave speeches that moved him to the very quick; he met foreign delegations, conducted negotiations, enacted strange laws that changed the face of the earth, and, after his death, modestly unveiled a monument to himself; or, suddenly, he would become an outstanding writer, whose every line tolled round the world like a prophetic bell, moving people's hearts, especially his own; or, abandoning great deeds, he would endow his face with captivating beauty, dress in the choicest suits, and conquer women's hearts in droves, breaking up marriages and running away with his lovers across every conceivable frontier, except the one of his imagination; or, he would saddle a rebel horse, break out the hidden sawed-off rifles, and lead a band of mindless men in a siege of the city, where he would shoot his way into these shops, pile his wagons high with these suits, these delicacies, and these pastries, and force a perfumed woman beneath him, like a captive.

The illusions described in this passage are of two types. One is material and instinctive – Stepan imagines himself a great lover and the happy pillager of all the sensual delights of the city. The other is intellectual – he sees himself as an effective propagandist, a brilliant statesman, or a famous writer. What is peculiar about these intellectual illusions is that Radčenko appears as both object and as subject in each of them.

This existential dualism, or reification, is particularly evident in Stepan's career as a writer. The initial impulse to try his hand at writing comes from his identification with the writers who appear onstage at the *soirée littéraire* he attends. He continues writing out of a sense of duty and existential obligation, as he discovers when he shows Zos'ka one of his books:

'Оце ти написав?' сказала вона. 'Люди такі коміки! Все вони щось накручують, накручують...'
    'Так покинути?' спитав він.
    'Ні, вже пиши, коли почав.'
    Він і сам це чудово розумів. Треба писати, коли почав! Ця книжечка обернула йому письменство в обов'язок, у вимогу, в слово чести, що він мусів додержати. (Kostjuk, 184 / *Misto*, 161 / BUL, 455)

'Did you write this?' she asked. 'People are so funny. They're always after one thing or another.'
    'Should I give it up, then?' he asked.
    'No, once you've started, keep writing.'
    He understood this perfectly himself. He must keep writing, now that he has started. This book had made writing an obligation for him, a demand, a word of honour that he had to live up to.

He views his own writing through the eyes of others. At the editorial offices of the journal he is happy when the other writers acknowledge his presence and is very proud of having participated in their debate, even though the only opinion he expressed was 'I think so, too' (Kostjuk, 176 / *Misto*, 154 / BUL, 447). The most significant manifestation of Stepan's tendency to reify people, however, is found in his presentation of fictional characters. Eventually, after rereading his stories, Stepan himself recognizes this feature of his writing:

Окремі хиби турбували його, чималі огріхи в побудові й страшенна прикрість від змісту. Про що, властиво, він писав? Ніде, протягом сотні сторінок не здибав він людини – того, що мучиться й прагне, що божевільні пориви зароджує в болі, того, що нидіє і буяє, плазує і підноситься на верховини. Він не знайшов у тих сторінках сумного карлика з велетенським розумом, дрібного звіря, що тягне на щуплих раменах вічний тягар свідомости; не знайшов чарівної дитини, що так мило плаче й сміється серед барвистих цяцьок існування, жорстокого войовника, що вміє вбивати й умирати за свої мрії, суворого поборника за далекі дні, невтомного гінця в майбутнє. І ця відсутність вразила його. Навіщо ж ці твори, коли людське серце в них не б'ється? Мертвими видались йому тепер ці оповідання, де людина зникла під тиском річей та ідей, від неї створених і для неї призначених. (Kostjuk, 245 / *Misto*, 212 / BUL, 507)

Specific faults troubled him: substantial flaws in construction and a terrible embarrassment over the contents. What, exactly was he writing about? Nowhere in the space of hundreds of pages had he encountered a person – one who suffers and struggles, who generates insane impulses out of pain, who languishes and soars, crawls and scales heights. He didn't find in these pages a sad dwarf with great wisdom, a tiny animal who carries on its narrow shoulders the eternal weight of consciousness; he didn't find a charming child who cries and smiles so sweetly among the colourful toys of existence, the ruthless warrior who knows how to kill and be killed for his dreams, the stern conqueror of future days, the tireless messenger into the future. And this absence distressed him. What good are these works if the human heart does not beat in them? They now seemed dead to him, these stories, in which people disappeared under the weight of things and ideas, created by them and for them.

By endowing Stepan with a career as a writer, Pidmohyl'nyj was following the general outline of his model, Maupassant's *Bel-Ami*, in which Georges Duroy becomes an important journalist. He was also following the outline of his own biography, with the significant difference that, unlike Radčenko, he had embarked on his career as a writer before he came to Kiev. The connection between Radčenko and Pidmohyl'nyj offers important clues for an analysis of *Misto*. Radčenko's early stories are highly symbolic and melodramatic. Indeed, his stories reflect his view of the Revolution and civil war, which he sees as a giant mass movement, in which одиниці були непомітні часточки, зрівнені в цілому й безумовно йому підпорядковані, де люди знеособились у вищій волі, що відібрала їм особисте життя і разом з ним усі ілюзії незалежности. Тим то героями його оповідань зовсім природньо ставали речі, що в них могутня ідея побіжно втілювалась. І справді, носіями дії в нього самі з себе робились панцерний потяг, зведений з реєк, спалений маєток, або здобута станція, що стояли проти людського колективу, як виразні особи. (Kostjuk, 135–6 / *Misto*, 120 / BUL, 413)

individuals were invisible particles, levelled in the larger whole and mindlessly subordinated to it; where people were depersonalized in a higher will, which had stripped them of their own life and, along with it, of all illusions of independence. Thus, quite naturally, the heroes of his works were things, in which the mighty idea was superficially embodied. Indeed, of their own will, the carriers of the action in his stories were a derailed armoured train, a burnt-out estate, or a captured station that had all stood against the human collective as distinct individuals.

It would be unfair to suggest that this description applies to Pidmohyl'nyj's own early stories, but the symptoms exaggerated here for comic effect are not so distant from the melodramatic and impressionistic symbolism that characterized most Ukrainian short stories, including his own, in the first half of the decade. Pidmohyl'nyj also parodies contemporary writing in the description of Stepan's screenplay, which conforms to a formula based on five required elements: (1) social conflict, (2) lovers from opposite sides, (3) another woman (from the same side), (4) smoke and bullets, and (5) justice victorious.[34]

Thus, although comic reflections on Radčenko's writing are designed to spotlight his development as a writer, they also reveal Pidmohyl'nyj's view of the structural and stylistic issues that distinguish his later works from his earlier writing. Fundamentally, however, their significance lies on the philosophical plane. A twentieth-century novel in which the hero is himself a writer is virtually guaranteed to be an existential search for harmony – witness the works of Joyce, Gide, Mann, and Sartre. Radčenko's quest to write a novel about people is stimulated by a desire not merely to overcome the technical limitations of the immature writer or even to transcend the stylistic bias of a passing era, but rather to bridge the gap between thought and life. Stepan's ability to write a novel about people will represent his ability both to overcome the faults in his writing and to conquer the divide between reason and matter. It will be a victory over bad writing and bad faith.

Between Reason and Irrationality

Another thematic link between *Misto* and *Bel-Ami* is the attention given to social issues. Both novels realistically portray a period of significant social transformation. Indeed, to a certain extent, they both present the same situation: After the disruption of war and the disillusionment of defeat, a new generation of young men enter the city in order to make their career and fortune at the centre of power and action. The society depicted in *Bel-Ami* reflects the scars left by the Prussian invasion of 1870, the disillusionment and cynicism of a generation that experienced, along with the young patriot Guy de Maupassant, a rude military and emotional awakening. On the eastern side of Europe, the events of 1917–1920 brought enormous changes to the Russian Empire. Nowhere were those years more turbulent, and nowhere did they leave a greater residue of disillusionment, on the one hand, and a greater sense of opportunity, on the other, than in Ukraine. In the mid-1920s, a generation of young men who had left their villages and seen a much bigger, but not very attractive, world during the war years were now streaming into the cities to make their fortune. Pidmohyl'nyj and Radčenko were both part of that stream.

The social background depicted in Pidmohyl'nyj's novel has often been taken as the primary subject of the work. The novel's title, *The City*, combined with its attention to social questions, convinced many readers that Pidmohyl'nyj's chief intention was the analysis of a social transformation. The author himself explained his purpose in words that make clear his interest in social issues but simultaneously suggest that those issues form the background for a larger thematic concern:

Написав *Місто*, бо люблю місто, і не мислю поза ним ні себе, ні своєї роботи. Написав ще й тому, щоб наблизити, в міру змоги, місто до української психіки, щоб сконкретизувати його в ній. І коли мені частина критики закидає 'хуторянську ворожість' до міста, то я собі можу закинути тільки невдячність проти села. Але занадто довго жили ми під стріхами, щоб лишитись романтиками їх.[35]

I wrote *Misto* because I love the city and because I do not imagine myself or my work outside of it. I wrote it also in order to bring the Ukrainian psyche closer, to the extent that is possible, to the city, to make the city a concrete element of that psyche. And when some of the critics accuse me of having a 'provincial aversion' to the city, I can only accuse myself of ingratitude towards the village. But we have lived under thatched roofs too long to continue romanticizing them.

Perhaps the most intriguing aspect of the social theme in *Misto* is the difference between Pidmohyl'nyj's treatment of it here and his treatment of the city-versus-village theme in his earlier works. Radčenko, like many of Pidmohyl'nyj's village-born heroes, finds a great deal to disapprove of in the city. But the alignment of forces in *Misto* is different from what it was in 'Povstanci,' for example. In his short stories Pidmohyl'nyj typically depicted a conflict between reason and irrationality, intellect and instinct, order and chaos, civilization and the magic of the night, and the city and the village (or, more specifically, the steppe). All the elements on either side of the conflict were grouped together. In *Misto* such groupings have disappeared; the configuration of forces has changed. Stepan, the village boy, is a pedant who complains about disorder in the city. He is an intellectual who first seeks a degree in economics and then becomes a writer. This is a far cry from *Otaman* Kremnjuk, who would destroy the cities to preserve the greater glory of the steppe.

Radčenko is a village boy trying to make good in the city, and thus it is hardly surprising that he has adopted urban values. But the city dwellers he meets continually disappoint him: They do not live up to the model of urban life that he had created in his imagination. His landlady milks her own cows. Andrij Venedovyč, the Latinist, is a relic from a previous century, and the various urban bureaucrats he encounters are no different from their incompetent country cousins. The city is not what Radčenko expected it to be. Indeed, it turns out to be a symbolic relative of the steppe.

In the final pages of the novel, Stepan remembers the magic charm of the steppe at night and sets out on a futile quest to return, with Nadijka, to the village. But the sense of a force greater than man can be found in the city, too. Indeed, he has already experienced it, in the print shop of the Deržavne vydavnyctvo Ukrajiny, where he is the editor of a journal:

Але найбільше любив він машиновий відділ – широкий, кругойдучий коридор, де низкою стояли присадкуваті варстати, висуваючи важкого щелепа за кожного оберту маховика. Тут міцніше тхнуло випарами фарби з накотних валів, чути було глухий шелест стиснутого між металом паперу, рівне зідхання коліс і свист моторів у дерев'яних футлярах. В цьому безкінечному строкатому шумі, що глушив людську мову й ходу, билось могутнє серце міста. Тут він був у його грудях, бачив залізну систему його тканин, чув голос його, пізнавав його потайну істоту. Зачарування, мрійність охоплювала його, і прислухаючись до розбіжного стукоту, обіймаючи разом його складові частини, він поволі вбирав у себе цей блискучий рух, зливався з ним, поринав у нього, переймаючись його легкістю й поривом. В ту мить йому воскресло давнє почуття незмірності вночішнього степу, завмерлого спокою рівнин під неозорим мінливим небом, що він споглядав самотньою дитиною з захватом і тремтінням. І як тоді, невиразні бажання колихалися у нім, мов хлюпіт легкої хвилі по шелесткому піску. (Kostjuk, 209 / *Misto*, 182 / BUL, 476)

But he loved the machine room the best – the wide, circular corridor with the squat presses standing in a row, pushing out the heavy bed for every revolution of the rotor. The smell of vapours from the inking rollers was stronger here. You could hear the faint rustle of the paper as it was pressed between metal, the even sighs of the rollers and the whistle of the motors in their wooden cases. In this endless uneven noise, which silenced the sound of human speech and footsteps, beat the mighty heart of the city. Here he was in its breast, he could see the steel system of its weave, hear its voice, discover its secret being. Enchantment and dreaminess overcame him, and, listening to the spreading sound, embracing at once its various components, he slowly assimilated into himself this polished motion, became one with it, immersed himself in it, amazed at its lightness and its impulse. At that moment he felt again the immeasurability of the steppe at night, the dead calm of the plain beneath the boundless changing sky, which he had experienced with rapture and trembling as a lonely child. Now, as then, vague desires swayed within him, like the gentle lapping of small waves on a rustling beach.

Stepan's encounter with the magic of the night in the power and noise of the machines of the city runs counter to the exclusive alignment of that force in his early stories with the steppe and the village. In *Misto*, Pidmohyl'nyj still portrays a conflict between reason and irrationality, but he no longer embodies it in the city – village polarity. In other words, in the tradition of Balzac and Maupassant, Pidmohyl'nyj has created a city that is a complete universe unto itself, in which reason and irrationality, order and chaos, civilization and the magic of the night, and good and evil forces of various kinds coexist in eternal conflict.

Although the new alignment of forces brings Pidmohyl'nyj's Kiev closer to Maupassant's Paris, it does not bring Radčenko any closer to Duroy. In the thematic structure of their respective novels, the two characters play very different roles and end up in very different situations. Ironically, this difference is nowhere more evident than in the final link between the two characters, an identical scene in both novels.

Misto ends with an ambiguous situation. Pidmohyl'nyj, like Maupassant, deliberately avoids making explicit judgments. Radčenko has discovered that he cannot return to the past, that he cannot go back to the village with Nadijka. He has also discovered that Rita is once again in Kiev, but only until the fall. He can enjoy a passionate physical relationship with her without fear of a lengthier or more serious involvement. Overjoyed at this prospect, Stepan goes home in a state of exuberant self-confidence:

Не чекаючи ліфту, хлопець притьмом збіг на шостий поверх, і до кімнати ввійшовши, розчинив вікна в темну безодню міста. Воно покірно лежало внизу хвилястими брилами скель, позначене вогняними краплями, і простягло йому з пітьми горбів гострі, кам'яні пальці. Він завмер від сласного споглядання цієї величі нової стихії і раптом широким рухом зронив униз зачудований поцілунок.
   Тоді, в тиші лямпи над столом, писав свою повість про людей. (Kostjuk, 281 / *Misto*, 242 / BUL, 538)

Without waiting for the elevator, the boy ran headlong up the stairs to the sixth floor, entered his room, and threw open the windows onto the dark abyss of the city. It lay submissively below in cliff-like waves marked with dots of fire, and out of the darkness of its hills, sharp stone fingers stretched out to him. He stood immobilized in sensual contemplation of the magnitude of this new force, then suddenly, with a grand gesture, he threw an enchanted kiss out below.
   Then, in the silence of his desk lamp, he wrote his novel about people.

In the corresponding scene in *Bel-Ami*, Duroy has come home from Forestier's dinner party, where he has just been given a job at the newspaper, and his first assignment. He tries to write his article about Algeria, but soon finds that he does not know how to begin. He goes to his window, which looks out over the railway tracks of the Chemin de fer de l'Ouest, where they emerge from the tunnel leading to the Batignolles station. His good humour is restored by the whistle of a train shooting out of the tunnel:

Alors, ressaisi par l'espoir confus et joyeux qui hantait toujours son esprit, il jeta, à tout hasard, un baiser dans la nuit, un baiser d'amour vers l'image de la femme attendue, un baiser de désir vers la fortune convoitée. (*B-A*, 276)

Then abandoning himself once more to the vague, cheerful optimism which never deserted him, he blew a kiss at random into the night, a kiss of love for the woman for whom he was waiting, a kiss of longing for the wealth which he desired. (*Friend*, 64)

The correlation between these two scenes goes beyond similarity. The ambiguous ending of Pidmohyl'nyj's novel needs an extrinsic clue to shed light on its significance. Duroy's kiss over the railway tracks provides that necessary evidence. Duroy and Radčenko are both in their rooms, writing, but whereas the former is failing to make a start, the latter is in fact writing. (The imperfective aspect of the verb in the last sentence of *Misto* leaves open the question of whether the work will end successfully.) In both scenes, the kisses are sensual, not abstract symbols of good spirits. But whereas Georges is imagining his ideal woman, Stepan has just been with Rita – in other words, the former is merely dreaming of success, whereas the latter has some tangible evidence of it. Georges is inspired by the whistle of a train, a symbol of sexual and personal aggressiveness. For him, success requires conquering enemies and overcoming obstacles. Stepan, by contrast, is being welcomed, perhaps seduced, by the outstretched fingers of the submissive city. For him, success has always come easily, of its own accord. His triumph at the end of the novel, if it may be called that, is the result of a harmony and balance between him and the city, and between his instincts and his reason.

Throughout the novel, Pidmohyl'nyj has depicted his hero in conflict with himself. The resulting dualism is evident in various traits and situations. Stepan's general bad faith, his village boy's hostility to the city, his muddled relationships with women, his uncertainty over his career choice, his vacillation between identification with the past and commitment to the present – all are symptoms of an internal conflict. But that conflict is most vividly revealed in the subjects of Stepan's stories. As George Shevelov points out in an important essay about *Misto*, 'writing about people' is not a meaningless goal.[36] In the course of the novel, as Stepan gradually comes to see the flaws in his early stories and the shortcomings of his initial view of the city, the word *people* slowly acquires a privileged position at the thematic centre of the novel. His inability to write about people is a result of the dualism within him, which does not allow him to see people for what they are, but, instead, forces them into the images of his own mental and emotional conflicts. The realization that Nadijka is not what he thinks she is leads Stepan to a psychological awakening.

In an essay on the poetry of Maksym Ryl's'kyj, Pidmohyl'nyj laments that poet's incongruous mixture of realism and romanticism, which he ascribes to a divided psyche. His advice to Ryl's'kyj is simple: 'Будь цільний, поете!' (Poet, be whole!).[37] Radčenko's new-found inspiration springs from precisely such a wholeness. In the oxymoronic silence of his desk lamp, Stepan can finally write about people. With that incongruous image, Pidmohyl'nyj illuminates in language what Stepan has experienced in his psyche – a union of incompatible elements. The narrator's rhetorical figure stands as a token of the unity Stepan has, at least for the moment, found.

CHAPTER FIVE

Nevelyčka drama
Philosophical Roots

Although Pidmohyl'nyj neither abandoned nor forgot the lessons he learned from Maupassant, in *Nevelyčka drama* his development as a writer took him beyond the influences that had nourished his talent earlier. New directions in style, construction, and theme characterize Pidmohyl'nyj's second novel.

Nevelyčka drama does, of course, have stylistic links with *Misto* and earlier works, but they are balanced by new and different techniques. For example, although the objective method has not disappeared, it has been modified. The novel is set in Kiev, and the city is still just as real as it was in *Misto*. As in the latter, the streets have real names. Marta lives on Žyljans'ka, Jurij's apartment is on P"jatakova (today's Saksahans'koho), and L'ova lives on Arsenal'na (which is not to be confused, in fact and in the novel, with Arsenalu). In addition to the street names, Pidmohyl'nyj mentions such well-known landmarks as the university, Xmel'nyc'kyj Square with the monument to the hetman in front of the Cathedral of St Sophia; and the dramatically situated Church of St Andrew, with its high, cast iron stairs and tiled patio. George Shevelov makes an important point when he calls *Nevelyčka drama* a 'chamber' novel by comparison with *Misto*, which he considers a 'social' novel. But he exaggerates when he asserts that Pidmohyl'nyj depicts his heroes 'against an abstract, black backdrop.'[1] In fact, the background is rich in realistic detail: It depicts not only an actual physical setting, but also the political, cultural, and intellectual atmosphere of the times. Among the popular notable figures mentioned in the novel are Hermann Keyserling, Kierkegaard, Nietzsche, Schopenhauer, and the poet Volodymyr Sosjura. Perhaps the most notable of the notable figures mentioned in the novel is Emil Fischer (1852–1919), the German organic chemist who won a Nobel prize in chemistry in

1902 and, as Pidmohyl'nyj's narrator explains in the novel, discovered a method for synthesizing polypeptides. The accuracy and timeliness of the discussion of protein synthesis is an easily overlooked but significant indicator of this novel's underlying realism.

Other signs of the objective technique are discernible in Pidmohyl'nyj's use of pathetic fallacy and consonant focalized narration. In *Nevelyčka drama* the tangible correlatives of the characters' psyches are limited to the weather and the three apartments in which almost all the action takes place. The chamber-novel quality that Shevelov points out is an important reflection of the inability of the characters to establish human relationships, to break out of the intellectual and emotional cubicles in which they exist. The action takes place during the winter of 1928, and the season contributes to a sense of physical and spiritual isolation. Ironically, spring arrives just as Marta reaches her emotional nadir.

The most important link between the physical and spiritual worlds in the novel is the clearly implied comparison between the scientific models of digestion devised by Jurij Slavenko, the male protagonist of the novel, and the fictional world in which he lives. Slavenko's decision to use himself and his students as experimental subjects becomes a symbol of the primacy of matter over spirit. He deliberately equates himself with an experimental subject, an ingested protein that has been broken down into its component amino acids, which are then synthesized into new proteins of a standard type, having a specific, practical function. Slavenko as a person is reduced to a geometric formula, the symbolic equivalent of a polypeptide chain. A similar dehumanization occurs on the other side of the novel's thematic and dramatic divide. Marta Vysoc'ka, the female protagonist, sees her life through a succession of romantic literary images. Her illusions about the willfulness and originality of her aspirations are eventually dispelled by the discovery that what she perceives as her most original and most willful act – breaking off with Jurij at the peak of their happiness – is also only a familiar literary trope. In short, Marta's idealism is no less dehumanizing than Jurij's pragmatism.

Like Maupassant's later novels, *Nevelyčka drama* does not adhere rigidly to the constraints of indirect narration. Although the bulk of the novel is a focalized third-person narrative, the fact that emotion is its chief subject means that the narrator inevitably must speak directly about the thoughts and feelings of the characters. The smooth surface of the narrative veneer is further and more seriously disturbed by the narrator's lengthy discourses on scientific matters. Chapter 7, for example, entitled 'O, Bajaderko, ty čaruješ mene' (Bajadere,[2] you enchant me), is written almost entirely in the narrator's voice and explains at some length and in considerable technical detail the general principles of organic chemistry as regards proteins, peptides, and amino acids. Although this explanation is by no means irrelevant to the novel, it is differentiated by its narrative texture from the rest of the work. In short, the narrative voice of *Nevelyčka drama* is occasionally very dry, heavy-handed, and intrusive. Although Pidmohyl'nyj has not lost his characteristic irony (witness the chapter titles), it is less evident here than in *Misto*.

The mixed objective and subjective narrative technique of *Nevelyčka drama* is at work in the opening passage:

В густому лісі, де вона вступила з гострим щемінням у серці, з напруженням свіжого тіла й бажань, стояла тиша і вогкість. Жодного шелесту, свисту чи шарудіння – важкий ліс цей був мертвий, бездушний за серпанком ранкового повітря. Вона не чула своїх кроків по землі, так ніби пливла все вперед, далі, вглиб гущавини, і суворі стовбури, здавалось, розступались перед нею нескінченною алеєю, стелили їй шлях туди, де прагнула вона в своєму легкому поході.

Вона вийшла на взлісся. Невидиме сонце, десь із-за її спини, поклало широкий промінь на степи, і от на пагорку побіч себе вона побачила церкву. Вона спинилась, і її серце пристрасно закипіло в передчуттях, кожним ударом припинаючи її до місця. Бо від церкви з горба врочисто сходив чернець. Ось підвів він заросле обличчя і, малий віддалік, щокроку зростав, заступаючи церкву і обрій. Вона чекала з надією й страхом, його наближення почуваючи як грозу.... Ось він підніс руку до її грудей, і ту ж мить позад його жахливого тіла постали тисячі нестерпних дзвонів, витягуючись у безконечний колючий звук, що в боліснім коливанні його вона впала у безвість.

Марта раптом розплющила очі й машинально схопила рукою будило. (Bojko,[3] 25–6 / *Nevelyčka drama*, 12–13 / BUL, 539)

The dense forest [which she entered] with a sharp tremor in her heart and a tense body full of desire was still and damp. Not a rustle, whistle, or crackle was to be heard; the heavy forest was dead and heartless behind the veil of the [morning] air. She could not hear her footsteps on the ground and, as it were, floated further and deeper into the thicket while stern tree trunks seemed to step aside in front of her in an endless avenue leading to where she craved to go with her easy walk.

She came to the edge of the forest. The invisible sun, somewhere behind her, cast a wide ray across the steppe and on a hill nearby she saw a church. She stopped and her heart stirred wildly in anticipation, nailing her to the spot with its every beat. For a monk was moving solemnly down from the church on the hill. Now he raised his bearded face and, [small from a distance, he grew with every step,] hiding the church and horizon. She waited with hope and fear, feeling his approach as if it were a storm. Now he was raising his hand to her breasts and at that moment from behind his horrible body there sounded thousands of bells stretching out in an endless piercing sound which enveloped her like a wave, plunging her into darkness.

Marta suddenly opened her eyes and automatically reached for the alarm clock. (*Touch*, 17)[4]

From a narrative perspective, the technique employed in this passage is a combination of objectivity and sleight of hand. What seems at first to be objective description limited by the perspective of the protagonist soon proves to be the effect of a ploy. The alarm clock rings, and the pretence of narrative objectivity is disclosed. Maupassant's *contes fantastiques* and Pidmohyl'nyj's own 'Vanja' use a similar device, but in *Nevelyčka drama* the effect is more dramatic. The play on objectivity in 'Vanja' comes at the very end of the story, so it does not affect the preceding narration. In Maupassant, the mixing of diegetic levels is generally restricted to such formal devices as the framed narrator and the diary. By using the device to open his novel, Pidmohyl'nyj creates an ironic narrative distance between the elements of each pair of the three figures in the narrative situation – the author (narrator), the reader, and the character. The effect of the device is to prod the reader to read the story from a wider philosophical perspective. That effect is itself an ironic trick: One of the novel's themes is the dehumanizing effect of studying rather than experiencing life.

Even before the alarm clock rings and the two levels of reality collide, the narrator abandons Maupassantian objectivity for a Proustian subjectivity. Pidmohyl'nyj's use of subjectivity in this passage has the effect of bridging the gap between author, reader, and character. The ringing of the alarm clock is thus made more dramatic because it awakens both Marta and the reader. Marta's dream is described from the perspective of her mental understanding, not her direct perception. The reader is told how the protagonist has accepted or interpreted her perceptions, not what the visual images were. Pidmohyl'nyj describes Marta's total experience of the landscape rather than merely cataloguing visual perceptions. Marta enters a thick, humid, silent forest. She experiences the soundlessness of her footsteps and the opening of a path through the trees. She sees a monk walking down a hill towards her, but she experiences sunlight from a sun she cannot see. The monk grows larger with his every step. These are her impressions, not her perceptions. Of course,

Nevelyčka drama

dream reality has no clear definition, and the whole experience of dreaming can be considered an event that happens to Marta and is, therefore, categorically objective. Even in that case, however, the narrative technique used here is far different from the visually oriented narration of *Bel-Ami* and *Misto*.

The symbolic elements in Marta's dream are also a reflection of the tendency of the narrative towards subjectivity. Unlike the symbols in *Misto* (the razor, for example) the dark forest and the monk descending from the church on the hill are projections from Marta's mind, rather than material correlatives of her emotional state. The dream with which *Nevelyčka drama* begins is the result of a psychoanalytic method of character depiction.

The general reliance on Freudian psychoanalysis in the creation of characters in Nevelyčka drama is a significant development in Pidmohyl'nyj's writing. The presence of Freudian ideas is not new in itself. The repressed sexuality of many of the young male characters in the early stories is based on a primitive application of Freudian principles. Similarly, Tamara Hnida in *Misto* is a finely crafted example of the explosive force of repressed female sexuality. But it is only in *Nevelyčka drama* that a series of Freudian ideas is reflected in the behaviour and make-up of the entire cast of characters. Pidmohyl'nyj's essay on Nečuj-Levyc'kyj offers insight into the nature of this psychoanalytic approach.[5]

In that essay, citing French and Russian translations of the works of Freud and Ernest Jones, Pidmohyl'nyj defends Freudian psychoanalysis against its popular detractors. The detractors, he argues, often allow themselves to be guided by an incomplete understanding of the subject and a 'natural' prejudice against it. The prejudice is natural, he argues, 'because psychoanalysis is "an analysis of the depths (of the psyche)," a painful disclosure of everything that is hidden in the dark depths of a person's being. What it brings into view appears, at first sight, so ugly, frightening, and unworthy of a person that the first reaction to its assertions is seldom other than sharply negative.'[6] Furthermore, argues Pidmohyl'nyj, the popular understanding of psychoanalysis as a reduction of everything to the level of 'vulgar sexuality' is based on misunderstanding of and a lack of familiarity with Freud's works. His own application of Freudian psychology, however, is sharply focused on the Oedipal complex.

Pidmohyl'nyj suggests that both the writings and the life story of Ivan Levyc'kyj, the leading figure in nineteenth-century Ukrainian prose, attests to the Oedipal instincts that dominated his personality. Working from Levyc'kyj's autobiography, from his stories and novels, and from literary-biographical studies of him by Serhij Jefremov and Jurij Meženko, Pidmohyl'nyj attempts to show a pattern that could only be the result of an unresolved

Oedipal conflict. Among the elements to which he calls particular attention are Levyc'kyj's autobiographical account of his unusually cool relationship with his father – an Orthodox priest and a reclusive, though public-minded, man – and the death of his mother when Levyc'kyj was twelve. On this foundation, Pidmohyl'nyj proceeds to build a structure of psychoanalytic evidence consisting of Freudian slips, father-figure and mother-figure characters in Levyc'kyj's works, and his predilection for descriptions of the landscape – that is, for loving portraits of the mother-surrogate, mother nature. Similarly, Pidmohyl'nyj makes the case that literature and the Ukrainian language are also mother surrogates and explains Levyc'kyj's stubborn defence of his own peculiar orthography from that perspective. He also considers Levyc'kyj's pseudonym, Nečuj – that is, *ne čuj* (don't hear) – and the abundance of sibilant consonants in the titles of his works (*sssh!*) part of the author's problematical relationship with his father, who did not know that his son was a Ukrainian writer. Finally, Pidmohyl'nyj identifies Levyc'kyj's notorious fastidiousness, stubbornness, and miserliness as three components of an anal-eroticism that cloaks the intricacies of an Oedipal conflict.

Ivan Levyc'kyj was indeed an interesting man, and his writings offer a wealth of material that lends itself to Freudian interpretation. Pidmohyl'nyj's essay, however, is inadequate to that task. Levyc'kyj may well have been everything Pidmohyl'nyj says he was, but the methods used and the evidence presented in the essay are too impressionistic to convince a serious reader. Pidmohyl'nyj was a writer, not a psychoanalyst, and the real value of his essay on Levyc'kyj lies in what it tells us about his own methods for creating characters.

The techniques Pidmohyl'nyj sees at work in the construction of Levyc'kyj's characters are also evident throughout *Nevelyčka drama*. The attention given to the unconscious, particularly to dreams, is a measure of the importance of Freudian psychology in Pidmohyl'nyj's character construction. A second dream of Marta's, in which flower petals turn into sharp blades, is described towards the end of the fourth chapter. Her neighbour, David Semenovyč, has a sadistic erotic dream about Marta in which her leg is severed by a streetcar, an accident reminiscent of one that he had witnessed on the streets of the city.

In his autobiographical sketch, Levyc'kyj mistakenly refers to Turgenev's *Fathers and Sons* as 'Bazarov,' the name of the story's young protagonist. According to Pidmohyl'nyj, this slip is conditioned by Levyc'kyj's Oedipal antipathy to his father. In *Nevelyčka drama* Jurij Slavenko also makes frequent errors in the names of characters and in the titles of literary works. When he sets out with L'ova to meet Marta for the first time, he asks, 'Де ж живе ця Бісектриса, ця мадемуазель Помпадур?' (Bojko, 89 / *Nevelyčka drama*, 50 / BUL, 579; 'So where does she live, this Bisectrix, this Mademoiselle Pompadour?' [*Touch*, 52]). As Jurij Bojko points out in the notes to his edition of the novel, there are two mistakes here. The word *bisektrysa* (bisectrix) denotes a line that bisects an angle. What Slavenko means to say is 'Beatriča' – that is, Dante's Beatrice, the literary embodiment of the idealized woman. The second mistake lies in referring to the Marquise de Pompadour, the famous mistress of Louis XV, as 'Mademoiselle.'[7] Jeanne Antoinette Poisson was Madame d'Étoiles before she became Louis's mistress and a marquise. But Bojko is missing the point when he suggests (in a footnote) that this error reveals Slavenko's ignorance: An ignorant man, or even a well-educated scientist, would not refer to Louis XV's mistress by any name whatsoever, let alone by one in which the only error is in her marital status. This is not ignorance but a deliberately, if somewhat crudely, contrived Freudian slip.

The first error, calling Beatrice 'Bisectrix,' is a simple malapropism. It has little psychological value but rather serves to reinforce the fact, already established by several other blunders in the biochemist's literary allusions, that Slavenko is not well acquainted with literature and that his mind is focused instead on scientific matters. Its real value, however, lies in camouflaging the significance of 'Mademoiselle Pompadour.' This second mistake, by virtue of its proximity to the first, is likely to be taken as yet another bit of lexical confusion or, perhaps, as a simple error of fact. Slavenko's association of a woman he has never met with the mistress of a French king actually reveals that he is unconsciously preoccupied with the role of women on an instinctive level. By calling her 'mademoiselle,' Slavenko emphasizes the sexual role of the king's mistress. Thus, it is not ignorance but libidinal instinct that informs Jurij's 'error.'

In his analysis of Levyc'kyj's personality, Pidmohyl'nyj deals with the relationship between the writer as a child and his parents, particularly his supposedly unloving father. The childhood relationship of characters to their parents is a significant element in the psychological background of Pidmohyl'nyj's own fictional characters, as is clear in the following description of Marta's unusual attachment to water:

Марта любила вмиватись, власне обтиратись холодною водою, а потім шорстким рушником до червоного тіла.... Вода була найбільша пристрасть її життя, бо виросла вона коло Дніпра, в Каневі, де річка широка і повновода. Батько її, вчитель сільський, до рибальства був дуже здібний, і сама вона, хлоп'ячий ухил у вдачі маючи, була за дитинства йому вірною і невтомною помічницею.

Between Reason and Irrationality

Там виробився в неї несвідомий погляд на воду, як на виключну, питому стихію життя, і відчуття води, як невичерпного джерела прагнення і сили. Тому зима, коли спиняється рух великої рідини, завжди здавалась дівчині мертвою і лихою.

Отож, до цього вранішнього процесу, такого звичайного й загально обов'язкового, вона потай додавала ту внутрішню, непомітну на чуже око любосність, що часто становить глибоке підґрунтя людських звичок, ту любосність, що народжується із давніх забутих дій, із юнацьких нерозвинених прагнень, обертаючи звичку в неодмінний ритуал життя, підносячи її, щоденну й непомітну, до високої ролі основ особистости. І воду вона уявляла завжди холоднуватою, як вода вечірньої річки, коли в перших сутінках ночі юрбою йдуть дівчата з хлопцями на берег і купаються там нарізно, на кілька кроків віддалік. Підлітком вона зазнавала радісного почуття сорому й визивности, біжучи від скинутої одежі до води, де рятувалась від гострих у пітьмі хлоп'ячих поглядів. І в цьому був цілий клубок заборонности, бо батько не схвалював її вечірніх купань з дівчатами. (Bojko, 28 / *Nevelyčka drama*, 14 / BUL, 541)

Marta loved to wash herself in cold water and then to [rub her body dry] with a rough towel till it was all red ... Water was her greatest passion in life. She had grown up near the Dnieper, in Kaniv, where the river is wide and full. Her father, a village school teacher, was very fond of fishing and [as a child she, a tomboy, had been his faithful and tireless assistant.] It was [there] that she developed [an unconscious] attitude toward water, as to a special, elemental force of life and the source of all craving and power. So to her winter, [when the flow of the great liquid stopped,] always seemed dead and evil.

Thus to her daily [regimen] she secretly added [an inner voluptuousness,] unnoticed by any outsider, a voluptuousness [that] often forms the deep substratum of human habits, a voluptuousness born in old, forgotten [acts, from] youthful undeveloped desires, turning habit into the steady ritual of living, [raising this daily, unnoticed habit to an important role as the cornerstone of a] personality. She imagined water always to be cool like an evening stream, when in the dusk [groups of] boys and girls go together to the river bank and swim, [separately,] in the water, [only] a few feet apart. As [an adolescent] she had felt a joyful pang of shame and daring when she ran from [her cast-off clothes to the water, hiding there from the eyes of the boys peering through the dusk.] There was a web of prohibition spun around [this scene, because] her father did not approve of her evening swims [with the girls.] (*Touch*, 19)

Marta's peculiar attachment to the Dnieper River is a product of her experiences on the river as a young girl.[8] (In this connection it is worth noting that Jurij does not know how to swim.) The narrator's description, which apparently reflects Marta's recollection, juxtaposes two separate incidents: fishing with her father and bathing with her friends, both boys and girls. The latter is evidently a recollection of adolescent sexual awakening. The two remembered scenes are linked by two elements: the river itself and the figure of Marta's father, who is represented in the second scene as a parental prohibition. Pidmohyl'nyj is creating a realistic psychological background for his protagonist. Marta's adult sexuality is tied to her childhood attachment to her father, which is inextricably bound up with water. Later she will tell Jurij that she wants her first sexual experience to be in Kaniv, in a boat on the river. Marta's unrealistic romantic idealism finds its source, at least in part, in a sexual fixation on her father.

Pidmohyl'nyj also explores the relationship between other characters and their parents. Jurij Slavenko has an elderly mother living alone in the Podil district. Although he does not allow her to visit him in his quarters, he dutifully sends her money every month and, when his unfulfilled sexual needs develop into a persistent problem, he seeks her advice. Jurij's father is not mentioned in the novel, but we know he was a member of the intelligentsia.[9] Iren Markevyč's relationship with her parents is friendly but tepid. Unlike Marta, she does not idealize her father, a portly professor and practitioner of internal medicine, whose two great passions are hot tea and the word *čudovo* (wonderful). Her time of youthful rebellion against her parents' bourgeois values is apparently over, and she is content to play a tedious and cynical waiting game that will eventually lead to marriage with Slavenko. About L'ova Rotter's parents the reader learns very little, except that his father, like L'ova, was a medical assistant. Like Marta, L'ova comes from Kaniv. Dmytro Stajnyčyj is the youngest of four sons born to a blacksmith and a laundress from Perejaslav. Although he is now a well-educated engineer, Dmytro still cherishes his father's simple, honest, and stern values. Marta's boss, Bezpal'ko, however, complains that his own son berates him for his opinions, but also says that he is not offended because he used to treat his own father the same way.

Pidmohyl'nyj used Levyc'kyj's notorious fastidiousness as an argument to support his diagnosis of an Oedipal complex. Indeed, the three traits associated in Freudian theory with repressed analeroticism – orderliness, parsimony, and obstinacy – are often found in Pidmohyl'nyj's characters. This is not to say that all Pidmohyl'nyj's fastidious characters should be read as Oedipal homosexuals. Pidmohyl'nyj's suggestion that Levyc'kyj's love of flowers was a sign of homosexuality says more about Pidmohyl'nyj than it does about Levyc'kyj. Similarly, Slavenko's and Markevyč's exactness reveals more about their author's technique of psychological character construction than it does about their infantile sexual fantasies. In both cases, however, these characteristics are depicted as fundamental personality traits rooted in the character's sexual self-identification. They are not merely Dickensian quirks that identify and enliven dull secondary characters.

Professor Markevyč's life revolves around immutable schedules. He drinks tea at eight and warm milk at ten. His daily round of patients and lectures is carefully planned in advance. His lectures themselves are prepared in detail and, although he never looks at his notes, he would be unable to lecture if they were not in his jacket pocket. His daughter has inherited some of her father's orderliness. She keeps a lamp by every piece of furniture in her room, but never allows two of them to be on at the same time. Both Iren and her father, however, appear chaotic and disorganized by comparison with Jurij Slavenko. His apartment, though filled to overflowing with books, is impeccably organized. The books are arranged by subject. His writing table is exceedingly neat, it is not even cluttered by an inkwell, since he writes with a mechanical pencil. In his first report after spying on Slavenko, Professor Markevyč quotes Jurij's neighbours to confirm that he keeps so rigidly to his schedule that you could set your watch by him. His daily ration of cigarettes is prepared for him by his chambermaid every morning. In the sixth chapter of the novel, when Jurij realizes he must do something to satisfy his sexual desires, he decides to propose to Iren:

Професор [Славенко] глянув на годинника – було початок на восьму. До десятої він зможе зробити так звану пропозицію, а потім до дванадцятої ще й трохи попрацювати. (Bojko, 132 / *Nevelyčka drama*, 76 / BUL, 606)

The professor [Slavenko] looked at his watch; it was a little after seven. He could propose by ten and then do a couple of hours of work before midnight. (*Touch*, 75)

The symbolic embodiment of Slavenko's orderliness is his neighbour's cat, Narcissus. The identification is negative. Slavenko sees the cat, who steals his food, as a complete nuisance. After he falls in love, however, his behaviour towards the cat changes, as he explains to Marta:

'Існування цього сусідського кота, за приблизним обрахунком, коштує мені близько червінця місячно, але я терпів його, щоб не

сваритися з сусідами, що на нього моляться. Я міг тільки ненавидіти його і давати йому крадькома стусана. Погляд мій на цього кота не змінився: це викінчений злодій, нахаба і грубіян. Але від якогось часу, не дуже давнього, я відчув, уяви собі, велику приязнь до нього! Я, коли хочеш, зрозумів його! Йому нудно, цими крадіжками він скрашує одноманітність свого побуту. Тепер я вільно допускаю його в свою кімнату. Він скаче на стіл, заривається в мої папери й спить.'
(Bojko, 167 / *Nevelyčka drama*, 97 / BUL, 628)

['The existence of the neighbour's] cat costs me [approximately] one ruble a month in stolen food, but I have suffered this so as not to quarrel with the neighbours who worship him. I could only hate it and whack it occasionally. My view of this cat has not changed; it is a thief, an insolent brute. Yet, for some time I have felt, if you can imagine it, great friendliness towards it. And if you like, I have understood it. He's simply bored and by stealing he makes his life more interesting. Now I let him wander freely into my room. He jumps on my desk, buries himself in my papers, and falls asleep.' (*Touch*, 95)

Slavenko offers this explanation as an analogy for his changed attitude towards poetry. A serious aesthetic theory lies just beneath the surface here. However, the relaxation of Jurij's strict orderliness during the time he is enchanted with Marta underscores the psychological link between sexuality and fastidiousness. As in his analysis of Levyc'kyj, Pidmohyl'nyj adopts the Freudian view of extreme orderliness as part of an anal-erotic complex. Jurij's relationship with Marta releases the repressed sexual energy that was being diverted into anal-erotic orderliness.

Another significant element of Pidmohyl'nyj's psychoanalytic reading of Levyc'kyj's works is the attention he calls to abstract surrogate mothers, specifically, nature, language, and literature itself. In *Nevelyčka drama*, there are no landscapes to parallel Levyc'kyj's, but a similar transference is suggested by Marta's attachment to Kaniv. Both she and L'ova come from that city, and they are both hopeless romantics. This 'geographic psychology' is further strengthened by the association of Kaniv with Ševčenko and, consequently, of both Marta and L'ova with Ukrainian national consciousness, represented principally by language preference: Marta and L'ova are advocates of Ukrainian; Slavenko and the Markevyčes speak Russian. The question of language is raised often in the novel, and it is identified specifically as one of Marta's attractions for Slavenko and one of the tools Iren uses to recapture him. The linkage between language and sexuality is paralleled by a similar tie between the arts and sexuality. Iren is associated with music, Marta with literature; both women use their art as a lure to snare Jurij. It is significant that the only man in the novel who is well-versed in literature is Bezpal'ko ('the fingerless one'), a romantic anti-pragmatist who sends flowers to Marta anonymously.

The role of language in *Nevelyčka drama* is greater than the aforementioned psychological associations might suggest. It belongs to a cluster of motifs that together form the thematic structure of the novel. Within this structure, the motif of language operates on two distinct levels, as the principal element of national identity and as a medium of communication. In the early days of their relationship, Marta and Jurij do not speak much:

Тобто, звісно, говорили, але коли б за стенограмою їхньої розмови хтось схотів би судити про мовний розвиток людей, то вжахнувся б кричущої вбогости їх лексикону. Різні вигуки, особові займенники першої і другої особи однини та до них відміна одного дієслова в одному тільки часі – от і вся була основа їхніх перших розмов. (Bojko, 158 / *Nevelyčka drama*, 92 / BUL, 622–23)

[That is, they spoke, of course, but if someone were to judge the development of human languages on the basis of a stenographic transcript of their conversations, that person would be shocked by the deafening] paucity of [their] vocabulary. [Various exclamations, the personal pronouns of the first and second person singular, and the conjugation of one verb in only one tense – these were the foundation of their early conversations.] (*Touch*, 90)

The narrator's commentary raises the issue of the function of language. The narrator sees language in the same light in which Slavenko sees digestion. Its elegance and efficiency do not impress him; he is interested in the mechanics of its functioning. Love, the synthetic product of two pronouns and one verb, is not a subject to occupy his interest. Communication occurs without recourse to the subtleties and intricacies of language.

A different view of language is presented in connection with Jurij's detailed exposition of his biochemical research. Marta listens to the stream of language, but what she understands does not correspond to what Slavenko has said:

Від розмов їй у пам'яті лишалось чимало спеціяльних термінів, що їх вона якось особливо плекала, силкуючись не забути, хоч і не розуміючи їх. Насамоті дівчина часто їх повторювала і, немов граючись, увособлювала їх. **Глюкоза** видавалась їй перекупкою, **алянін** уявляла гарненьким білявим хлопчиком, **глікоколь** – страшенним пустуном,

тирозин – людиною небезпечною, **триптофан** – кумедним тюхтієм. Почувала до цих невідомих речовин велику ніжність, бо вони від нього походили, з його уст, з його душі, і вони лишались, коли він відходив, роблячи його самого реальнішим під час відсутности, навіть розраджували її самотність, коли вона ввечері його чекала. (Bojko, 185 / *Nevelyčka drama*, 108–9 / BUL, 640)

These conversations left in her memory many terms, which she [cultivated in particular, straining not to forget them,] though she did not understand them. Alone, she often repeated them and played with them, lending them different personalities. **Glucose** was for her a huckstress; **alanine**, a nice blond boy; **glycol**, a spoiled brat; **tyrosine**, a dangerous fellow; **tryptophan**, a comic good-for-nothing. She felt quite tender towards these unknown substances, [because they emanated from him, from his lips, from his soul] and they stayed with her after he left, making him more real during his absences, cheering her solitary hours in the evenings while she was waiting for him. (*Touch*, 104)

This dualism between a functional and an extra-functional perception of language is not unique to *Nevelyčka drama*; examples of a similar dualism appear in *Misto*, as well. There, the scientific approach to language is ridiculed in the description of Stepan's language exam before the Ukrainization commission:

Другого дня вранці Степан уже з'явився перед українізаційний ареопаг, де його піддано **під** чи взято **на** іспит, залежно від мовних переконань кожного з членів. І після того, як із зізнання підсудного точно встановлено, що ablativus auctoris в українській мові ніким, ніде й ніколи не може бути вживаний, що для переведення розвантаження мови дієслівні речівники мусять бути старанно й невхильно обходжувані; після того, як він, вгорі названий і зазначений, виявив цілковите розуміння, чому людина ходить **по** вулицях у справах **на** адресу **з** наказу **за** основними правилами мови, – його висвячено на лицаря українізації першого розряду. (Kostjuk, 110–11 / *Misto*, 100 / BUL, 392)

Early the next day Stepan appeared before the Areopagus of Ukrainization, where an informal examinational conversation took place **between** or **among** the members of the board and **he** or **him**, depending on the linguistic theories of each of the members of the board. Next the defendant confirmed that according to all the relevant authorities of grammar, infinitives were to never be split, and sentences were not to end in prepositions, even if there seemed to be good reason for them to. Having spent some time analysing the prohibitions against dangling participles, it was concluded that as a matter of fact the theory that it seemed likely that in many cases various and sundry expressions could often be deleted from a sentence with no discernible effect on its meaning was true. Finally, after explaining why the word *which*, that is a non-restrictive pronoun, should be distinguished from the word *that* which is often, mistakenly, used in its place and why it is better to maintain verbal parallelism on both sides of the word *than* than not to, Stepan was proclaimed a Knight of Ukrainization.[10]

The opposite view of language, as a mirror of the non-rational, is also evident in *Misto*, particularly in names. Stepan changes his name to 'Stefan' because it sounds less mundane. Earlier the narrator had described Nadijka's two roommates, one of whom was named Hanna and the other Njusja, 'тобто так само Ганна, тільки у вищім ступні' (that is, also Hanna, but to a higher degree; Kostjuk, 43 / *Misto*, 44 / BUL, 335).

In both *Misto* and *Nevelyčka drama*, language is presented from two opposing perspectives: on the one hand, as a vehicle for the output of the rational mind, and on the other hand, as a reflection of emotions and unconscious feelings. As a thematic motif, however, this dualism in language is necessarily part of a larger dualism that encompasses all human experience.

The heavy reliance on Freudian characterization is part of an overall pattern of increased attention to structure and technique in this novel. As in previous works, Pidmohyl'nyj employs parallelism and juxtaposition as a major weapon in his arsenal of organizational devices. Indeed, these techniques are more common in *Nevelyčka drama* than in any of Pidmohyl'nyj's earlier works. All the male characters in the novel, for example, are meant to be measured by the same yardstick. The fact that all the men, with the exception of Professor Markevyč, are Marta's suitors is only the beginning. Their personalities, including Professor Markevyč's, all combine two mutually incompatible ingredients – pragmatism and idealism. Their actions as well as their frequent expression of their personal values, are meant to be analysed and measured on the same scale. L'ova Rotter is at one end of that scale, and Dmytro Stajnyčyj is at the other. The women in the novel are also measured on a continuum. Marta and Iren Markevyč obviously represent a study in contrasts, but the minor female characters are shown to occupy specific niches on the scale between them. Lina, the secretary in the office of the Tobacco Trust where Marta works, exists only to enter into a loveless marriage at the end of the first chapter of the novel. In the few sentences he devotes to her, Pidmohyl'nyj makes clear that Lina's practical reasoning is the opposite of Marta's idealism. She is getting married, Lina says of herself, because:

Його батьки виїжджають, а нам лишають помешкання. Він служить, я служу, якось можна жити.... (Bojko, 39 / *Nevelyčka drama*, 20 / BUL, 547)

His parents are moving and they're leaving us their apartment. He's working, [I'm working, we can manage somehow.] (*Touch*, 25)

In thematic structure, *Nevelyčka drama* is a very symmetrical and even mechanistic work. The novel is clearly divided between Marta, a romantic dreamer in pursuit of emotional ideals, and Jurij, a pragmatic scientist who bows only to reason and efficiency. The two figures quickly become flagposts marking opposite poles in a philosophical debate. Each of them represents one side in a long list of juxtaposed qualities. Marta is to Jurij as irrationality is to rationality, as instinct is to reason, as the unconscious is to the ego, as feelings are to intellect, as art is to science, as faith is to knowledge, as hope is to destiny, as spontaneity is to planning, as freedom is to duty, as the language of the heart is to the language of the mind. Their love affair is an excuse for a dramatized debate rather than a fictional love story. There is even a clear suggestion of circularity. At the end of the novel L'ova leaves Marta asleep in her bed; at the beginning of the novel she had just awakened from an erotic dream. Perhaps the novel presents only one instance in a recurring cycle.

A number of other parallels between the two main characters underscore the careful symmetry of the novel's thematic debate. Marta and Jurij are both pursued by another person who is very similar to them. L'ova, like Marta, is a hopelessly romantic dreamer. Iren, like Jurij, is a pragmatist. Although Jurij marries Iren at the end of the novel, he is not attracted to her, just as Marta is not attracted to L'ova. Marta and Jurij are drawn to each other because they are opposites, and because otherwise there would be no debate. They each have a particular interest that typifies their nature: Jurij is a research scientist, Marta a reader of literature. Science and art are explicitly offered as competing models for an evaluation of human existence. In the course of the novel, both are found lacking.

In an important personal admission, Jurij tells Marta that science can never answer its own questions. In the large unknown that science resolves, there always remains a smaller unknown. Like a child who wants to discover how a toy works, the scientist destroys what he is trying to understand, and still achieves only an incomplete answer. The goal of Jurij's own research is synthetic protein. In his own pragmatic view, the utility of synthetic protein lies in the production of synthetic food which would eliminate hunger. But the practical application of the solution is not realizable. For the foreseeable future, artificial food will be more expensive and more difficult to produce than natural food. In other words, Jurij's very pragmatic and utilitarian science is, in fact, an academic exercise grounded in naive idealistic dreams.

On the other side of the thematic divide, Marta is explicitly modelling her life and her ambitions on the literary works she reads. Early in the novel she tells L'ova that she wants to fall in love senselessly, 'like in a novel.' Later, she chooses to demonstrate her love for Jurij by making a supreme sacrifice. She will do what no other lover, in fact or in fiction, has ever done: She will abandon her lover at the pinnacle of their happiness. But her gesture proves futile. Jurij, it turns out, has been looking for a way out of their relationship; what is worse, however, Marta learns that her sacrifice is not original – it was done in Henrik Ibsen's *Kjaerlighedens Komedie* (Love's Comedy). Literature, here a material synecdoche for abstract, irrational idealism, offers a model for human experience that turns out to be unreliable and false. Just as reason fails on its own terms because it cannot answer all the questions it sets out to resolve, so, too, does imagination fail to fulfil its own promise because, the hope it offers turns out to be illusory.

The explicit dualism that lies at the heart of *Nevelyčka drama* recalls the Nietzschean distinction between the Apollonian and the Dionysian. In general terms, Nietzsche's influence on Pidmohyl'nyj is hardly in doubt. Indeed, the influence of Nietzsche's works and ideas, at least in a popular, diluted form, is quite pronounced in Ukrainian and Russian culture during the first three decades of the twentieth century.[11] In the works of Ukrainian writers from this period, from Kobyljans'ka and the Moloda muza group of poets, through Vynnyčenko and Lesja Ukrajinka, to Jurij Janovs'kyj and Mykola Bažan, reflections of Nietzschean ideas form a continuous stream. Unfortunately, these reflections often show only a general and indirect familiarity with the works of the German philosopher. In the case of a writer as familiar with western European culture and as philosophically inclined as Pidmohyl'nyj was, there is reason to assume a deeper and more direct relationship could have existed. In the absence of biographical and other non-belletristic evidence, however, Pidmohyl'nyj's debt to Nietzsche can only be extrapolated from his novels and stories.

There are a number of direct allusions to Nietzschean and his ideas in Pidmohyl'nyj's works. His name is mentioned on a number of occasions, and, as we have seen earlier, the epigraph to 'Problema xliba' quotes aphorism number 180 from his *Human, All Too Human*.[12] In an earlier story, 'Sobaka,' the protagonist, Tymerhej, a university student, finds himself facing a choice, as he puts it, 'between Kant and borsch, Nietzsche and sausage.'

Both stories in which Nietzsche's name occurs deal with the problem of hunger and the extremes to which it drives humans. The protagonists of these stories are men of reason, moderation, and understanding. The unnamed first-person narrator of 'Problema xliba' is an intellectual who politely refuses a prostitute's proposition and then discusses with her the market forces that affect her business. After beating an old watchman who catches him stealing, he returns to speak to the man, only to find that he has killed him.

Hunger drives these characters to commit act that, under normal circumstances, they would condemn. The desire for self-preservation transforms them from rational, civilized human beings into beasts driven by the survival instinct. They undergo, in varying degrees, characteristically Nietzschean transformations. The bourgeois intellectual who once observed traditional social values becomes an egotistical opportunist who scorns them. The student of abstract philosophy tears down the wall of books behind which he has been hiding and is inspired to rethink his ideas in the light of his new sense of the physical urgency of life.

It is important to note, however, that in the stories themselves, these transformations occur in the context of circumstances that cast them in an ambivalent, in not negative, light. The intellectual's new ethics permit murder and stealing. The philosopher's new ideas are the hallucinations of a weakened mind. However directly these stories reflect Nietzsche's ideas, Pidmohyl'nyj is certainly not accepting them uncritically.

In addition to the stories in which Nietzsche is named explicitly, a few others contain apparent allusions to his ideas, either in the use of specific terms or in the depiction of certain situations. For example, in his soliloquy in 'Na seli' Petro refers to a Nietzschean slaves' rebellion, in this case against the daylight, which Petro associates with socialism.[13] Allusions to Nietzsche's superman can be found in Pidmohyl'nyj's early stories as well as in *Misto*. Serhij Dančenko in 'Vijs'kovyj litun' and Jevhenij Pereponenko in 'Prorok' seem to be guided by Nietzschean images and ideas. These isolated examples do not, however, constitute a discernible pattern. In order to trace the influence of Nietzschean ideas on the thematic structure underlying Pidmohyl'nyj's works, we must apply a model suitable for charting that influence.

In his study of the influence of Nietzsche's thought on four modernist writers – Lawrence, Malraux, Gide, and Mann – John Burt Foster categorizes Nietzsche's legacy to them under four major headings: (1) polaristic thinking,

(2) psychologies of inadequacy and creativity, (3) cultural crisis, and (4) power and life.[14] These four topics are not separable building blocks that can be assembled and disassembled. Rather, they are interrelated variables in a single equation, that, in combination, offer a useful scheme for analysing the nature of Nietzsche's influence on a writer's thematic universe.

In *Nevelyčka drama* Pidmohyl'nyj presents fictional reality in terms of strict polarities. The distinction between Apollo and Dionysus is at the thematic centre of the novel. The structural parallels between Marta and Jurij underscore the tendency to present issues in terms of polar oppositions. Polar oppositions were also common in Pidmohyl'nyj's previous works. In *Misto*, for example, Stepan is caught in a psychic struggle between two opposing forces. On the one hand, there is Stepan the village activist, who will study at the university and return to help improve social conditions in the village; on the other, there is Stefan the newly discovered writer, whose native skills and energy point to personal fulfilment in a successful literary career. Other polarities extend beyond the protagonist. The city-versus-village theme in *Misto* and in the earlier stories also reflects polar thinking. In *Nevelyčka drama* this theme has evolved into conflict on another level – between the proletariat and the bourgeoisie. None of the characters in the novel is a villager. Marta and L'ova are from Kaniv, but this village has literary rather than agricultural associations. Neither character's parents were farmers. Discussions of the role of the bourgeoisie and the value of culture in society recur throughout the novel. In an afterword, Pidmohyl'nyj himself calls attention to this issue:

> У цьому романі я писав про міщанство. Писав тому, що воно здається мені не тільки гідним зневаги, але й варте громадської уваги задля своєї небезпечності. Писав тому, що вважаю міщанство за одного з помітних ворогів нашої перебудови, за ворога тяжкого, дарма що причаєного, за щось подібне до іржі, що точить нишком залізо дверей, не даючи їм вільно розчинитися. (BUL, 780)

> In this novel I wrote about the bourgeoisie. I wrote about it because it seems to me not only deserving of scorn but also worthy of society's attention because it is dangerous. I wrote about it because I consider the bourgeoisie to be one of the notable enemies of our reconstruction, a difficult enemy although a hidden one; as something similar to rust, which stealthily eats away at the steel hinges of a door until it won't open freely any more.

As in his earlier comments about the social theme in *Misto*, Pidmohyl'nyj only hints at the real issue here. By describing the novel's thematic focus in terms of the official party view of social issues, he is camouflaging the real intellectual heart of the novel, which is less palatable politically. Nevertheless, the social polarity between the bourgeoisie and other classes is yet another instance of deliberately polarized relations in the novel.

On a different level, Pidmohyl'nyj's choice of Western (French) rather than Eastern (Ukrainian, Russian) models for his literary works points to another Nietzschean polarity. In the literary debate in Ukraine in the 1920s, the distinction between Europe and Asia was a standard topos. In general terms, this distinction accorded with Nietzsche's own delineation of the two continents.

Nietzsche devotes much attention to the individual's response to alienation. In his summary of Nietzsche's views regarding the psychology of inadequacy, Foster emphasizes three elements: *ressentiment*; the value of feelings of guilt, pity, and love; and the reversal of inadequacy into tragic affirmation. *Ressentiment* is Nietzsche's term for the loss of self-sufficiency. It is similar to the existential concept of bad faith, with the additional feature that Nietzsche's *ressentiment* leads to violence and a desire for revenge. This is in fact the state Stepan Radčenko finds himself in as his relationship with Zos'ka becomes intolerable. Pidmohyl'nyj expressly refers to Stepan's desire for 'endless slavery' (Kostjuk, 272 / *Misto*, 235 / BUL, 530) and his 'slave revolt' (Kostjuk, 146 / *Misto*, 129 / BUL, 422), a Nietzschean concept associated particularly with the psychology of inadequacy. Further examples of such inadequacy are Bezpal'ko and Dmytro Stajnyčyj, both of whom seek revenge (the latter in physical cruelty) when Marta turns down their proposals.

Other Pidmohyl'nyj characters display the 'weakness' characteristic of inadequacy. Whereas for Schopenhauer pity is the supreme virtue, for Nietzsche pity, along with guilt and ideal love, is a symptom of slave morality, a refuge for those frightened by life. In characterizing pity, love, and guilt as weaknesses, Nietzsche does not suggest that cruelty and insensitivity should be virtues, but only that pity and guilt are unproductive emotions that should not be held up as virtues in themselves. L'ova Rotter in *Nevelyčka drama* and Vasjurenko in 'Syn' are two of many Pidmohyl'nyj characters for whom pity is an unproductive and unhealthy emotional crutch. They are unable to face up to inadequacy, a gesture that Nietzsche calls tragic affirmation. In facing up to inadequacy the individual discovers – in contrast, as it were – that life itself is worth affirming. This is the tonic value of inadequacy, a peculiar characteristic of the tragic genre, and a focal point of much of Nietzsche's analysis. In Western modernism and in other areas of

Nietzsche's influence, the affirmative elements of his philosophy are less often the vehicles of influence than are the negative elements. This is true of tragic affirmation, which can be seen in Malraux's novels, but not in those of the other three figures Foster discusses in his study.[15] Pidmohyl'nyj, too, shows few parallels to Nietzsche in the positive elements of his philosophy. Tragic affirmation is a part of the unity Stepan is seeking at the end of *Misto*, but it is not given much attention.

The notion that European culture was in the midst of a major transformation was popular in many circles at the end of the nineteenth and beginning of the twentieth century. In Nietzsche this idea finds particular expression in the notion of the superman, a token of the new personal psychology and new system of cultural values that he believes will replace the decadence and nihilism of his own time. Few writers, of those who were influenced by Nietzsche, adopted the idea of a superman, although it is often mentioned or alluded to, as in the conversation between Vyhors'kyj and Radčenko in the café (Kostjuk, 191–92 / *Misto*, 167–68 / BUL, 461). A more common vehicle for the idea was the consciousness, among characters in a fictional work, of an important break with the past. In both *Misto* and *Nevelyčka drama* the idea of breaking with the past plays an important role in the psychology of the protagonists. Stepan is continually contemplating the need for a break with the past, and he chafes under the burden it places on him. His attempt to return to the Nadijka he once knew and his ability to overcome that impulse – or, rather, the shock of the discovery he makes – are the central moments in his struggle with the past.

In *Nevelyčka drama* the past appears on both the personal and collective levels. Marta's memories of her father, L'ova's recollections of the war years and his first wife, Iren's experience of her 'first marriage,' and the presence of Jurij's mother are all markers of the individual past that each character tries to transcend. The historical past appears in the novel in two forms. Marxism, particularly in its Soviet implementation, is concerned with the transformation of both society and the individual. With the war and revolution receding into the past, the 1920s saw some genuine and many insincere illusions about the impending change in social and personal values. In *Nevelyčka drama* Pidmohyl'nyj depicts this sense of cultural crisis in the conversation among Marta's suitors, in the novel's fourth chapter. The men all have different views of what the new Soviet man and the new social order will be like. In this they reflect the general mood in postwar Europe. History also appears in the novel in a wider perspective. Among the subjects discussed by the characters in the novel is the mythical-historical Ukrainian past represented by such figures as Marusja Bohuslavka. Iren associates Marta with a 'Little Russian' mentality:

Мовою, культурою, політичною свідомістю вони росіяни, але десь там у душі їм ще лишились якісь спогади. Досить ці спогади підогріти, і їх обпадає національна романтика, вони відчувають себе нащадками запорожців, мріють Мазепою, Хмельницьким, Дорошенком та іншим старим маняттям. (Bojko, 219–20 / *Nevelyčka drama*, 130–31 / BUL, 663)

In their culture, language, and political consciousness they are Russians, but somewhere deep in their souls they still have memories. It's enough to warm up these memories a little and they are overcome with national romanticism; they declare themselves the heirs of the Zaporozhian Cossacks and they dream of Mazepa, Xmel'nyc'kyj, Dorošenko and other such old rags. (*Touch*, 123)

Specifically Ukrainian history underlies a second cultural crisis which lies just beneath the surface of the novel. The year is 1928. It is ten years since an independent Ukraine was born and then destroyed. The Ukrainization program of the 1920s is running into political opposition and obstacles. Despite the important progress made during the last decade, the future of Ukrainian culture in Ukraine, particularly in the cities, is still in doubt. Ukrainian culture and the prevailing ideology of pragmatism are, it seems, mutually incompatible.

Perhaps the best-known principle of Nietzsche's philosophy, and the most misunderstood, is his espousal of the Will to Power. Whatever political connotations this term may carry, its aesthetic reception among modernist writers tends to expressions of an affirmation of life. This affirmation, as Nietzsche himself suggests in his later writings, is identified with Dionysus – the procreative, life-affirming, and sexual Dionysus, not the Dionysus of aggressive energy and destruction.

From his first works to his last, Pidmohyl'nyj consistently focuses his attention on instinctual, sexual, and creative energies. In the cluster of thematic motifs that characterize his work, particularly the early stories, these energies are associated with revolutionary anarchism, hunger, dreamy romanticism, the night, and, especially, the steppe. This thematic cluster, defined earlier as the magic of the night, is essentially parallel to the Dionysian version of Nietzsche's Will to Power. The association becomes more precise in the two novels, where the differentiation between the magic of the night and its polar complement, reason, is sharply delineated. But the two novels are not thematically identical. Where in *Misto* Pidmohyl'nyj saw or at least envisioned the possibility of a harmony or unity between the two forces, in *Nevelyčka drama* the possibility is gone. At the end of the novel Jurij marries his fellow-pragmatist Iren, L'ova leaves Kiev with the memory of another failed romance, and Marta is left to fend for herself, back in a position similar to the one she was in at the beginning of the novel. Pidmohyl'nyj does not offer a judgment on the outcome of the story. Where the last lines of *Misto* were optimistic, the end of *Nevelyčka drama* is neutral. What will Marta feel when she awakes? Is she forever alienated by her unhappy love, or is she still a romantic dreamer? Will she find a new job and another man to love, or will she wallow in *ressentiment*? The end of the novel leaves open these possibilities. It does not leave open, however, the possibility of an affirmation of life, or a harmony of polar forces. In his second novel Pidmohyl'nyj has moved beyond Nietzsche to an existential position that no longer allows for idealized harmony or transcendent affirmation. There is only an honest and sober appraisal of an irresoluble conflict or a retreat into rational or emotional illusions.

Pidmohyl'nyj's second novel reveals a new approach to questions that had occupied him throughout his career. The magic of the night is a presence throughout his creative oeuvre. In *Nevelyčka drama* this force has become one aspect of a Nietzschean polarity, whereas in earlier works it was less clearly defined. The conflict between reason and instinct is a personal preoccupation for Pidmohyl'nyj. Its significance goes beyond acquired theories and influences. It is a strongly felt personal view of the human condition. But it is also something of a cultural stereotype.

At the end of the first chapter of *Misto* Stepan settles down for the night on the workbench in the Hnidyjs' shed and assures himself that all is well and that his situation is at worst comic. He knocks on the wall to the cows on the other side, laughs, and opens his eyes. Through the window above a chimney, a bright new moon shines (Kostjuk, 20 / *Misto*, 25 / BUL, 316). A few pages later, at the end of the second chapter, Stepan is in the same place, looking at the same scene, but now he sees smoke spreading from the chimney across the grey sky. This somewhat ominous device is reminiscent of the moon in Gogol's Dikanka stories, whether the bright moon over the Dnieper in 'A Terrible Vengeance' or the one that slips out of the devil's pouch as he flies in and out of the chimney in 'Christmas Eve.' The allusion, if such it is, raises the question of recurrent cultural topoi. An essential cultural truth in the Ukrainian ethos is the notion of mediation between two worlds. This idea, which sometimes figures in etymologies of the name 'Ukraine,' is historically conditioned. From the time of Kievan Rus', Ukraine has been a middle ground between other forces or interests, whether they be East and West, Byzantium and the north, Poland and Russia, or Russia and the steppe. A parallel cultural myth can be detected in a number of Ukrainian writers, in whose work rational and irrational forces coexist within a single psyche. This structure underlies the dualism between the adjusted and non-adjusted self that George Grabowicz sees in his important study of Ukraine's foremost romantic poet, Taras Ševčenko.[16] This is also the pattern Grabowicz sees at the heart of Gogol's mythical view of the curse in Ukrainian history.

> The internal, mythical explanation of the origins of the curse is formulated on the most basic of dichotomies, that between man and woman. The opposition between the world of man and woman devolves ultimately upon the difference between two different forms or modes of social existence – the warlike, 'nomadic,' aggressive life of the Cossacks, and the settled, peaceful, and agricultural life of the other strata of the Ukrainian people. And it is in the breakdown of the boundaries and the rules of coexistence between these two forms of Ukrainian life that Gogol' intuits and then mythically projects the beginnings of the inevitable fall of the Cossack Ukraine.[17]

A similar dualism informs George Luckyj's discussion of the polarity between Ševčenko and Kuliš.[18] All of these dualisms, but particularly the one in Gogol, are important because they reflect a historical perception of the role of Ukrainian culture. Although Pidmohyl'nyj does not expressly address issues bearing on the future political or social development of Ukraine, concern for the future development of Ukrainian culture is often just beneath the surface of his works. Thus, in his early works, Ukrainian culture, identified with the instinctive forces of the magic of the night, is a lost and hopeless proposition. It will be plowed up like the steppe by the forces of civilization and reason, or shot in the back like a deranged prophet by a frightened sceptic. In some of the stories of the middle period, and especially in *Misto*, Pidmohyl'nyj redistributes the forces of fate between reason and night's magic. It is no coincidence that Stepan Radčenko is a Ukrainian writer. The unity he finds on a personal level promises a new era for Ukrainian culture. The future is not quite so bright in *Nevelyčka drama*. The dualism that characterizes Pidmohyl'nyj's view of the Ukrainian ethos remains polarized. The bright future has reverted to an unproductive continuity.

The focus on irrational forces is not an exclusively Ukrainian idea. The notion of a cultural dualism between reason and irrationality is also evident in Russia, particularly in the late nineteenth and early twentieth centuries, when so many eyes in Russia were looking towards the West. This is evident in much of Russian literature from this period. Pidmohyl'nyj's early works were compared to one such writer, Leonid Andreev.

Between Reason and Irrationality

The major parallel between Andreev's works and the stories in Pidmohyl'nyj's *Tvory: Tom 1* lies in the focus on a dark, instinctive side of human psychology, what Conrad's Mr. Kurtz finds in 'The Heart of Darkness,' both in the jungle and in his own heart: The horror, the horror! Unlike Conrad, however, Andreev's heroes find the darkness in the midst of natural beauty. As Aleksander Zakrževskij observes, Andreev presents a world in which the darkness must be accepted because only the darkness can extinguish that satanic fire in which the whole world is being destroyed.[19] This view, which focuses on a Schopenhauerian pessimism, was characteristic of Andreev's reception by his more insightful contemporaries. Pidmohyl'nyj's stories, particularly those in which a young man is frightened by the discovery of his own sexuality or by the destructive hatred that springs up in him, present a similar psychological situation.

The comparison between Andreev and Pidmohyl'nyj is instructive. While the overt depiction of the irrational is similar in both writers, the underlying dualism is not. The basic polarity in Pidmohyl'nyj is between reason and irrationality. As James Woodward explains, for Andreev the dualism is between the empirical and the transcendent.

> His works show a dualistic conception of reality, a polarization of metaphysical unity and harmony and phenomenal diversity and discord ... The term 'first reality' is employed by Andreyev to denote the ephemeral, the world of man's empirical existence, a world dominated by the principle which Schopenhauer termed the *principium individuationis*. On this plane man is a prisoner within the walls of his individuality, and his intellect is the instrument by means of which he endeavors to pierce them. But its struggles are eternally frustrated; its powers do not extend beyond the 'first reality.' The whole impetus of Andreyev's thought is towards the establishment of contact with the 'other plane,' the transcendence of the empirical *ego*.[20]

The difference between Pidmohyl'nyj and Andreev hinges on the fact that both poles of Pidmohyl'nyj's thematic continuum are empirical. For Pidmohyl'nyj, there is no transcendent.

The fundamental problem that preoccupied Pidmohyl'nyj from his first known story, 'Važke pytannja,' dated March 1917, to his second novella, *Povist' bez nazvy*, which he was working on at the time of his arrest in 1934, was the conflict between reason and irrationality. This dualism is the hub from which all of his creative output emanates: all of Pidmohyl'nyj's thematic preoccupations can be derived from or related to this central concern. Even the technical devices and the literary techniques he adopts can be seen as a natural outgrowth of his focus on this dualism.

The polarity between reason and irrationality is not a fixed and immutable relation. The dualism Grabowicz reveals in Gogol is not identical to the dualism he reveals in Ševčenko or to the dualism that Luckyj sees between Ševčenko and Kuliš or between Ševčenko and Gogol. They are all, nonetheless, related to a larger cultural polarity that is characteristic of Ukrainian literature. Also related to this larger cultural polarity is the dualism that informs Pidmohyl'nyj's works. But this dualism itself changes over time. In his earliest stories Pidmohyl'nyj paid scant attention to reason. His interest was focused on the magic of the night. In *Tvory: Tom 1* the magic of the night appears as a mixture of loosely related forces. In stories such as 'Važke pytannja,' 'Dobryj boh,' and 'Prorok' it is embodied in the sexual energy and social rebelliousness of young men. In 'Hajdamaka' and 'Na seli' it is more closely associated with the natural beauty and power of the steppe, with political anarchy, and with Ukrainian national aspirations. In 'Vanja' and later 'Ivan Bosyj' and 'Povstanci,' the magic of the night becomes a force unto itself: a powerful instinctual energy that blends discrete portions of all the ingredients found in the other stories.

In all of Pidmohyl'nyj's early stories, however, the dualism is only implied. The actual focus is one-sided. The absence of a clearly defined opposite to the magic of the night is not auspicious. The technical and intellectual deficiencies of the stories in *Tvory: Tom 1* are largely a matter of this imbalance. To the degree that the second pole in this dualism remains undefined, Pidmohyl'nyj's stories are intellectually vague and seem more plausibly to be imitations of Andreev. 'Vanja,' however, gives the second pole a much clearer outline and thereby enjoys a considerable aesthetic benefit.

The key to Pidmohyl'nyj's success in defining the polar complement of the magic of the night is literary realism. The tradition of French realistic prose from Balzac to Maupassant and beyond offers a good model for the depiction of abstract problems in an exclusively empirical world. Maupassant, in particular, depicts complex psychological issues within the limits of a tangible universe. Even in his *contes fantastiques* Maupassant restricts the fantastic to psychological elements or at least to elements that need not exceed psychological explanations. In 'La Petite Roque,' for example, the elements of the fantastic are kept firmly within the dimensions of the protagonist's psyche. The bulk of the thematic argument is presented through various technical devices, most notably parallelism and juxtaposition. 'Vanja' is also built on juxtapositions of parallel situations. The complement of the magic of the night is depicted in the encounter with the man-eater in the gully, where reason, courage, and the light of day dispel night's magic.

Through the course of his career, Pidmohyl'nyj moved towards a clearer definition of the two poles of his thematic dualism. Inevitably, these definitions benefited from his contact with Maupassant. Instinctive male sexuality was illuminated by a greater focus on the sexual role of women. Abstract images of order and stability were clarified in portraits of typical bourgeois values. The technical lessons of Maupassant's objective method were complemented by his interpretation of Schopenhauerian pessimism. Narrative technique helped define thematic issues. Yet Pidmohyl'nyj's understanding of his thematic material differed from Maupassant's.

With the benefit of twenty years during which the ideas of Nietzsche and Freud achieved exceptionally wide currency, Pidmohyl'nyj redefines Maupassant's Schopenhauerian pessimism into a Nietzschean positivism, which itself is transformed into existential empiricism.[21] The development of Stepan Radčenko in *Misto* from a writer of symbolic stories about things to an author of a novel about people is a reflection of Pidmohyl'nyj's own development on the thematic level. In his early stories the magic of the night appears as a powerful force that takes possession of his characters. In *Nevelyčka drama*, night's magic has become part of the characters themselves. It is no longer a vague mixture of sexual instinct and social anarchy. It is Marta Vysoc'ka, the romantic dreamer. Both poles of the dualism are now defined as Nietzschean categories. Where the polar opposite of the magic of the night was absent in *Tvory: Tom 1*, in *Nevelyčka drama* it is an equal partner in the structure of the novel and personified in the biologist. Reason, the thematic complement to the magic of the night is firmly established as the rational, scientific, orderly, and pragmatic universe of Jurij Slavenko's existence.

CHAPTER SIX

The Last Works
A Final Synthesis

Although Pidmohyl'nyj's last two known works, 'Z žyttja budynku No. 29,' and *Povist' bez nazvy*, are unusual in a number of ways, they also confirm Pidmohyl'nyj's development as a writer along the path set by his earlier works. Prominent among the new features is, first, the matter of genre. Pidmohyl'nyj's two previous works were novels. With the exception of journalism and translations (but even there, he was translating novels), he had abandoned short prose after 1925. It seems, however, that he was now ready to return to the short story and the novella, the latter a genre he had tried earlier without marked success. Perhaps the difficult political circumstances of the early 1930s explain the return to shorter genres. These circumstances are themselves an important feature of Pidmohyl'nyj's last known short story, published on 27 June 1933, in *Literaturna hazeta*.

'Z žyttja budynku No. 29'[1] is an account of man's inhumanity to man. It tells a story not unlike those found in the works of Oles' Hončar, the most popular Ukrainian writer of the 1970s and 1980s, who often focuses on the conflict between human and institutional values. In Pidmohyl'nyj's story the administrators of a housing project, in order to facilitate building renovations, decide to evict an elderly woman from her apartment and to resettle her in a room next to the furnace in the basement. Part of the justification for her eviction is that as the wife of a former high functionary under the tsars and, as a class enemy, she does not deserve sympathy or special consideration. When she is informed of the decision, she refuses to cooperate. Three days later she is found dead in her apartment, suffocated by a gold coin lodged in her throat. Among her possessions, the building committee chairman tells a friend, is a quantity of gold coins, which she had begun to swallow to avoid their being discovered; a number of letters in French to various anti-communist leaders; and a jug of gasoline with which she had apparently meant to burn down the building.

'Та це просто божевільна!' скрикнув голова ревізкому.
'Можливо. Але класово божевільна.'[2]

'But this is simple insanity!' cried the chairman of the auditing committee.
'Perhaps. But it is class insanity.'

Not since his early story 'Komunist' had Pidmohyl'nyj allowed himself to challenge the reigning government and its ideology so openly. But the political reality of the early thirties was, in fact, much worse than what Pidmohyl'nyj depicted in his story. Moreover, it is important to observe that even in a story as melodramatic and political as 'Z žyttja budynku No. 29,' Pidmohyl'nyj is still writing about the issues that concern him most profoundly. Indeed, the conversation between the bureaucrats in the story is precisely about the balancing of material and metaphysical values, or more specifically, the illusion of values derived from practical and abstract motives. The chairman of the auditing committee embodies the conflicting values both in his pronouncements and in his behaviour:

'Я особисто стою на тому, що про зручність людини в наших радянських умовах треба дбати скрізь і повсякчасно, товаришу Вивірко.'
  Голова ревізкому глянув на голову ЖК і вибачливо посміхнувся. Тоді добув з кишені в пальті цигарника.
  'Але ці люди,' провадив він, запалюючи між словами, 'ці люди ... приносять ... приносять сюди силу бруду, болота, вони дихають, плюють, харкають нарешті, а ваші співробітники, що сидять по сім з половиною годин, мусять цим повітрям дихати.'
  'Курять сильно, от біда,' прикинув рахівник, виходячи. 'Є об'ява, що заборонено, а вони шмалять. А то було б нічого.'
  'Ви перший курите,' сказав голова ЖК з притиском. 'Ви перший систематично порушуєте постанову.'
  'Палити заборонено відвідувачам, а я належу, сказати б, до адміністрації,' сухо відказав голова ревізкому.[3]

'Personally, I think that in our Soviet conditions it is incumbent on us to consider the comfort of the individual at all times and in all places, Comrade Vyvirka.'

The Last Works

The chairman of the auditing committee glanced at the chairman of the building committee and smiled apologetically. Then he pulled a cigarette case from his coat pocket.

'But these people,' he continued, lighting his cigarette between words, 'these people ... bring ... bring in piles of dirt and mud, they breathe, spit, and blow their noses, while your co-workers, who sit here for seven and a half hours, must breathe in this air.'

'They smoke like chimneys, that's the problem,' added the accountant as he walked out of the room. 'There's a sign that says smoking is prohibited, but they smoke anyway. If it weren't for that, it'd be okay.'

'You yourself smoke,' said the chairman of the building committee pointedly. 'You are first among those who systematically break the regulation.'

'Visitors are not allowed to smoke, but I'm part of the staff,' answered the chairman of the auditing committee dryly.

Double standards that distinguish the man from mankind were a hallmark of Soviet communism; they are also elementary projections from the thematic foundation of Pidmohyl'nyj's works. The political explicitness of this story is unusual for Pidmohyl'nyj, but its topicality and theme are not.

The title of Pidmohyl'nyj's last known work represents another unusual feature. In full, it reads: *Povist bez nazvy, do toho ž cilkovyto nejmovirna, vyhadana vid počatku do kincja avtorom, ščob pokazaty sutyčku dejakyx pryncypiv važlyvyx dlja našoho dnja i majbutn'oho* (A Tale without a Title, Moreover a Completely Unbelievable One, Invented from Beginning to End by the Author in Order to Demonstrate the Conflict of Certain Principles Important in Our Time and in the Future). This ponderous, medieval-sounding title has a twofold function: to call attention to itself and to alert the reader to the presence of an intellectual subject. Implicit in it is the question, What is this story actually about? It is an effective device.

Thematically, *Povist' bez nazvy* develops Pidmohyl'nyj's familiar ideas. The story is about a Kharkiv journalist, Andrij Horodovs'kyj, whose real name is Rudčenko. One day while in Kiev to settle some details about the publication of his new book, Horodovs'kyj catches a glimpse of a woman on the street. The woman captivates him and he starts to follow her, but he quickly gets hold of himself and stops. Nevertheless, the woman's image continues to haunt him, even after he returns home to Kharkiv. He decides to take advantage of an upcoming vacation to return to Kiev to search for her. In Kiev, he implements a systematic plan to find the woman. In the course of his search he meets two men: Anatolij Petrovyč Paščenko, a professor of physics, and Jevhen Bezpal'ko, an illustrator working on the dust jacket of Horodovs'-

kyj's book. His encounters with Bezpal'ko and Paščenko further strengthen his resolve to find the woman who so captivated him. The story ends with Horodovs'kyj still searching for the woman.

As the title suggests, the story is built around a number of conflicting ideas. The most important of these are chance and fate, randomness and determinism. The central event in the story, Horodovs'kyj's glimpse of the woman in Kiev, precipitates a crisis precisely because it is a random event. His attraction to the woman overpowers him because his initial impulse was an instinctive response, beyond his physical and mental control. Generally, Horodovs'kyj's relations with women have been governed by mutual self-interest. His mistresses in Kharkiv – his neighbour, Zinajida Myxajlivna, and Tonja, the stenographer – meet specific needs in his life. His relations with them are built on a very ordered and rationally governed passion. The woman in Kiev, by contrast, reminds him of an episode eleven years earlier, when, en route to Moscow, he spent a night beside a young woman in a field near a village railway station. While the woman slept, he, a naïve and sexually inexperienced eighteen-year-old, had kissed her hands, her hair, and her eyes, and had wept with joy from the pure emotion of his spontaneous passion. The woman in Kiev rekindles in him that feeling of purity and spontaneity.

Horodovs'kyj's response to spontaneous passion is characteristically measured, orderly, and restrained. After initially following the woman a short distance, he submits to the authority of his superego, which appeals to his sense of shame and self-respect. A few days later the passion overwhelms him again, propelling him back to Kiev, but once there he begins to develop elaborate, systematic plans to find the woman. At first he believes that the woman will respond to his mere presence in Kiev 'as to the insistent, sharp ring of a telephone' (*Nevelyčka drama*, 289 / BUL, 267). 'Surrendering to the voice of faith and chance' (*Nevelyčka drama*, 290 / BUL, 267), he sets off on a streetcar, his gaze fixed on the sidewalks, where he expects to see the woman. But he soon realizes that he can observe only one side of the street. He rides to the end of the line and back in order to see both sides, but then realizes that he is seeing only half the street once again, since in the time that has elapsed the people on both sides of the street have changed. This relentless logic assaults his confidence in finding the woman and leads to a state of existential alienation and paranoia:

Тепер він стояв біля опери, але мусив зробити зусилля, щоб пізнати місцевість так, ніби за ці два дні з часу, як він проходив тут востаннє, в місті сталися катастрофічні зміни. Будинки справляли враження гумових, немов готові були відскакувати геть, якщо він спробує наблизитися, і люди проходили мимо так байдуже і відчужено, немов тільки для того, щоб спинитися за рогом і підстерігати тисячами злорадісних очей його дальші заходи. (*Nevelyčka drama*, 290–1 / BUL, 268)

Now he was standing by the opera but he had to make an effort to recognize the area, as if in the two days since he had walked here last the city had undergone catastrophic changes. The buildings gave the impression that they were made of rubber and seemed ready to jump away if he tried to come near. And the people who walked past seemed indifferent and estranged, as if their real intention was to stop around the corner and observe his next move with a thousand malevolent eyes.

This state of alienation and despair lasts six days, until Horodovs'kyj meets Bezpal'ko and moves into the apartment the illustrator recommends. There, he meets Paščenko. After his first, long sleep in the new quarters, Horodovs'kyj awakes to a new consciousness, with a new, rational resolve to achieve his objective. Viewing his own situation through the eyes of an 'other,' he determines that he has merely changed 'dominants' in his life. 'З погляду свого прагнення він був досі інженером, потім журналістом, тепер став закоханим' (In terms of his aspirations, he had been an engineer, then a journalist, and now he had become a man in love; *Nevelyčka drama*, 297 / BUL, 275). Accepting the latter as his new identity, Horodovs'kyj draws up new plans.

Треба шукання ввести в систему, поставити його на більш-менш твердий ґрунт якогось розрахунку. Але для розрахунку потрібні дані! Їх він мав до смішного мало, але зараз, перевіривши ще раз якнайпильніше свої спогади, не міг сказати, що не має їх зовсім: по-перше, він був зараз певний, що незнайома, зустрінута ним, несла в правій руці портфель – отже, вона десь працює; по-друге, лишається незаперечним, що вона надзвичайно цікава і, як така, конче повинна мати певне коло знайомих, прихильників, може чоловіка чи коханця (це його не турбувало зовсім), з якими вона не може не відвідувати кіно, концертів і театрів. Установи й видовища – ось куди мусить бути скерована його увага. (*Nevelyčka drama*, 297 / BUL, 275–76)

The search needs to be systematized, to be put on the more or less firm foundation of some sort of calculation. But calculation requires data, and those were in laughably short supply. But now, reviewing his recollections once more in the minutest detail, he could not assert that there were no data at all. First, he was now certain that the unknown woman he had glimpsed was carrying a briefcase in her right hand – therefore she worked somewhere; second, it remained irrefutable that she was an unusually interesting woman and as such would certainly have a particular circle of friends, admirers, perhaps a husband or a lover (this did not bother him at all), with whom she certainly could not avoid frequenting the cinema, concerts, and theatres. Places of business and of popular entertainment – that is where he must direct his attention.

This apparently rational scheme runs into unusual obstacles. Pidmohyl'nyj signals the importance of the randomness motif by undermining normally predictable events. Horodovs'kyj implements his plan by reading the theatre schedule and setting off for what he considers the most promising performance. At the theatre, however, he discovers that a different play is being staged than the one that was scheduled, without any prior notice at the box office or any evident consternation on the part of the audience. In fact, Horodovs'kyj is mistaken about the date, having slept for thirty-six hours and thereby lost a day. But Pidmohyl'nyj's point is clear: Even the state of affairs we normally consider ordered is actually random. The concept of time that governs human affairs is merely a convenience. It has no intrinsic truth to support it and can easily break down, as it does for Horodovs'kyj.

The notion of apparent order masking actual chaos is central to the story. It appears in several episodes, but nowhere more clearly than in the description of people waiting for a streetcar in Kiev:

Трамвая не було досить довго, і Городовський, ставши в чергу, мав час розглянутися навколо. Передусім, супроти харківських звичаїв, ставання в чергу до трамвая було йому новиною, бо в столиці пасажири чекали вагонів юрбою, що здобувала місця штурмовим чином. Це свідчило, міркував він, про більшу активність харків'ян, тобто про меншу їхню культурність, коли вважати культурність за звичку стримувати природні порухи, підлягаючи правилу, що стримує їх. Адже природним порухом кожного індивіда, що має пересунутися трамваєм на певну віддаль, завжди буде бажання захопити собі місце у вагоні, який не може вмістити всіх охочих, і коли харків'янин доконує це навально, він користується первісним правом сили й спритності, а киянин, утворюючи чергу, шанує вже культурніше право першого займання. Хоч обидва ці способи всідання в трамвай були однаково несправедливі, бо в першому разі людина з найбільшою потребою їхати могла бути не найдужчою, а в другому разі – не найпершою в черзі, Городовський усе-таки потішився душею, почуваючи себе в приємній атмосфері ладу. (*Nevelyčka drama*, 273 / BUL, 250)

The streetcar did not come for quite a while, so Horodovs'kyj, having gotten in line, had a chance to look around. First of all, coming from Kharkiv, he was unacquainted with the custom of lining up to wait for a streetcar; in the capital, passengers waited for the trains in a mob and conquered their seats by storming the cars. This was evidence, he thought, of the greater vitality of Kharkiv residents, that is, of their lower level of civilization, if you consider civilized behaviour to be the habit of suppressing the natural instincts, subject to the rules that govern them. After all, the natural instinct of every individual who needs to travel some distance on the streetcar will always be to claim a seat in the car, which cannot accommodate all the passengers. When the Kharkiv resident charges for the seats, he is relying on the primordial right of strength and quickness, while the Kiev resident, by forming a line, is honouring the more civilized principle of first come – first served. Although both of these ways of getting on a streetcar were equally unjust – since the person with the greatest need to ride the streetcar might not, in the first case, be the strongest or in the second, the first in line – Horodovs'kyj still felt good to be in an atmosphere of pleasant orderliness.

But the good feeling does not last long. When the streetcar finally comes, the line suddenly breaks down and the passengers storm the car. What Horodovs'kyj observed was only a semblance of order.

Horodovs'kyj's sojourn in Kiev and his search for the unknown woman are an exercise in existential self-awareness. The orderly, rational journalist gradually discovers that his relationship to the world around him, like the line-up at the streetcar stop, is not governed by immutable laws of order and determinacy. Ironically, his realization comes as a result of his efforts to systematize chance. In attempting to create a program that will guarantee the repetition of a chance event (the encounter with the unknown woman), Horodovs'kyj comes to terms with the existential indeterminacy of the world he lives in. In the carefully planned structure of Pidmohyl'nyj's story, Horodovs'kyj's gradual reconciliation with existential indeterminacy is achieved through his encounters with two characters who are balanced at opposite ends of the continuum between chance and determinism.

The subject that is uppermost in the consciousness of the physicist Anatolij Paščenko is chance, or in his terminology, 'accident' (випадок). In his view, human beings are biological accidents who have falsely convinced themselves of the purposefulness and, consequently, the value of their lives, their ideas, and their actions. In the chapter entitled 'Deklaracija rezonera' (Declaration of a *Raisonneur*), Paščenko narrates his biography as a sequence of four accidents: his birth; the death of his sister, killed in a streetcar accident; the death of his brother and Paščenko's subsequent acquisition of the vial marked *Bandja*; and the meeting with Horodovs'kyj. Each of these accidents, except the last, and Paščenko's childhood observations of the functioning of the law and the courts, confirm his view of the insignificance of life, the nothingness of man, and the senselessness and pretentiousness of human reason.

Paščenko's account of the significance of his birth reveals that his pursuit of the irrational springs from a disillusionment with reason. In a passage reminiscent of the opening paragraphs of Laurence Sterne's *Tristram Shandy*, the physicist laments the accidental nature of his birth and, thus, of his being:

Яка-небуть тупиця, чванько від науки скаже вам з почуттям цапиної зверхности, що ви доконечно народилися від статевого єднання ваших батьків. Облиште! Доконечно народилося **щось**, а не **я**. Все має якусь реальну причину, скаже вам далі той самий науковий ферт. Ах, так? – скажу я: тим краще! Тоді визнайте, будь ласка, що коли б мій батько того вечора, як зародив мене, був, припустимо, трохи більше стомлений чи заклопотаний і відклав би цю справу на годину, на одну лише годину, – через годину вся сукупність причин – настрій батьків, а також їхні фізіологічні умови – були б уже інші, отже і наслідок був би інший, тобто мене як такого не утворилося б, утворилася б інша дитина, така сама випадкова, як і я, але інша, кажу вам, а я не існував би. От вам і доконечність! (*Nevelyčka drama*, 304 / BUL, 282–3)

Any blockhead of a conceited scientist will tell you with a sense of bull-headed superiority that you were necessarily born from the sexual union of your parents. Forget it! **Something** was necessarily born, but not **I**. Everything has an actual cause, that same pompous scientist will tell you. Is that so? Well, I say, all the better! In that case please admit that if, on the evening that he begot me, my father had been, let's say, a little more tired or worried and had put the matter off by an hour, by just one hour – then in that hour, the sum of all the causes, my parents' mood as well as their physiological condition, would have been different and, therefore, the result would have been different, too. Therefore, I would not have been created. Some other child would have been created – just as accidental as I but a different child – and I tell you, I would not exist. There's necessity for you!

The Last Works

Whereas the circumstances of his birth convince him of the nothingness of his being, his sister's death teaches him the insignificance of life. We all live, concludes Paščenko, only inasmuch as we have not yet been run over by a streetcar. Moreover, abstraction is not a source of abiding values. Human intellect and reason cannot overcome the basic senselessness of man's existence. Paščenko recalls accompanying his father, a lawyer, to the courtroom, where he was struck by the illogical nature of the proceedings.

Уявіть собі – дорослі люди, очевидно, більш-менш розумні прокурор, судді, присяжні, адвокати. Вони розглядають справу. Але як? Зовсім диким, несподіваним чином! Замість того, як це було б природно, нормально для розумних людей, щоб **один** обізнався з справою, вдумався в неї і розв'язав її, потрібен, розумієте, цілий синедріон, де один говорить одне, другий зовсім протилежне, потрібні всі ці промови, докази, напади і оборона, ніби це футбольна гра, де комусь треба забити гол! Ви тільки вдумайтеся в це, але глибоко до кінця, і ви зрозумієте те, що зрозумів я: нікчемство, злидні людського розуму, якого не вистачає навіть на те, щоб самостійно розв'язати справу про якийсь там злочин. І після цього той самий розум береться пояснити світ. Яка нісенітниця! (*Nevelyčka drama*, 307 / BUL, 285–6)

Imagine, grown-ups, obviously more or less intelligent people – the prosecutor, judges, jurors, lawyers. They are examining a case. But how? In some wild, unexpected manner! Instead of having **one person** study the matter, think about it carefully, and resolve it, as would be natural and normal for intelligent people, we need, you understand, a whole synedrion, where one person says one thing and another says the complete opposite; we need all these speeches, evidence, attacks, and defences, as if this were a soccer match and somebody were trying to score a goal. Just think about it, but deeply and completely, and you'll realize what I realized: the baseness, the poverty of human reason, which isn't even capable of independently solving a matter regarding some trivial crime. And then this same mind attempts to explain the world. What nonsense!

The third accident in Paščenko's life is its real turning point. The sudden death of his brother, who had been exiled from Russia and spent some time in Asia before returning home after the outbreak of the Revolution, leaves the physicist with the task of disposing of his brother's possessions. Among them he finds and keeps a vial containing a substance that turns out to be hashish. His brother, a zealous communist, certainly did not use the drug. But Paščenko experiments with it and comes to a remarkable conclusion:

Світ збудований таким ідіотським чином, що сприйняття його, який він насправді є, можливо тільки за допомогою наркотику.... Це пізнання можливе наперекір розумові, через усунення його, через те, що ми безпосередня частина світу всупереч тому, що ми розумні. Злитися з світом у його безконечності й вічності – ось дійсний шлях світопізнання. (*Nevelyčka drama*, 310–11 / BUL, 289–90)

The world is constructed in such an idiotic manner that it can be perceived as it truly is only with the help of narcotics ... This perception is possible despite reason, through its elimination, because we are an immediate part of the world in spite of our reason. To become one with its infinity and eternity – this is the true path to understanding the world.

But now the vial of hash is running out. Paščenko has measured out his remaining doses: In seven days he will have used up all the drug. He will then go to a site he has prepared for this purpose outside the city limits, where he will bury himself alive, the purpose and goal in his life having been completed.

The last accident in Paščenko's life – the meeting with Horodovs'kyj – is very different from the first three. Whereas his earlier accidents had offered lessons in the pervasiveness of chance, the last one is not a lesson at all, but rather a revelation of the physicist's unwillingness to abide by the lessons he has learned. His need to tell his story to someone, which he does when he meets Horodovs'kyj, is a symptom of his bad faith. It is a symptom of his unwillingness to accept the meaninglessness of his existence. He, as an individual, is still driven to leave his personal mark on the world. He cannot escape from a world where life is a soccer match and the object is to score an intellectual goal.

Horodovs'kyj's reaction to Paščenko's narrative about his life leaves no doubt as to the dissimilarity of their views. The next morning Horodovs'kyj visits his co-tenant and explodes in a tirade of abuse. He calls Paščenko a dog who takes pleasure in smelling and eating human faeces. He tells the physicist that he is a failure as a human being, a conceited fool who wanted to become a god but could not live up to his own expectations. Horodovs'kyj's evaluation of Paščenko is to a certain degree justified, but the insults he hurls at him are a clear indication that Paščenko's views have affected him deeply. He senses that his response is excessive and wonders why he is so upset by his neighbour's baseness. Then he realizes that Paščenko's search for a meeting with someone is not unlike his own.

This explicit link between the physicist and the journalist is a textual marker of the vital thematic connection between these characters. By juxtaposing Horodovs'kyj and Paščenko, Pidmohyl'nyj exposes the fundamental principle that he announced in the title of the work and explores one aspect of it. Paščenko's assertion of the insignificance of existence is never seriously questioned in the story. His response to that insignificance is to retreat into randomness. But life governed by chance alone is no better than death. For Horodovs'kyj, and for Pidmohyl'nyj, Paščenko's is not an adequate or acceptable response. The difference between the journalist's and the physicist's views is epitomized in the images they use to describe the daily lives of the mass of humanity. Paščenko's is similar to Camus's image of Sisyphus, but without the heroic noble context. For him, man is like an ant that toils at pushing along balls of manure. The only possible achievement is the accumulation of more balls of material or spiritual manure. Horodovs'kyj, by contrast, relies on an idea reminiscent of Goethe's *Faust*. He recalls the response of a prominent professor of engineering, at the apex of his career, when asked if he was satisfied with his profession. No, he replied, because what he had already accomplished was so much greater than what remained for him to accomplish. When a man no longer has hope, he is dissatisfied.

At the opposite end of the spectrum from Paščenko is the illustrator Bezpal'ko. Whereas the physicist is a disciple of chance, the artist is a paragon of determinism. (This irony is very characteristic of Pidmohyl'nyj). The physicist is a recluse from life, living alone in sparsely furnished rooms and avoiding contact with people. The illustrator is an affable man who lives with his family in an overcrowded apartment. Whereas Paščenko has reduced his physical and material needs to a minimum, Bezpal'ko is a moderate epicurean (Horodovs'kyj is able to wear down his insistence on sharing a bottle of wine only by feigning a serious digestive disorder). Like his intellectual counterpart, Bezpal'ko tells Horodovs'kyj his life story. Unlike the hash-smoker, however, the illustrator views his life in terms of the relationship between his art and his everyday existence. When Horodovs'kyj admits he is not married and has no children, Bezpal'ko laments that condition:

Це жахливо. Ви не знаєте більшої половини життя. Безліч переживань для вас пропадає зовсім. Я теж з цього починав, як і кожний, звичайно. Присвятити себе мистецтву, тільки мистецтву, щоб ніщо не заважало, воля, незалажність і таке інше. Одно слово, виступив у костюмі весталки. Так що я знаю, яка холодна кімната нежонатого. Брр! Заходиш, як у морг, і ніяке мистецтво тебе не гріє. Моя весталочка змерзла, зажурилася і з горя бу-бух, стала вакханкою. Сторч головою. І закрутилося: спідниці, кучері, теплі

коліна, млость, як у Володимира Сосюри. Я розказую вам і сам не вірю: невже це справді було? Неймовірно! Міраж, *фата моргана*. І знову пустка, холод, той самий морг. Тоді я зажурився вдруге і піднісся до Бажана. Пам'ятаєте:
Кінчається ночей вільготне половіння
І ясний зір достиг багатий урожай.
В чарованих гаях ти, дівчино, шукай
Собі ядерного і чистого насіння.[4]

Тобто одружився. Зверніть увагу, все це я проробив, як у підручнику діамату: теза, антитеза, синтеза. І вийшло правильно. Треба тільки дуже закохатися. Щоб ця жінка стала для вас усім *conditio sine qua non*, та й тільки. І коли ця жінка скаже вам 'так,' ви відчуєте себе удавом, який проковтнув кроля і якому більше нічого не треба. Ну, ось і я. (*Nevelyčka drama*, 319 / BUL, 298–9)

That's terrible. You don't know the greater half of life. You are completely missing countless experiences. I also began from that, of course, as everyone does. To devote yourself to art and to art alone, so that nothing interferes – freedom, independence, and all that. In a word, I stepped out in the robes of a vestal. So I know how cold the bachelor's rooms are. Brr! You walk in, as if into a morgue, and no art can warm you. My vestal shivered, worried, and out of misery – ka-bam – she became a bacchanalian. Head first. And everything began to spin in my head: skirts, locks of hair, warm knees, languor – as in Volodymyr Sosjura's poems. I'm telling you and I can't believe it myself – was it really so? Unbelievable! A mirage, *fata morgana*. And then again, emptiness, cold, that same morgue. Then I got worried again and I rose to Bažan. You remember:
The nights' moist blossoming ends
And the rich harvest of bright stars is ripe.
In magic groves, girl, seek
For yourself an inner and pure seed.

In other words, I got married. Notice, I went through all this as in a textbook on dialectical materialism: thesis, antithesis, synthesis. And it came out right. You only have to fall deeply in love. So that this woman becomes for you the whole *conditio sine qua non* and nothing more. And when this woman says "yes," you will feel like a snake that has swallowed a rabbit and needs nothing more. Well, there I am.

Indeed, Bezpal'ko is the sated reptile who seeks nothing more in life. He has ordered and systematized all aspects of his life to minimize the disturbing effects of chance. To the degree that his happy family life interferes with his art, he has devised a schedule of separate vacations. The family apartment is divided between living space and studio. Bezpal'ko even changes clothing when he moves from his role as an artist to his role as a family man, and vice versa. His life and his art are kept separate. This separation is reflected in his art as well. He paints sunny landscapes of childish cheerfulness. In his works there is no reflection of life or people as they really are. There is only the eternal joy and beauty of nature. His artistic credo, which he borrows from Oscar Wilde, is that life creates art and art creates life. It is the second half of the formula that is important for Bezpal'ko.

Bezpal'ko's attitude towards art is the thematic link that ties him to Horodovs'kyj. As a former bohemian idealist who has become a respectable pragmatist, he has travelled in the opposite direction from Horodovs'kyj. Horodovs'kyj, before he glimpses the woman in Kiev, is the journalistic equivalent of the sated illustrator. His work is routine and uninspired and kept separate from his personal life, which consists primarily of occasional sex. Perhaps prompted by the recognition of his accomplishments as reflected in his forthcoming book, Horodovs'kyj begins thinking more seriously about his work, about its intellectual and creative significance. The woman in Kiev becomes a symbolic embodiment of this new-found idealism. But unlike the illustrator, who marries the woman and swallows the rabbit, Horodovs'kyj is left to pursue a distant and almost hopeless ideal. Pidmohyl'nyj offers no comment on this situation, and the story ends (if we may assume that Pidmohyl'nyj meant to end it here) with Horodovs'kyj still searching. The clear implication is that the search is eternal and hopeless, but not futile. The human existential condition is to exist between chance and fate; to accept life, as Bezpal'ko does, but without sacrificing ideals; to acknowledge truth without despairing of life. At the end of the story, when Horodovs'kyj discards the illustrator's painting, ignores Paščenko, and sets out to attend a play and two movies, he is choosing precisely such a course.

The theme of the story is most clearly evident in the characters, as we have just seen. It is also evident on other levels, notably that of imagery. A few images, such as that of a snake who has swallowed a rabbit and that of insects pushing balls of manure, have been noted above. A number of other images help clarify the theme and demonstrate Pidmohyl'nyj's technique. Chapter 2 begins with the voice of the narrator breaking the fictional illusion of the story and offering an unusual simile:

Ця повість почалася, власне, трохи раніше у вагоні поїзда Дніпропетровськ – Київ. Городовський не міг заснути вночі, ... лежав,

стараючись слухати невпинний стукіт коліс та розмірені поштовхи вагона. Але ці звуки, що мали навіяти йому потрібний сон, зливалися поступово у невиразний гуркіт, що тоншав і видовжувався, як дріт між вальцівницями, аж поки не починав рватися і зникати геть.
(*Nevelyčka drama*, 269 / BUL, 245–6)

This novella actually began a little earlier, in a coach of the Dnipropetrovs'k-Kiev train. Horodovs'kyj could not fall asleep that night ... he lay, trying to listen to the ceaseless clatter of the wheels and the measured lurches of the coach. But these sounds, which were supposed to induce the sleep that he needed, gradually blended into an indistinct rumbling, which thinned and lengthened, like a wire between rollers, until it began to break and disappear.

The image of a wire drawn taut between rollers is unexpected and jarring, particularly since it seems to emanate directly from the narrator's consciousness, rather than from circumstances in the story. This effect is, of course, deliberate. Pidmohyl'nyj mirrors Horodovs'kyj's alienation from his environment by disrupting the fictional illusion and the smooth flow of the narrative. But the industrial image turns out to be Horodovs'kyj's, rather than the narrator's. A few paragraphs later we learn that the journalist was in Dnipropetrovs'k to report on a breakdown in the rolling-mill of a steelworks there. The industrial image clearly derives from his consciousness. The narration in this passage, as in Pidmohyl'nyj's earlier works, is focalized. The image is a good metaphor for the alienation that besets Horodovs'kyj in the first half of the story. A model of predictability and order, derived from human reason, is perceived to be senseless when imposed on an unruly world. Like the stretched wire, and like the reader's perception that the focalization of the narrative through its protagonist has been abandoned in this passage, Horodovs'kyj's mental constructs snap when they encounter unpredictable reality.

Travel, in various modes and different circumstances, has an important place in the novella, both on the level of image and in a wider context. Three of Horodovs'kyj's trips are given specific attention: the train ride from Dnipropetrovs'k to Kiev, the plane trip from Kharkiv to Rostov, and the trip from Hadjač to Moscow when he was eighteen years old. Each of these trips reflects a significant event in Horodovs'kyj's life. Collectively, they are a metaphor for his existential quest for self-fulfilment.

On the train to Kiev the night before he glimpses the woman, Horodovs'kyj is restless. The financial security he will gain from the publication of his book obliges him to give serious consideration to his plans for the future. For some time now he has contemplated taking time off to write 'a big and, for him, unusually important thing, in which he could honestly foresee a reflection of the meaning of his life up to this point' (*Nevelyčka drama*, 270 / BUL, 248). As he stares out the window at the expanse of the steppe, he analyses his past and contemplates his readiness to pursue this grand ambition. His anxiety stems from his uncertainty about the future. He is abandoning his predictable fate as a journalist for the vagaries of chance in an uncertain project.

A few days later, when he is flying out of Kharkiv on his way to Rostov he is struck by the view of the city from the air. It reminds him of the view of Moscow that he had seen from the roof of a freight train eleven years earlier. During the flight he dreams about that earlier train ride. He recalls his youthful enthusiasm, his idealism, and his intention to make his mark on the world. But what he remembers best is the explosion of confused feelings of desire and loneliness. His public-spirited ambition is derailed by the sexual allure of a young woman sleeping on the grass beside him. He goes on to Moscow, but he remembers mostly what happened en route. For Horodovs'kyj and for Pidmohyl'nyj, life is to be found not at the destination but along the way. Reality lies in the chance personal experiences beside the station, not in the planned accomplishments at the end of the trip.

The existential symbolism of planes and trains and the philosophical contrasts between the characters in *Povist' bez nazvy* show that, in this last known work, Pidmohyl'nyj is still pursuing the themes he had set out in his two earlier novels. Building on the fundamental dualism between the rational and the irrational, which in this novella appear as fate and chance, he continues to search for ways of reconciling these forces. But there is no bridge across this divide. There is no synthesis that can integrate chance and determinism, desire and memory, love and sex, creativity and understanding, Kiev and Kharkiv, or any of the other polarities that Pidmohyl'nyj enlists in the expression of his basic theme. There is, however, honesty, persistence, and an appreciation of human values. These are the qualities that will guide Horodovs'kyj in his search for the woman he glimpsed.

In its structural and stylistic properties, as in its theme, *Povist' bez nazvy* develops further the principles Pidmohyl'nyj had adopted in his earlier works. The parallels and juxtapositions characteristic of his earlier writing are still evident here, for example, in the threefold juxtaposition of the protagonist and the two supporting characters. But on the level of continuity, Pidmohyl'nyj is experimenting with new ideas. He does not abandon the causal, sequential logic of composition that had worked well in *Misto* and *Nevelyčka drama*, but he modifies this structure, in keeping with the thematic focus, to allow for greater subjectivity in the unfolding of the plot. The novella begins *in medias res*. Horodovs'kyj is in the apartment recommended by Bezpal'ko and Paščenko pays him a visit. Chapters 2 through 7 recount the story up to the point at which Horodovs'kyj meets Bezpal'ko and learns about the apartment. Chapter 8 opens with Horodovs'kyj once again awakening, as in the first chapter, this time after a good rest following Paščenko's initial visit. It is not immediately apparent that the intervening six chapters replace more than a single day. Individual chapters follow distinct units of the plot. Chapter 2 recounts Horodovs'ky's thoughts during the train ride to Kiev. Chapter 3 describes the chance meeting with the woman in Kiev the next day. The fourth chapter shows him returning to daily rituals in Kharkiv. In chapter 5 we see him restless and uneasy. In the sixth chapter he gets on a plane to Rostov. Chapter 7 describes his first six days in Kiev. Each chapter is a complete and objectively delimited segment of the story, but the focus is generally on Horodovs'kyj's emotional and psychological state.

The subjectivity evident in theme and structure is also reflected in the stylistic details of the novella. In *Povist' bez nazvy* Pidmohyl'nyj introduces significant modifications to the objective method. We have already noted the intrusion of the narrator at the beginning of chapter 2 and the deliberate but false suggestion of a break in focalization. Pidmohyl'nyj is developing in the direction of greater narrative complexity. The objective method is no longer the backbone of his technique, but rather an anchor around which it circles and against which it can bounce off and be measured. This greater reliance on technical innovation, on narrative tricks and devices, is most evident in the author's foreword[5] to the novella:

> Від автора
>
> Коли хто прийде до мене, скажи, що немає вдома. Скажи, що він давно вже в парку. А якщо спитають, що він робить там такої глибокої осені, коли вітри вже видули, мабуть, від підніжжя дерев згірклу жовтизну, скажи, що обмислює своє переднє слово до читачів.
>
> О, мій любий і дорогий читальнику, – скажи, мислить він, загортаючи в пальто свій малокровний тулуб, – як прагну я від тебе теплого вітання! Як хочеться мені застерегти тебе від прикрих помилок щодо короткої повісті, що ти знайдеш, перегорнувши цю сторінку! Як хочеться запевнити тебе словом честі, що події, описані в ній, ніколи не відбулися, і постаті, які ти в ній побачиш, ніколи не існували. Ти зробив би найбільшу честь моєму хистові, якби прийняв їх за живі і дійсні, але я вважаю […]

The Last Works

Бо хоч що хай каже письменник, хоч якого спокійного до твоїх вироків він буде удавати з себе, а, повір мені, ніщо його так не зогріває, як твоя зичлива увага. Навіть коли він, як похмурий Михайль,[6] загрожував тобі презирством, і тоді він був не байдужий до того, як купував ти його книжки. (*Nevelyčka drama*, 264 / BUL, 762)

From the Author

If someone comes to see me, tell them I'm not home. Say that he's been in the park for a long time now. And if they ask what he is doing there so late in autumn, when the wind has likely blown the bitter yellowness out from under the trees, say that he is thinking about his preface to the reader.

Oh, my dear lovely reader – say that he's thinking, as he wraps his anemic body in his coat – how I long for a warm greeting from you! How I want to protect you from unpleasant errors regarding the short novella that you will find when you turn this page! How I want to assure you with my word of honour that the events depicted there never happened and that the characters you will see there never existed. You would do my talent the greatest honour if you accepted them as living and real, but I think [... *a portion of the text may be missing or the ellipsis may be intentional*]

Because, no matter what the writer says, no matter how calm he pretends to be about your judgments, believe me, nothing warms him like your benevolent attention. Even when, like the dour Myxajl', he threatened you with contempt, even then he was not indifferent, when you were buying his books.

Although Pidmohyl'nyj addressed an ironic epigraph to the reader in 'Problema xliba' (indeed, he is, I believe, referring to that epigraph in the passage just quoted), this particular text reveals an entirely new dimension of his prose. The conscious shift from the first to the third person and then back again, the flaunting of conventional sentiment and its ironic negation, the reference to a contemporary writer and the subsequent tense shift that marks a self-reference – these are devices that break with realist conventions and undermine the basic logic of the objective method.

Pidmohyl'nyj is gradually moving in the direction of post-modern narrative poetics. But the change is only slight. Realism and the objective method, techniques borrowed largely from the western European novel of the previous century, are still the nucleus around which his narrative revolves. Pidmohyl'nyj's departures from the grammatical and perspectival rules of this method are a very significant break with tradition, but they still constitute only a challenge to the old technique, not yet an autonomous new one.

Between Reason and Irrationality

Viewed as a whole, the body of Valerijan Pidmohyl'nyj's known works is a monument to psychological realism. Ironically, this nineteenth-century technique makes Pidmohyl'nyj an important innovator in Ukrainian literature. Soviet orthodoxy notwithstanding, realism is a poorly represented movement in Ukrainian prose. The ethnographic realism of Panas Myrnyj or Ivan Nečuj-Levyc'kyj represents only one aspect of realist prose. In their works, as in the works of western European writers, realism is largely visual. For both groups of writers realism is also a partner in political efforts to identify, illuminate, and correct various social ills plaguing their respective societies. But for the Ukrainian realists, the political agenda is populism. The individual is not the centre of attention and the technical repertoire of their works allows for only a very limited and primitive psychological portraiture. The psychological realism of late nineteenth- and early twentieth-century western European literature is not widespread in any period of Ukrainian prose, including the 1920s. Pidmohyl'nyj, Vynnyčenko, Les' Martovyč, and Ivan Franko wrote works that can be described as psychological realism. Presumed realists, such as Kocjubyns'kyj and Janovs'kyj, are modernists *par excellence*. The bulk of prose from the 1920s, particularly the novels of the second half of the decade, is either old-fashioned populist realism or experimental modernism.

In the explosion of energy that characterized the cultural climate in Ukraine in the 1920s, the emergence of the novel as a successful popular genre was perhaps the most important indicator of the good health of the creative environment. Much has been said about the political dimensions of this explosion, but the aesthetic history of Ukrainian literature in the 1920s has yet to be written. In the absence of such an overview it is difficult to assess the relative place of an individual writer of the period. Furthermore, cultural development was cut off in the 1930s, and Pidmohyl'nyj's works, like those of many of his contemporaries, were not republished in Ukraine until recently. Thus, Pidmohyl'nyj's influence in Ukrainian literature has been slight. The intellectual prose of the 1980s, particularly the novels of Valerij Ševčuk, demonstrate a conscious debt to Pidmohyl'nyj, but this influence is neither exclusive nor systematic. What Pidmohyl'nyj's influence might have been under different circumstances is entirely speculative; given the importance of psychological realism in the development of the twentieth-century philosophical novel in Western literature, however, it seems safe to assume that it would have been important. Unrealized influence notwithstanding, the accomplishments of this writer stand on their own. In the brief and difficult decade and a half of his literary career, Pidmohyl'nyj produced a literary *œuvre* of exceptional quality and value that deserves the continued attention of generations of readers and scholars.

Notes

Introduction

1 Many of the facts of Pidmohyl'nyj's biography are common knowledge and can be found in a number of sources. Through the untiring efforts of Volodymyr Mel'nyk, many new facts about his life have recently been uncovered. Thus, the most complete and factually most reliable account of Pidmohyl'nyj's life is Volodymyr Mel'nyk's *Valer"jan Pidmohyl'nyj* (Kiev: Znannja, 1991).
2 A copy of his graduation certificate is reproduced in Volodymyr Mel'nyk, 'Najbil'š intelektual'no zahlyblenyj,' *Literaturna panorama, 1990* (Kiev: Dnipro, 1990) 159.
3 Letter to the author dated 24 September 1992.
4 *Žovten': zbirnyk* (Kharkiv: Vseukrlitkom, 1921) 156.
5 Quoted in Vasyl' I. Pivtoradni, *Ukrajins'ka literatura peršyx rokiv revoljuciji (1917–1923 rr.)* (Kiev: Radjans'ka škola, 1968) 94n2.
6 Jurij Smolyč, *Rozpovidi pro nespokij nemaje kincja* (Kiev: Radjans'kyj pys'mennyk, 1972) 101.
7 Holodajko [pseud.], 'Lyst z Kyjeva,' *Nova Ukrajina* 1922, 6: 33.
8 The stories were listed under the following titles: 'Sobaka,' 'Smert',' 'V epidemičnomu baraci,' 'Ostap Šaptala,' 'Povstanci,' 'Komunist,' 'Mynule,' 'Za den',' 'Kolysanka,' and 'Koxannja.' 'Mynule,' 'Kolysanka,' and 'Koxannja' are unknown.
9 Stefan Karol' [Mykola Xvyl'ovyj], 'Xudožnij materijal v *Novij Ukrajini*,' *Červonyj šljax* 1923, 2: 309. Also in *Mykola Xvyl'ovyj: Tvory v p"jat'ox tomax* (Baltimore: Slovo & Smoloskyp, 1978–86) 4: 562.
10 *Radjans'ke literaturoznavstvo* 1989, 8: 19.

11 *Červonyj šljax* 1923, 2: 281. Reprinted in Valerijan Pidmohyl'nyj, *Misto*, ed. Hryhorij Kostjuk (New York: Ukrajins'ka vil'na akademija nauk u SŠA, 1954) 284–5.
12 *Červonyj šljax* 1923, 4–5: 289–90. Reprinted in Leonid Bilec'kyj, 'Umovy literaturnoji praci na Ukrajini (1917–1926),' *Nova Ukrajina* 1927, 10–11: 70–1.
13 *Červonyj šljax* 1924, 1–2: 261.
14 The policy of Ukrainization, an attempt to make the culture and language of Ukraine Ukrainian, was adopted and implemented during the second half of 1923, in keeping with the resolutions on the national question adopted by the Twelfth Party Congress, in April 1923.
15 See Volodymyr Vynnyčenko, *Ščodennyk*, vol. 2 (Edmonton: Canadian Institute of Ukrainian Studies, 1983) 17, 213.
16 *Červonyj šljax* 1924, 1–2: 4–33.
17 'Trahedija nepotribnoji trahyčnosty,' *Červonyj šljax* 1924, 4–5: 264–72.
18 *Červonyj šljax* 1924, 4–5: 283.
19 *Žyttja j revoljucija* 1925, 8: 7–13.
20 'Na stepax' (an excerpt from the *povist' Dnipro*), *Nova hromada* 1924, 35: 11–12.
21 See 'Postanova Politbjuro CK KP(b)U pro ukrajins'ki xudožni uhrupovannja, vid 10/IV 1925 roku,' in A. Lejtes and M. Jašek, comps., *Desjat' rokiv ukrajins'koji literatury (1917–1927)*, 2nd ed. (Kharkiv: Deržavne vydavnyctvo Ukrajiny, 1930) 559–60. An English translation appears under the title 'Resolution of the Politbureau of the Central Committee of the CP(b)U on Ukrainian Literary Groupings,' in George S. N. Luckyj, *Literary Politics in the Soviet Ukraine, 1917–1934*, rev. and updated ed. (Durham, N.C.: Duke University Press, 1990) 277–8.
22 Leonid Čerevatenko, 'Vse, čym duša bolila,' *Jevhen Plužnyk: Poeziji* (Kiev: Radjans'kyj pys'mennyk, 1988) 40–1.
23 He is, however, cited as a writer hostile to the ideology of the Communist Party in a speech to the Politburo of the Central Committee of the Communist Party (bolshevik) of Ukraine on 20 September 1926, by its First Party Secretary, Lazar Kahanovyč. The speech is reproduced in *Mykola Xvyl'ovyj: Tvory v p"jat'ox tomax*, 5: 558–65.
24 Descriptions and detailed analyses of the Literary Discussion can be found in the works of two expert s on the subject, George Luckyj and Myroslav Shkandrij: See Luckyj, *Literary Politics in the Soviet Ukraine* (particularly chapter 5, pp. 92–111); Myroslav Shkandrij, 'Introduction: Mykola Khvylovy and the Literary Discussion,' in Mykola Khvylovy, *The Cultural Renaissance in Ukraine: Polemical Pamphlets, 1925–1926* (Edmonton: Canadian Institute of Ukrainian Studies, 1986) 1–30; and Myroslav Shkandrij, *Modernists, Marxists and the Nation: The Ukrainian Literary Discussion of the 1920s* (Edmonton:

Canadian Institute of Ukrainian Studies Press, 1992).
25 *Šljaxy rozvytku sučasnoji literatury* (Kiev: Kul'tkomisija Misckomu UAN, 1925) 37. For an interesting alternative view of Pidmohyl'nyj's speech at the public debate (a speech that he did not finish, because, as a note to the stenographic transcript explains, 'he wasn't feeling well'), see 'Šljaxy rozvytku ukrajins'koji literatury,' a parody of the debate by Omel'ko Buc, reproduced in *Mykola Xvyl'ovyj: Tvory v p"jat'ox tomax*, 5: 480–2.
26 Volodymyr Mel'nyk, 'V očax vidbylosja stolittja,' *Literaturna Ukrajina* 15 October 1992.
27 *Kul'tura i pobut* 8 August 1926.
28 'Vse, čym duša bolila,' 64–5.
29 Larysa Masenko, 'Zahublenyj skarb,' Valerijan Pidmohyl'nyj and Jevhen Plužnyk, comps., *Rosijs'ko-ukrajins'kyj frazeolohičnyj slovnyk*, (Kiev: Kobza, 1993) 3.
30 'Bez sterna (Maksym Ryl's'kyj),' *Žyttja j revoljucija* 1927, 1: 39–53.
31 Vjačeslav Brjuxovec'kyj, *Mykola Zerov* (Kiev: Radjans'kyj pys'mennyk, 1990) 22.
32 Preface, *Vybrani tvory* by Ivan Nečuj-Levyc'kyj, (Kiev: Čas, 1927) 1: v–viii.
33 'Ivan Levyc'kyj-Nečuj (Sproba psyxoanalizy tvorčosty),' *Žyttja j revoljucija* 1927, 9: 295–303.
34 Reported in Čerevatenko, 'Vse, čym duša bolila,' 41–2.
35 Review of *Opovidannja*, by Tymofij Borduljak (Vetlyna) (Kharkiv: Knyhospilka, 1927), *Žyttja j revoljucija* 1927, 7–8: 187–88.
36 'Panajit Istrati v Kyjevi,' *Žyttja j revoljucija* 1928, 2: 166–9.
37 Vasyl' Čaplenko, 'Dvoje v odnij kimnati,' *Blyz'ke j daleke ta inši tvory* (New York: privately published, 1978) 60–9.
38 Olena Zvyčajna, 'Kryve dzerkalo,' *Avangard* (Official Journal of the Central Committee of the Ukrainian Youth Association) 1955, 5–6: 63–72.
39 Olena Zvyčajna, *Ty: Povist' iz žyttja ukrajinciv u zolotoverxomu Kyjevi v 1927–29 rokax* (Munich: Ukrajins'ke vydavnyctvo, 1982), ch. 18.
40 *Gorod*, trans. B. Elysavetskyj (Moscow: Gosizdat, 1930).
41 Plans for the translation of unspecified works are mentioned in *Červonyj šljax* 1929, 1: 245, and in Orest Zilynskyj, ed., *Sto padesát let česko-ukrajinskych literárních styku, 1814–1964* (Prague: Svět Sovětu, 1968) 56.
42 'Pys'mennyky u proletars'koho studenstva,' *Literaturna hazeta* 15 March 1929: 7.
43 'Xiba ce misto?' *Literaturna hazeta* 15 March 1929: 7.
44 Rabičev, 'Kul'turna revoljucija ta zavdannja profspilok u haluzi kul'troboty,' *IV Vseukrajins'kyj z"jizd profspilok, 1–8 hrudnja 1928 r.: Stenohrafičnyj zvit* (Kharkiv: n.p., 1929) 332–47.
45 Bohdan Kravčenko [Krawchenko], 'Nacional'ne vidrodžennja ta robitnyča kljasa na Ukrajini v 1920–yx rokax,' *Sučasnist'* 1984, 1–2: 114.

46 *Červonyj šljax* 1929, 3: 144–6.
47 Borys Antonenko-Davydovyč, 'Spohad pro pryjom Stalinom ukrajins'koji delegaciji 1929 roku,' *Sučasnist'* 1984, 7–8: 4–12.
48 *Universal'nyj žurnal* 1929, 1: 45. Reprinted as the Afterword to the novel *Misto*, in *Misto* (Kiev: Molod', 1989) 441.
49 *Slovo i čas* 1991, 2: 22–5, and *Literaturna Ukrajina* 31 January 1991.
50 *Žyttja j revoljucija* 1930, 3: 5–76; 4: 4–38; 5: 9–55; and 6: 30–66.
51 See Mel'nyk, *Valer"jan Pidmohyl'nyj*, 34.
52 Leonid Čerevatenko, 'Z žyttja lyxoho suspil'stva,' *Dnipro* 1991, 2: 177–8.
53 'Šljax na holhofu,' *Vitčyzna* 1991, 1: 150–8.
54 *Vitčyzna* 1991, 2: 94–105. In subsequent references, this issue of the journal is identified as *Vitčyzna*.
55 *Družba narodov* 1989, 9: 185–92.
56 *Tractatus de Intellectus emendatione*.
57 This may be a misprint. Perhaps Pidmohyl'nyj was referring here to Natalija, his sister.
58 Pidmohyl'nyj is referring to Cicero's first oration against Catiline, which begins: 'Quousque tandem abutêre, Catilina, patientiâ nostrâ? Quamdiu etiam furor iste tuus nos eludet? Quem ad finem sese effrenata jactabit audacia? (How far, O Catiline, wilt thou abuse our patience? How long shall thy frantic rage baffle the efforts of justice? To what heights meanest thou to carry thy daring insolence?)' (*Select Orations of Marcus Tullius Cicero*, trans. William Duncan [London, 1816] p. 114–15).

Chapter One

1 *Tvory: Tom 1* (Katerynoslav: Ukrajins'ke vydavnyctvo v Sičeslavi, 1920); henceforth identified in the text as *Tvory*.
2 *Misto: Roman, opovidannja*, ed. Raisa Movčan and Valerij Ševčuk (Kiev: Molod', 1989); henceforth identified in the text as *Misto*. Note that citations from Pidmohyl'nyj's early stories are true to their original publication in 1920 in *Tvory: Tom 1*.
3 *Valer"jan Pidmohyl'nyj: Opovidannja, povist', romany*, comp. Volodymyr Mel'nyk, Biblioteka Ukrajins'koji Literatury series (Kiev: Naukova dumka, 1991); henceforth identified in the text as BUL.
4 As, for example, in *Česnist' z soboju*.
5 V. Junoša [Petro Jefremov], 'Poet čariv noči,' *Vyr revoljuciji: Zbirnyk* (Katerynoslav, 1921) 95.
6 The Ukrainian word translated here as 'madness' is шаленство, which is defined as 'insanity; madness; extreme anger; excessive emotionality.' In the previous excerpt, the Ukrainian word translated as 'madness' was скаженина,

which has the primary meaning of 'a viral infectious disease of mammals (i.e., rabies),' but can also mean 'insanity; madness; excessive emotionality.'

Chapter Two

1 The term *novella* is used in the English sense of 'short novel' rather than the Italian sense of 'short story.'
2 *Povstanci j ynši opovidannja* (Prague: Nova Ukrajina, 1923); henceforth identified in the text as *Povstanci*.
3 Volodymyr Mel'nyk describes the sentry's words as the plea of a peasant's soul ('волання хліборобського єства') ('"Povstanci" Valer"jana Pidmohyl'noho,' *Prapor* 1990, 7: 95). This interpretation stems from Mel'nyk's sociological reading of the work.
4 The actual number of sections in the work depends on the edition. The 1922 Leipzig edition has nineteen sections, whereas the version included in both the BUL edition and the collection entitled *Misto: Roman, opovidannja* (Kiev: Molod', 1989) has sixteen. The version in *Problema xliba*, 2nd ed. (Kharkiv: Knyhospilka, 1930) has eighteen. I follow the Leipzig edition in dividing the sections. In the BUL and *Misto* [1989] editions, this would involve splitting sections 2, 5, and 14.
5 Yuri Tkach uses the simple past tense in his translation: 'By eight in the morning the patients finished breakfast and the ward rounds began.' 'In the Infirmary,' *Before the Storm: Soviet Ukrainian Fiction of the 1920s*, ed. George S. N. Luckyj (Ardis: Ann Arbor, 1986) 131.
6 *Ostap Šaptala: Povist'* (Kharkiv: Vseukrlitkom, 1922); henceforth identified in the text as *Šaptala*.
7 *Nevelyčka drama: Roman, povisti*, comp. Klavdija Frolova (Dnipropetrovs'k: Promin', 1990); henceforth identified in the text as *Nevelyčka drama*. Quotations from *Ostap Šaptala* are referenced to both the original edition (1922) and this one, but are true to the original edition.
8 Tzvetan Todorov, *The Poetics of Prose*, trans. Richard Howard (Ithaca: Cornell University, 1977) 116.
9 To be fair, it should be noted that Todorov is concerned with units of text that correspond to propositions in formal logic; in other words, he is thinking of clauses and sentences. Todorov calls longer blocks of a story 'sequences.' Although he describes types of sequences, he does not discuss the relations between them. Nevertheless, it is apparent that the same categories that describe the relations between propositions also describe the relations between sequences.
10 J. Hillis Miller calls parallelism repetition. See his *Fiction and Repetition* (Cambridge: Harvard University Press, 1982).

11 Stream-of-consciousness narration is a technique that deliberately challenges temporal sequence as a structural relation by allowing any sequence to masquerade as a temporal one.
12 Pidmohyl'nyj calls it one of his better works in an autobiographical blurb dated 5 March 1924. The portion of that blurb reproduced in *Literaturna Ukrajina* 31 January 1991, does not contain the comment.
13 The grand duke was the brother of Nicholas II.

Chapter Three

1 An example is the dispute between Arthur Lovejoy and René Wellek regarding Romanticism.
2 (Littleton, Colo.: Ukrainian Academic Press, 1975). Ukrainian original: *Istorija ukrajins'koji literatury* (New York: Ukrainian Academy of Arts and Sciences in the U.S., 1956).
3 (The Hague: Mouton, 1969). See also René Wellek, 'Closing Statement' in *Style in Language*, Proceedings of the Conference on Style held at Indiana University in 1958, ed. Thomas Sebeok (Cambridge: MIT Press, 1960) 408.
4 'Style and Its Image,' *The Rustle of Language* [Le bruissement de la langue], trans. Richard Howard (Oxford: Basil Blackwell, 1986) 99.
5 See chapter 1, p. 29.
6 Friedrich Nietzsche, *Werke in Drei Banden* (Munich: Karl Hanser Verlag, 1954) 3: 562.
7 Marion Faber with Stephen Lehmann, trans., *Human, All Too Human*, by Friedrich Nietzsche (Lincoln, Nebr.: University of Nebraska, 1984) 119.
8 Gérard Genette, *Narrative Discourse*, trans. Jane Lewin (Ithaca, NY: Cornell University Press, 1980); originally published as a part of his *Figures III* (Paris: Éditions du Seuil, 1972).
9 Dorrit Cohn, *Transparent Minds: Narrative Modes for Presenting Consciousness in Fiction* (Princeton: Princeton University Press, 1978).
10 Indeed, focalization and harmony are largely overlapping categories. I have deliberately exaggerated the differences between them for analytic purposes.
11 V. Junoša [Petro Jefremov], 'Poet čariv noči,' *Vyr revoljuciji: Zbirnyk* (Katerynoslav: 1921) 95.
12 *Tretja revoljucija: Opovidannja* (Kiev: Knyhospilka, 1926); henceforth identified in the text as *Tretja*.
13 M. Dolengo [Myxajlo Klokov], 'Trahedija nepotribnoji trahyčnosty,' *Červonyj šljax* 1924, 4–5: 266.
14 Dolengo, 'Trahedija,' 267.
15 See chapter 1, p. 32.
16 Junoša, 'Poet čariv noči,' 96.

17 Actually, Maxno's poem in the story is not by Pidmohyl'nyj, but by Jevhen Plužnyk. See Leonid Čerevatenko, ed., *Jevhen Plužnyk: Poeziji* (Kiev: Radjans'kyj pys'mennyk, 1988) 117, 360–1.
18 For more information about the 1921–2 famine, see Kazuo Nakai, 'Soviet Agricultural Policies in the Ukraine and the 1921–1922 Famine,' *Harvard Ukrainian Studies* 1982, 1: 43–61.
19 *Syn: Opovidannja z časiv holodu*, ed. Serhij Pylypenko, 2nd ed. (Kharkiv: Deržavne vydavnyctvo Ukrajiny, 1925). This 31-page edition, which came out in the Biblioteka seljanyna, Krasne pys'menstvo (The Peasant's Library, Belles-lettres) series, had a press run of 15,000 copies.
20 For a discussion of the relationship between hunger and lust in Pidmohyl'nyj's stories, as well as of the influence of Freudian theory, see A. Muzyčka, 'Tvorča metoda Valerijana Pidmohyl'noho,' *Červonyj šljax* 1930, 10: 109–14.
21 See, for example, M. Motuzka, 'Selo j misto v tvorčosti V. Pidmohyl'noho,' *Krytyka* 1928, 6: 34–50.
22 See his '"Povstanci" Valer"jana Pidmohyl'noho,' *Prapor* 1990, 7: 94–5; and his *Valer"jan Pidmohyl'nyj: Do 90-riččja vid dnja narodžennja* (Kiev: Znannja, 1991), particularly the chapter 'Na perexresti mista i sela' [At the crossroads of city and village], pp. 21–30.
23 For a different explanation, see Volodymyr Mel'nyk, *Valer"jan Pidmohyl'nyj*, 26.

Chapter Four

1 Two items recount public discussions of Pidmohyl'nyj and his novel: 'Pys'men-nyky u proletars'koho studentstva (Zbory v INO 2 bereznja 1929 roku),' *Literaturna hazeta* 15 March 1929; and Rabičev, 'Kul'turna revoljucija ta zavdannja profspilok u haluzi kul'troboty,' *IV Vseukrajins'kyj z"jizd profspilok 1–8 hrudnja 1928. Stenohrafičnyj zvit* (Kharkiv: 1929) 332–347.
2 *Misto*, ed. Hryhorij Kostjuk (New York: Ukrajins'ka vil'na akademija nauk u SŠA, 1954); henceforth identified in the text as Kostjuk.
3 Junoša, 'Poet čariv noči,' 94.
4 *Žovten': Zbirnyk* (Kharkiv: Vseukrlitkom, 1921) 156.
5 Jurij Smolyč, 'Pidmohyl'nyj,' *Vitčyzna* 1972, 2: 93.
6 Volodymyr Mel'nyk, *Valer"jan Pidmohyl'nyj* (Kiev: Znannja, 1991) 5.
7 A chapter of my dissertation is devoted to those connections. See Maxim Tarnawsky, 'Valerijan Pidmohyl'nyj, Guy de Maupassant, and the Magic of the Night,' PhD diss., Harvard University, 1986.
8 Mahdalyna Laslo-Kucjuk, '*Misto* V. Pidmohyl'noho i francuz'kyj roman XIX stolittja,' *Šukannja formy* (Bucharest: Kryterion, 1980) 143.
9 The plot of *Bel-Ami* itself is borrowed, or rather adopted, from a long tradition

of parvenu stories, from among which the best-known character is perhaps Balzac's Lucien de Rubempré. A number of specifics link Maupassant's novel to Balzac's works, particularly to the second half of *Les Illusions perdues*. Milton Chaikin, in his 'Maupassant's *Bel-Ami* and Balzac' (*Romance Notes* 1 [1960]: 109–12), has catalogued some of those similarities, of which the most apparent are the following: In both novels women are the rungs and journalism the ladder that the protagonists ascend. They indulge in similar corrupt practices and enjoy similar benefits as a result (in the theatre, for example). Many details link the two heroes: their attention to clothes and food, acceptance of money from sexual partners and free services from prostitutes, duelling, ennobling name changes, and an ambiguous relationship with family in the provinces.

10 These parallel scenes are discussed in Laslo-Kucjuk, *Šukannja formy*, 161–2.
11 He is thinking of the Polish king Stefan Batory, 1575–86.
12 Laslo-Kucjuk, *Šukannja formy*, 154.
13 *Problema xliba*, 2nd ed. (Kharkiv: Knyhospilka, 1930) 5. The text of the preface is reprinted in the notes to *Misto*, p. 444.
14 Dolengo, 'Trahedija nepotribnoji trahyčnosty,' 269–70.
15 For a further discussion of the parallels between *Misto* and Pidmohyl'nyj's earlier works, see Petro Jefremov, 'Pro roman V. Pidmohyl'noho *Misto*,' *Pluh* 1928, 9: 66-72.
16 'Le Roman,' *Guy de Maupassant: Romans* (Paris: Albin Michel, 1959) 840-1.
17 Leonard Tancock, trans., *Pierre and Jean*, by Guy de Maupassant (Harmondsworth: Penguin, 1979) 32–3.
18 For a further discussion of Pidmohyl'nyj's description of Kiev, see Andrij Nikovs'kyj, 'Pro *Misto* V. Pidmohyl'noho,' *Žyttja j revoljucija* 1928, 10: 111.
19 Among them, M. Motuzka, 'Selo j misto v tvorčosti V. Pidmohyl'noho,' *Krytyka* 1928, 6: 36, and Myxajlo Mohyljans'kyj, 'Ni mista, ni sela,' *Červonyj šljax* 1929, 5-6: 274.
20 Laslo-Kucjuk, *Šukannja formy*, 155.
21 For further discussion of the influence of Schopenhauer on Maupassant see: Micheline Besnard-Coursodon, *Étude thématique et structurale de l'oeuvre de Maupassant: Le Piège* (Paris: Nizet, 1973) 65-100; René-Pierre Colin, 'Maupassant et le "saccageur de rêves,"' *Schopenhauer en France: Un Mythe naturaliste* (Lyon: University of Lyon Press, 1979) 193-202; Pierre Cogny, *Maupassant, l'homme sans dieu* (Brussels: La Renaissance du Livre, 1968) 17-63; G. Hainsworth, 'Schopenhauer, Flaubert, Maupassant: Conceptual Thought and Artistic "Truth,"' *Currents of Thought in French Literature* (New York: Barnes & Noble, 1966) 165-190; Kurt Willi, *Déterminisme et liberté chez Guy de Maupassant* (Zurich: Juris Druck, 1972) 61–5 and passim; and chapter 2 of André Vial, *Guy de Maupassant et l'art du roman* (Paris: Nizet, 1954) 111–249.

22 'Auprès d'un mort,' in *Maupassant: Contes et nouvelles*, ed. Louis Forestier, 2 vols, Bibliothèque de la Pléiade (Paris: Gallimard, 1974-9) 1: 728.
23 *The Complete Short Stories of Guy de Maupassant*, 3 vols. (London: Cassels, 1970) 3: 709.
24 *Guy de Maupassant, Chroniques*, Series 10:18, 3 vols. (Paris: Union Générale d'Éditions, 1980) 1: 127-33.
25 In her *Étude thématique et structurale de l'oeuvre de Maupassant: Le Piège* (Paris: Nizet, 1973).
26 Actually, the passage is from *Hagigah* 16A, in the *Mo'ed* seder. In the Soncino translation the passage reads as follows: 'Six things are said of human beings: in regard to three, they are like the ministering angels, and in regard to three, they are like the beasts. "In regard to three, they are like the ministering angels": they have understanding like the ministering angels; and they walk erect like the ministering angels, and they can talk in the holy tongue like the ministering angels. "In regard to three, they are like beasts': they eat and drink like beasts, and they propagate like beasts, and they relieve themselves like beasts." (*The Babylonian Talmud: Seder Mo'ed*, ed. Rabbi I. Epstein [London: Soncino Press, 1938] 102).
27 Basia Gulati, trans., *Thaïs*, by Anatole France (Chicago: University of Chicago Press, 1976) 119.
28 On the evening Musin'ka first approaches Stepan, he has been studying statistics, a science that 'unerringly calculates how many chances everyone has of falling under a streetcar, contracting cholera, or becoming a genius' (Kostjuk, 85 / *Misto*, 78 / BUL, 370).
29 Laslo-Kucjuk, *Šukannja formy*, 157.
30 Philippe Bonnefis, 'Comme Maupassant,' *Le Naturalisme: Colloque de Cerisy*, Series 10:18 (Paris: Union Générale d'Éditions, 1978) 287-315.
31 *Bel-Ami* in *Guy de Maupassant. Romans*, ed. Albert-Marie Schmidt (Paris: Albin Michel, 1959; reprint 1975); henceforth identified in the text as *B-A*.
32 Douglas Parmée, trans., *Bel-Ami*, by Guy de Maupassant (Harmondsworth: Penguin, 1975) 189; this translation is henceforth identified in the text as *Friend*.
33 For an interesting examination of Radčenko's bad faith (although it is not referred to by that term in the article), see Petro Lakyza, 'Istorija odnijeji kar"jery (Pro roman *Misto* V. Pidmohyl'noho),' *Na meži: Literaturni syluety* (Kharkiv: Deržavne vydavnyctvo Ukrajiny, 1930) 35-68.
34 Commenting on the writing of *Misto*, Pidmohyl'nyj noted that the novel began as a screenplay. See *Misto*, 441.
35 'Moja ostannja knyha,' *Universal'nyj žurnal* 1929, 1: 45; cited in *Misto*, 441.
36 Jurij Šerex (George Shevelov), 'Ljudyna i ljudy (*Misto* Valerijana Pidmohyl'-noho),' in his *Ne dlja ditej* (New York: Prolog, 1964) 83-96.

37 Valerijan Pidmohyl'nyj, 'Bez sterna (Maksym Ryl's'kyj),' *Žyttja j revoljucija* 1927, 1: 53.

Chapter Five

1 'Bilok i joho zaburennja,' *Literaturna hazeta* (Munich) 3.9 (Sept. 1957): 1; English translation: 'A Disturbance in the Protein,' in George S. N. Luckyj and Moira Luckyj, trans., *A Little Touch of Drama*, by Valerian Pidmohylny, (Littleton, Colo.: Ukrainian Academic Press, 1972) 10.
2 An allusion to Imre Kalman's operetta *Die Bajadere*.
3 Valerijan Pidmohyl'nyj, *Nevelyčka drama*, ed. Jurij Bojko (Paris: Perša ukrajins'ka drukarnja y Franciji, 1956); henceforth identified in the text as Bojko.
4 Luckyj and Luckyj, trans., *A Little Touch of Drama*; henceforth identified in the text as *Touch*. With the translators' permission, I have made changes in some passages (contained in square brackets) to render a more literal translation.
5 'Ivan Levyc'kyj-Nečuj (Sproba psyxoanalizy tvorčosty),' *Žyttja j revoljucija* 1927, 9: 295–303.
6 'Ivan Levyc'kyj-Nečuj,' 295.
7 This assumes that the 'mademoiselle' refers to the historical marquise rather than, by transference, to Marta.
8 Compare this with Pidmohyl'nyj's description of Levyc'kyj's attachment to the Ros' River area in 'Ivan Levyc'kyj-Nečuj,' 301–2.
9 Slavenko's background, in contrast to Dmytro Stajnyčyj's, is described as including 'a generation or two of intellectual labour' (Bojko, 114 / *Nevelyčka drama*, 65 / BUL, 595; *Touch*, 66).
10 In order to convey the gist of the passage, I have substituted analogous examples from English grammar for those in the Ukrainian text.
11 The resurgence of interest in Nietzsche since the 1970s, particularly among post-structuralist literary critics, has led to the popular acceptance of certain views about the meaning and significance of his thought that differ dramatically from the view of his philosophy that prevailed sixty years ago. Recently, serious attention has been given to the question of Nietzsche's influence at that time in Russia and in the Soviet Union, including Ukraine. The fruits of this attention can be found in the following works: Bernice Glatzer Rosenthal, ed., *Nietzsche in Russia* (Princeton: Princeton University Press, 1986); Edith W. Clowes, *The Revolution of Moral Consciousness: Nietzsche in Russian Literature, 1890–1914* (Dekalb, Ill.: Northern Illinois University Press, 1988); and in the papers presented at the conference on Nietzsche's Influence on Soviet Culture, held at Fordham University, Bronx, NY, in June 1988. Two earlier studies, one focusing on Russia and the other on Poland, offer a wealth

of information: Ann Marie Lane, 'Nietzsche in Russian Thought 1890–1917,' PhD diss., University of Wisconsin – Madison, 1976, and Tomasz Weiss, *Fryderyk Nietzsche w pismiennictwie polskim lat 1890–1914* (Cracow: Polska Akademia Nauk, 1961).

12 See chapter 3, p. 75.
13 In 1919, when Pidmohyl'nyj's story was written, the irony of comparing the dehumanizing effects of socialism with Nietzsche's views on the effects of Christian morals was, perhaps, less evident than it is today.
14 John Burt Foster, Jr, *Heirs to Dionysus: A Nietzschean Current in Literary Modernism* (Princeton: Princeton University Press, 1981) 39–144.
15 Foster, *Heirs to Dionysus*, 81.
16 George G. Grabowicz, *The Poet as Mythmaker* (Cambridge, Mass.: Harvard Ukrainian Research Institute, 1982) 1–16.
17 George G. Grabowicz, 'The History and Myth of the Cossack Ukraine in Polish and Russian Romantic Literature,' PhD diss., Harvard University, 1975, 495.
18 Jurij Luc'kyj, 'Šče do temy "Ševčenko i Kuliš,"' *Sučasnist'* 1985, 11: 15–24.
19 Aleksander Zakrževskij, *Podpol'e: Psyxologičeskija paralleli* (Kiev: Iskusstvo i pečatnoe dělo, 1911) 21.
20 James B. Woodward, *Leonid Andreyev: A Study* (Oxford: Clarendon, 1969) 29.
21 For more on Pidmohyl'nyj's existentialism, see Maxim Tarnawsky, '*Nevtomnyi honets v maibutnie*: An Existential Reading of Valeriian Pidmohylny's *Misto*,' *Journal of Ukrainian Graduate Studies* 1979, 2: 3–19, or the Ukrainian translation of that essay, 'Nevtomnyj honec' v majbutnje: Ekzystencial'ne pročytannja *Mista* Pidmohyl'noho,' *Slovo i čas* 1991, 5: 56–63.

Chapter Six

1 The title of the story in *Literaturna hazeta* is apparently unclear. Others have read it as 'Z žyttja budynku.' Leonid Čerevatenko, who is responsible for the publication of the story in *Dnipro* (1991, 2: 178–82), cites the authority of Tajisa Kovalenko, the sister of Jevhen Plužnyk's wife, for adding the number of the building to the title.
2 Valer"jan Pidmohyl'nyj, 'Z žyttja budynku No. 29,' *Dnipro* 1991, 2: 182 / BUL, 240.
3 Pidmohyl'nyj, 'Z žyttja budynku No. 29,' 178–79 / BUL, 233.
4 From Mykola Bažan's 'Rozmaj-zillja III,' 1926.
5 In the BUL edition the piece is called 'a fragment of a preface' and is relegated to the endnotes.
6 Myxajl' Semenko, the futurist poet.

Bibliography
Works by and about Valerijan Pidmohyl'nyj

Works by Pidmohyl'nyj

BOOKS

Tvory. Tom 1. Katerynoslav: Ukrajins'ke vydavnyctvo v Sičeslavi, 1920. 168 pp.
  Contents: 'Starec',' 'Vanja,' 'Važke pytannja,' 'Prorok,' 'Hajdamaka,' 'Dobryj boh,' 'Na seli,' 'Na imenynax,' 'Did Jakym.'
Ostap Šaptala. Povist'. Kharkiv: Vseukrlitkom, 1922. 118 pp. 3,000 cop.
V epidemičnomu baraci. Narys. Leipzig: Ukrajins'ka nakladnja, 1922. 47 pp.
  (Contains a brief introduction about Pidmohyl'nyj by Vasyl' Vernyvolja [Simovyč]).
Povstanci j ynši opovidannja. Prague: Nova Ukraina, 1923. 47 pp. Contents: 'Povstanci,' 'Ivan Bosyj,' 'Probljema xliba.'
*Syn. Kiev: Nova hromada, 1923. 35 pp. 1,000 cop. (Reprint from *Nova Hromada* 1923, no. 9.).
*Vijs'kovyj litun: Opovidannja. Kiev: Červonyj šljax, 1924. 168 pp. 3,000 cop.
  Contents: 'Vijs'kovyj litun,' 'Istorija pani Jivhy,' 'Problema xliba,' 'Sobaka,' 'V epidemičnomu baraci.'

To the best of my knowledge, the listing of works by Pidmohyl'nyj in this bibliography is comprehensive. The entries are annotated, where possible, to include such information as page length, number of copies printed, and, in the case of collections, the contents of the book. In the listing of works about Pidmohyl'nyj, page references given in square brackets and preceded by the abbreviation VP indicate pages that deal specifically with Pidmohyl'nyj. An asterisk indicates that the publication was unavailable to me.

Bibliography

Syn: Opovidannja z časiv holodu. Ed. Serhij Pylypenko, 2nd ed. Biblioteka seljanyna, Krasne pys'menstvo [The Villager's Library, Belles-lettres] series. Kharkiv: Deržavne vydavnyctvo Ukrajiny, 1925. 31 pp. 15,000 cop.

Tretja revoljucija: Opovidannja. Kiev: Knyhospilka, 1926. 48 pp. 4,000 cop.

Problema xliba. Kiev: Masa, 1927. 218 pp. 3,000 cop. Contents: Peredmova (Preface), 'Sonce sxodyt',' 'Tretja revoljucija,' 'Syn,' 'Vijs'kovyj litun,' 'Istorija pani Jivhy,' 'P"jatdesjat verstov,' 'Problema xliba,' 'Sobaka,' 'V epidemičnomu baraci,' 'Smert'.'

Misto. Kiev: Knyhospilka, 1928. 256 pp. 4,000 cop. Second printing: 1929. 5000 cop.

Problema xliba. 2nd ed. Kharkiv: Knyhospilka, 1930. 169 pp. 5,000 cop. Contents: As in the 1929 edition (above), with the exception of 'Smert'.'

Syn. Kharkiv: Deržavne vydavnyctvo Ukrajiny, 1930. 36 pp. 20,000 cop.

Tretja revoljucija. Ed. Svjatoslav Hordyns'kyj. Lviv: Ukrajins'ke vydavnyctvo, 1942. 162 pp. Contents: Peredmova (Preface), 'Sonce sxodyt',' 'Tretja revoljucija,' 'Syn,' 'Problema xliba,' 'Sobaka,' 'V epidemičnomu baraci,' 'Povstanci.'

Misto. Ed. Hryhorij Kostjuk. New York: Ukrajins'ka vil'na akademija nauk u SŠA, 1954. 298 pp.

Nevelyčka drama. Ed. Jurij Bojko. Paris: Perša ukrajins'ka drukarnja u Franciji, 1956. 342 pp.

Misto: Roman, opovidannja. Ed. Rajisa Movčan and Valerij Ševčuk. Kiev: Molod', 1989. 447 pp. Contents: *Misto*, 'Dobryj boh,' 'Hajdamaka,' 'Vanja,' 'Starec',' 'Na imenynax,' 'Did Jakym,' 'Na seli,' 'V epidemičnomu baraci,' 'Sobaka,' 'Problema xliba,' 'Istorija pani Jivhy,' 'P"jatdesjat verstov,' 'Syn,' 'Vijs'kovyj litun,' 'Sonce sxodyt',' 'Tretja revoljucija.'

Nevelyčka drama: Roman, povisti. Comp. Klavdija Frolova. Dnipropetrovs'k: Promin', 1990. 325 pp. Contents: *Nevelyčka drama, Ostap Šaptala, Povist' bez nazvy*.

Istorija pani Jivhy: Opovidannja, povist'. Comp. Vitalij Kocjuk. Kiev: Veselka, 1991. 173 pp. Contents: 'Vanja,' 'Istorija pani Jivhy,' 'Hajdamaka,' 'Povstanci,' 'Za den',' 'Ivan Bosyj,' 'P"jatdesjat verstov,' 'Syn,' 'Z žyttja budynku,' *Ostap Šaptala*.

Valer"jan Pidmohyl'nyj: Opovidannja, povist', romany. Comp. Volodymyr Mel'nyk. Biblioteka Ukrajins'koji Literatury series. Kiev: Naukova dumka, 1991. Contents: 'Dobryj boh,' 'Hajdamaka,' 'Vanja,' 'Starec',' 'Na imenynax,' 'Did Jakym,' 'Na seli,' 'V epidemičnomu baraci,' 'Sobaka,' 'Problema xliba,' 'Ivan Bosyj,' 'Syn,' 'Vijs'kovyj litun,' 'Istorija pani Jivhy,' 'Sonce sxodyt',' 'Tretja revoljucija,' 'Z žyttja budynku,' *Povist' bez nazvy, Misto, Nevelyčka drama*.

Bibliography

Russian translation:
Gorod. Trans. B. Elisavetskyj. Preface by A. Lejtes. Moscow: Gosizdat, 1930. 302 pp. 3,000 cop.

English translation:
A Little Touch of Drama. Trans. George and Moira Luckyj. Littleton, Colo.: Ukrainian Academic Press, 1972. 191 pp.

FICTIONAL WORKS PUBLISHED IN JOURNALS, ANTHOLOGIES, AND OTHER PUBLICATIONS

*'Hajdamaka' and 'Vanja.' *Sič* 1919, 1: 2–27.
*'Starec'.' *Sič* 1919, 2: 30–40.
*'Povstanci.' *Ukrajins'kyj proletar* 1920, 49/30.
*'Pered nastupom.' *Ukrajins'kyj proletar* 1920, 54/35.
*'V epidemičnomu baraci.' *Vyr revoljuciji: Zbirnyk.* Katerynoslav, 1921. 43–53.
'Sobaka.' *Žovten': Zbirnyk.* Kharkiv: Vseukrlitkom, 1921. 34–41.
*'Ostap Šaptala.' *Šljaxy mystectva* 1921, 2: 35–60.
*'Syn.' *Nova hromada* 1923, no. 9.
*(Under the pseudonym P. Valčuk). 'Komunist.' *Literaturno-naukovyj vistnyk* (Lviv) 1923, 1: 20–6.
'Povstanci.' *Nova Ukrajina* (Prague-Berlin) 1923, 1–2: 71–83.
'Problema xliba.' *Nova Ukrajina* (Prague-Berlin) 1923, 4: 48–56.
'Ivan Bosyj.' *Nova Ukrajina* (Prague-Berlin) 1923, 6: 1–7.
*'Istorija pani Jivhy.' *Nova hromada* 1924, no. 17.
'Na stepax (Uryvok iz povisti *Dnipro*).' *Nova hromada* 1924, no. 35.
'Vijs'kovyj litun.' *Červonyj šljax* 1924, 1–2: 4–33.
'Tretja revoljucija.' *Červonyj šljax* 1925, 6–7: 32–53.
'Ivan Bosyj.' *Kaljendar-al'manax 'Dnipro.'* Lviv: Ukrajins'ke tovarystvo dopomohy emigrantam z Velykoji Ukrajiny, 1925. 3: 16–22.
'Vijs'kovyj litun.' *Literaturno-naukovyj vistnyk* (Lviv) 1925, 7–8: 200–34.
'Sonce sxodyt'.' *Žyttja j revoljucija* 1925, 8: 7–13.
*'Starec'.' *Ridna mova* (A fourth-grade reader). Comp. V. Aranautov, O. Vodolažčenko, et al. Kharkiv: Deržavne vydavnyctvo Ukrajiny, 1927. Second printing: 1928.
'Bilja vohnju' (An excerpt from *Misto*). *Sjajvo. Dekljamator.* Comp. Mykola Zerov. Kiev: Sjajvo, 1929. 410–412.
'Nevelyčka drama.' *Žyttja j revoljucija* 1930, 3: 5–76, 4: 4–38, 5: 9–55, 6: 30–66.
*'Z žyttja budynku No. 29.' *Literaturna hazeta* 27 June 1933.
'Ivan Bosyj.' *Čotyry šabli.* Paris: Ukrajins'ke slovo, 1938. 5–13.

Bibliography

'Ivan Bosyj.' *Probojem* (Prague) 1941: 393–8.
'Ivan Bosyj.' *Avangard* (London) 1953, 8–9: 68–74.
'Ivan Bosyj.' *Rozstriljane vidrodžennja.* Ed. Jurij Lavrinenko. Paris: Instytut Literacki, 1959. 448–56.
'Ivan Bosyj.' *Xrestomatija z ukrajins'koji literatury XX stolittja.* Ed. V. Fedorenko and Pavlo Maljar. New York: Škil'na rada, 1978. 155–61.
Povist' bez nazvy, do toho ž cilkovyto nejmovirna, vyhadana vid počatku do kincja avtorom, ščob pokazaty sutyčku dejakyx pryncypiv važlyvyx dlja našoho dnja i majbutn'oho. Vitčyzna 1988, 2: 106–44.
'Problema xliba.' *Ukrajina* 21 February 1988.
'Za den'.' *Literaturna Ukrajina* 10 August 1989.
'Tretja revoljucija.' *Kyjiv* 1989, 10: 18–34.
'Povstanci.' *Prapor* 1990, 7: 65–84.
'Ivan Bosyj.' *Prapor* 1990, 7: 84–91.
'Komunist.' *Literaturna Ukrajina* 31 January 1991.
'Z žyttja budynku No. 29.' *Dnipro* 1991, 2: 178–82.
'Prorok.' *Vil'na dumka* 1992, 11-12: 9.

Russian translation:
'Tret'ja revoljucija.' Trans. E. Movčan. *Družba narodov* 1989, 9: 164–79.

English translations:
'The Problem of Bread' (Problema xliba). Trans. George and Moira Luckyj. *Modern Ukrainian Short Stories.* Ed. George S. N. Luckyj. Littleton, Colo.: Ukrainian Academic Press, 1973. 97–113 (parallel text).
'Ivan Bosyj.' Trans. Wolodymyr Slez. *Ukrainian Review* 32.2 (Summer 1984): 62–68.
'Vania.' Trans. Maxim Tarnawsky. *Journal of Ukrainian Studies* 10.2 (Winter 1985): 49–67.
'In the Infirmary' (V epidemičnomu baraci). Trans. Yuri Tkach. *Before the Storm: Soviet Ukrainian Fiction of the 1920s.* Ed. George S. N. Luckyj. Ann Arbor: Ardis, 1986. 131–50.
'The Problem of Daily Bread.' Trans. Oles Kovalenko. *Ukraine* 1988, 10: 29–31, 44.

German translations:
'In der Seuchenbaracke' (V epidemičnomu baraci). Trans. Anna-Halja Horbatsch. *Blauer November: Ukrainische Erzähler unseres Jahrhunderts.* Heidelberg: Wolfgang Rothe, 1959. 280–98.

Bibliography

'Iwan Bossyj.' Trans. Anna-Halja Horbatsch. *Ein Brunnen für Durstige: Die Ukraine in Erzählungen der besten zeitgenössischen Autoren*. Tübingen: Horst Erdmann Verlag, 1970. 81–9.

ARTICLES, LETTERS, AND MISCELLANEOUS PUBLICATIONS

A letter to the editors. *Červonyj šljax* 1923, 2: 281. Reprinted, with an error, in *Misto*, ed. Hryhorij Kostjuk, New York, 1954.
A letter to the editors. Valerijan Pidmohyl'nyj, Hryhorij Kosynka, and Teodosij Os'mačka. *Červonyj šljax* 1923, 4–5: 289–90.
Stenographic transcript of a public speech. *Šljaxy rozvytku sučasnoji literatury: Dysput 24 travnja 1925 r.* Kiev: Kul'tkomisija misckomu UAN, 1925. 35–8.
**Frazeolohija dilovoji movy*. Comp. Valerijan Pidmohyl'nyj and Jevhen Plužnyk. Kiev: Čas, 1926. 293 pp.
'Bez sterna (Maksym Ryl's'kyj).' *Žyttja j revoljucija* 1927, 1: 39–53.
**Frazeolohija dilovoji movy*. Comp. Valerijan Pidmohyl'nyj and Jevhen Plužnyk. 2nd rev. ed. Kiev: Čas, 1927. 296 pp.
'Ivan Levyc'kyj-Nečuj (Sproba psyxoanalizy tvorčosty).' *Žyttja j revoljucija* 1927, 9: 295–303.
Preface. *Ivan Nečuj-Levyc'kyj: Vybrani tvory*. 2 vols. Kiev: Čas, 1927. 1: i–xvi; 2: i–viii.
Review *Opovidannja*, by Tymofij Borduljak [Vetlyna]. (Kharkiv: Knyhospilka, 1927). *Žyttja j revoljucija* 1927, 7–8: 187–8.
'Panajit Istrati v Kyjevi.' *Žyttja j revoljucija* 1928, 2: 166–9.
*A response to critics of *Misto*). *Universal'nyj žurnal* 1929, no. 1.
*Review of *Majster Korablja*, by Jurij Janovs'kyj. *Hlobus* 1929, 3: 43.
Letters to his wife, mother, sister from the Solovecki Islands prison camp. Ukrainian translation of text. *Vitčyzna* 1988, 2: 94–105.
Letters to his wife, mother, sister from the Solovecki Islands prison camp. Original Russian texts. *Družba narodov* 1989, 9: 185–92.
Z lystuvannja (Letters to Illja Borščak, Mykola Zerov, and his wife). *Literaturna Ukrajina* 31 January 1991.
Letters to Mykola Zerov. *Slovo i čas* 1991, 2: 22–5.
'Lysty do Il'ka Borščaka.' *Vsesvit* 1991, 12: 178–80.
'Xarkiv-Paryž, 1930' (Letters to Il'ko Borščak). *Spadščyna* 1991, 2: 13.
Rosijs'ko-ukrajins'kyj frazeolohičnyj slovnyk: Frazeolohija dilovoji movy. Comp. Valer"jan Pidmohyl'nyj and Jevhen Plužnyk. Kiev: Kobza, 1993. 248 pp.
'Lysty Valer"jana Pidmohyl'noho do Troxyma Romančenka.' *Borysten* 1993, 2: 6-7.

Bibliography

TRANSLATIONS

From French:

Amp, P"jer [Hamp, Pierre (Pierre Bourillon)]. 'Vjaznycja' ['La Prison' (*Gens: Deuxième tableau*)]. *Červonyj šljax* 1925, 9: 66–75.
- 'Ščo stalosja?' ['Qu'est qui se passe?']. *Hlobus* 1925, 13: 301, 303.
- 'Pryhoda.' ['Tabagie' (*Gens: Deuxième tableau*)]. *Hlobus* 1925, 15: 344–45.
- *Ljudy: Opovidannja*. [*Gens* (selections from *Gens* and *Gens: Deuxième tableau*)]. Ed. Stepan Savčenko. Kharkiv: Deržavne vydavnyctvo Ukrajiny, 1927. 152 pp. 5,000 cop. Contents: 'P"jer Amp,' by S. Savčenko; 'Avtorova peredmova,' 'Madmuazel' Surir,' 'Paxučyj,' 'Hracija,' 'Kalytka,' 'Madam Emma,' 'Ljudyna z dobrym remestvom,' 'Klasovyj mil'joner,' 'Holjar,' 'Ščyryj respublikanec',' 'Senatorova pryhoda,' 'Na paryz'kij vulyci,' 'Zrazkovyj ahent,' 'Vjaznycja.' [Contents: 'Pierre Hamp,' by S. Savčenko; 'Préface,' 'Mademoiselle Sourire,' 'L'embaumé,' 'Gracieuse,' 'Au Guichet,' 'Mme Emma,' 'Un homme qui a un bon métier,' 'Le millionaire de classe,' 'Une barbe,' 'Un bon républicain,' 'Tabagie,' 'Accident,' 'Un agent bien noté,' 'La prison.']

*– *Opovidannja* [*Contes*]. Trans. Valerijan Pidmohyl'nyj and H. Vynohradova. Kharkiv: Literatura i mystectvo, 1931. 94 pp. 10,000 cop.

Bal'zak, Onore [Balzac, Honoré de]. *Horio* [*Le Père Goriot*]. Ed. Serhij Radzevyč. Kharkiv: Knyhospilka, 1927. 288 pp. 4,000 cop.

*– *Bidni rodyči. Kuzen Pons* [*Les Parents pauvres. Le Cousin Pons*]. Kharkiv: Deržavne vydavnyctvo Ukrajiny, 1929. 304 pp. 5,000 cop.

*– *Bidni rodyči. Kuzyna Beta* [*Les Parents pauvres. La Cousine Bette*]. Kharkiv: Deržavne vydavnyctvo Ukrajiny, 1929. 472 pp. 5,000 cop.

*Didro, Deni [Diderot, Denis]. *Vybrani tvory* [*Oeuvres choisies*]. Preface by Serhij Rodzevyč. Kharkiv: Radjans'ka Ukrajina, 1933. Vol. 1. *Černycja. Nebiž Ramo* [*La Religieuse. Le Neveu de Rameau*]. 308 pp. 4,000 cop. Vol. 2. *Žak fatalist i joho pan* [*Jacques le fataliste et son maître*]. 274 pp. 3,150 cop.

– *Nebiž Ramo* [*La Neveu de Rameau*]. In *Černycja. Nebiž Ramo*. Kiev: Deržavne vydavnyctvo xudožn'oji literatury, 1963. 171–244.

Djuamel', Žorž [Duhamel, Georges]. 'Lyst pro včenyx' ['Sur les savants' (*Lettres au Patagon*)]. *Žyttja j revoljucija* 1927, 6: 332–41.

– 'Lyst pro amatoriv' ['Sur les amateurs' (*Lettres au Patagon*)]. *Žyttja j revoljucija* 1927, 7–8: 81–90.

*Dode, Al'fons [Daudet, Alphonse]. *Lysty z vitrjaka: Opovidannja* [*Les Lettres de mon moulin*]. Kharkiv: Knyhospilka, 1926, 62 pp. 5,000 cop.

Frans, Anatol' [France, Anatole]. *Opovidannja*. [*Contes*] Ed. Stepan Savčenko. Kharkiv: Deržavne vydavnyctvo Ukrajiny, 1925. 237 pp. 5,000 cop. Contents: 'Anatol' Frans,' by S. Savčenko; 'Utopija,' 'Dobrodij Pižono,' 'Svjatyj Satyr,'

Bibliography

Huk, M. Review of *Tretja revoljucija*, by Valerijan Pidmohyl'nyj. *Kul'tura i pobut* 20 June 1926.
– Review of Prosper Merime, *Kolomba*, trans. Valerijan Pidmohyl'nyj. *Kul'tura i pobut* 7 May 1927.
Jakubovs'kyj, Feliks. 'Do kryzy v ukrajins'kij xudožnij prozi.' *Žyttja j revoljucija* 1926, 1: 40–8.
– 'Ukrajins'ka xudožnja proza v Kyjevi.' *Hlobus* 1927, 4: 55–8.
– Review of *Problema xliba*, by Valerijan Pidmohyl'nyj. *Krytyka* 1928, 1: 179–81.
– Review of *Misto*, by Valerijan Pidmohyl'nyj. *Komunist* 20 May 1928.
– *Syluety sučasnyx ukrajins'kyx pys'mennykiv.* Kiev: Kul'tura, 1928. 45–6.
*Jakubs'kyj, B. 'Sim rokiv (1917–1924).' *Žovtnevyj zbirnyk*. 1924. 87–103.
*– Review of Vol'ter, *Kandid*, trans. Valerijan Pidmohyl'nyj. *Proletars'ka pravda* 11 August 1927.
Jakymovyč, Tetjana. Review of Anatol' Frans, *Tvory*, vol 7, trans. Valerijan Pidmohyl'nyj. *Žyttja j revoljucija* 1933, 4–5: 111–13.
Jefremov, Petro. 'Pro roman V. Pidmohyl'noho *Misto*.' *Pluh* 1928, 9: 66–72.
– [Junoša, V.] 'Poet čariv noči.' *Vyr revoljuciji: Zbirnyk*. Katerynoslav, 1921. 93–101. Reprinted in his *Molytva Bohu nevidomomu*. Dnipropetrovs'k, 1993. 31–41.
Jefremov, Serhij. *Istorija ukrajins'koho pys'menstva*. Leipzig: Ukrajins'ka nakladnja, 1919. 2: 398–404.
Ju. G. 'Valerijan Pidmohyl'nyj.' *Avangard* (London) 1953, 8–9: 65–8.
*Kapustjans'kyj, Ivan. 'Učytel'stvo v ukrajins'kij literaturi.' *Šljaxy osvity* 1925, 4: 159.
Karol', Stefan [Mykola Fitil'ov, i.e., Mykola Xvyl'ovyj]. 'Xudožnij materijal v *Novij Ukrajini*.' *Červonyj šljax* 1923, 2: 304–11. Reprinted in *Mykola Xvyl'ovyj: Tvory v p"jat'ox tomax*. Baltimore: Slovo & Smoloskyp, 1978–86. 4: 555–65.
'Knigi, nerekomenduemye dlja zakupky v biblioteki.' Review of V. Pidmogil'nyj, *Gorod*, trans. B. Elisavetskyj. *Krasnyj bibliotekar* 1930, 2: 86. In Russian.
Kocjuk, Vitalij. 'Dar pravdy.' Preface to Valer"jan Pidmohyl'nyj, *Istorija pani Jivhy*. Kiev: Veselka, 1991. 3–10.
Kolesnyk, Petro. *Valerijan Pidmohyl'nyj*. Kiev: Literatura i mystectvo, 1931.
– 'Proty oportunistyčnoji krytyky.' *Žyttja j revoljucija* 1932, 4: 82–9.
– 'Ukrajins'ke opovidannja.' *Antolohija ukrajins'koho opovidannja v 4-ox tomax*. Ed. O.I. Bilec'kyj et al. Kiev: Deržavne vydavnyctvo xudožn'oji literatury, 1960. 1: 5–51 [vp 44].
Kolomijec', Lada. '*Misto* V. Pidmohyl'noho: problematyka ta strukturna orhanizacija.' *Slovo i čas* 1991, 5: 64–70
*– 'Malaja proza V. Pidmogyl'nogo.' *Raduga* (Kiev) 1991, no. 9. In Russian.
*– 'Specyfika xarakterotvorennja v romani V. Pidmohyl'noho *Misto*.' *Aktual'ni problemy sučasnoho literaturoznavstva ta movoznavstva*. Kiev, 1991.

Bibliography

- 'Osoblyvosti poetyky xudožn'oji prozy Valer"jana Pidmohyl'noho.' Avtoreferat dysertaciji [Dissertation absract]. Kiev: Kyjivs'kyj universytet im. Tarasa Ševčenka, 1992.
- 'Ukrajins'kyj renesans: U pošukax indyvidual'nosti.' *Slovo i čas* 1992, 10: 64–70.

*Korjak, V. 'Literaturnyj rik.' *Narodnij učytel'* 1926, no. 13.

Kostjuk, Hryhorij. 'Valerijan Pidmohyl'nyj.' Afterword. *Misto.* By Valerijan Pidmohyl'nyj. New York: Ukrajins'ka vil'na akademija nauk u SŠA, 1954. 283–93. Reprinted in his *U Sviti idej i obraziv.* New York: Sučasnist, 1983. 219–29.

Kovalenko, B. 'Literaturnyj Kyjiv.' *Hart – Kyjiv: Al'manax.* Kiev: Deržavne vydavnyctvo Ukrajiny, 1925. 111–52 [vp 137].

Kravciv, Bohdan. 'Valerijan Pidmohyl'nyj.' *Encyklopedija ukrajinoznavstva.* Vol. 2. Paris: Naukove tovarystvo imeni Ševčenka, 1970. 6: 2092.

Kravciv, S. Review of Prosper Merime. *Kolomba,* trans. Valerijan Pidmohyl'nyj. *Červonyj šljax* 1927, 7–8.

Kružok kritiki pri žurnale *Rost.* Review of V. Pidmogil'nyj. *Gorod* trans. B. Elisavetskyj. *Pravda* 17 February 1930. In Russian.

Lakyza, I. Review of *Problema xliba,* by Valerijan Pidmohyl'nyj. *Žyttja j revoljucija* 1927, 12: 358.

Lakyza, Petro. 'Do istoriji odnijeji kar"jery (Literaturni notatky do tvorčosty V. Pidmohyl'noho).' *Molodnjak* 1929, 4: 87–93; 5: 125–33. Reprinted in his *Na meži.* Kharkiv: Deržavne vydavnyctvo Ukrajiny, 1930. 69–101.

- 'Istorija odnijeji kar"jery (Pro roman *Misto* V. Pidmohyl'noho).' *Na meži.* Kharkiv: Deržavne vydavnyctvo Ukrajiny, 1930. 35–68.

Laslo-Kucjuk, Mahdalyna. 'Valerijan Pidmohyl'nyj.' *Ukrajins'ka radjans'ka literatura.* Bucharest: Mul'typlikacijnyj centr buxarests'koho universytetu, 1976. 65–71.

- '*Misto* V. Pidmohyl'noho i francuz'kyj roman XIX stolittja.' *Šukannja formy: Narysy z ukrajins'koji literatury XX stolittja.* Bucharest: Kryterion, 1980. 141–64.
- 'Arxitektonika romanu.' *Zasady poetyky.* Bucharest: Kryterion, 1983. 230–60 [vp 250–4].

Lavrinenko, Jurij. 'Valerijan Pidmohyl'nyj.' *Rozstriljane vidrodžennja. Antolohija 1917–1933.* Paris: Kultura, 1959. 443–7.

Lejtes, A. 'Peredislovie.' *V. Pidmogyl'nyj. Gorod.* Moscow: Gosizdat, 1930. 3–7. In Russian.

Lisovyj, P. Review of *Misto.* By Valerijan Pidmohyl'nyj. *Kul'tura i pobut* 26 May 1928.

Martyč, Juxym. *Dovha, dovha vesna. (V hostjax u Maksyma Ryl's'koho).* Kiev: Radjans'kyj pys'mennyk, 1969. [vp 63–68].

Bibliography

Mel'nyk, Volodymyr. 'Koly zahynuv Valer"jan Pidmohyl'nyj?' *Ukrajina* 1989, 43: 10–11.
- 'Ne izmenivšij sebe.' *Družba narodov* 1989, 9: 180–84.
- 'Svoho poklykannja ne zradyv.' *Literaturna Ukrajina* 10 August 1989.
- 'Valer"jan Pidmohyl'nyj povertajet'sja.' *Kyjiv* 1989, 10: 35–8.
- '"Povstanci" Valer"jana Pidmohyl'noho.' *Prapor* 1990, 7: 93–6.
- 'Na perexresti mista i sela.' *Slovo i čas* 1990, 11: 23–33.
- 'Najbil'š intelektual'no zahlyblenyj.' *Literaturna panorama, 1990.* Kiev: Dnipro, 1990, 157–70.
- 'Šljax na holhofu.' *Vitčyzna* 1991, 1: 150–8.
- 'Odyn z-pomiž peršyx.' *Literaturna Ukrajina* 31 January 1991.
- *Valer"jan Pidmohyl'nyj: Do 90-riččja vid dnja narodžennja.* Kiev: Znannja, 1991.
- '"Duže Vam vdjačnyj ščyro i tovarys'ky ...": Lysty Valer"jana Pidmohyl'noho do Mykoly Zerova.' *Slovo i čas* 1991, 2: 20–7.
- 'Na perexresti mista i sela (Roman V. Pidmohyl'noho *Misto* u krytyci 20-x rokiv).' *Dvadcjati roky: Literaturni dyskusiji, polemiky.* Kiev: Dnipro, 1991. 212–60.
- 'Valer"jan Pidmohyl'nyj.' *Valer"jan Pidmohyl'nyj: Opovidannja, povist', romany.* Kiev: Naukova dumka, 1991. 5–28.

Meženko, Jurij. Review of *Vol'ter. Kandid* trans. Valerijan Pidmohyl'nyj. *Žyttja j revoljucija* 1927, 9: 318–19.

Mohyljans'kyj, Myxajlo. Review of *Anatol' Frans. Opovidannja* trans. Valerijan Pidmohyl'nyj. *Žyttja j revoljucija* 1925, 9: 103–4.
- 'Ni mista, ni sela ... (Z pryvodu romanu Pidmohyl'noho *Misto*).' *Červonyj šljax* 1929, 5–6: 273–5.

Moroz-Strilec', Tamara. 'Universytet na domu.' *Vitčyzna* 1981, 11: 218–19.

Motuzka, M. 'Selo j misto v tvorčosti V. Pidmohyl'noho.' *Krytyka* 1928, 6: 35–50.

Movčan, Rajisa. 'Valerian Pidmohyl'nyj.' *Vitčyzna* 1988, 2: 92–4.
- 'Valerian Pidmohyl'nyj.' *Pys'mennyky radjans'koji Ukrajiny, 20–30 roky: Narysy tvorčosti.* Kiev: Radjans'kyj pys'mennyk, 1989. 305–28.
- 'Valer"jan Pidmohyl'nyj – perekladač.' *Vsesvit* 1991, 12: 178.

*Mus' [Mykola Samus']. Review of *Misto*, by Valerijan Pidmohyl'nyj. *Robitnyčyj žurnal* 1928, 6: 10.

Muzyčka, Andrij. 'Tvorča metoda Valerijana Pidmohyl'noho.' *Červonyj šljax* 1930, 10: 107–21; 11–12: 126–37.

*Myxajlec', Hryhorij. Review of *Tretja revoljucija*, by Valerijan Pidmohyl'nyj. *Plužanyn* 1926, 6–7.

Nazaruk, Bazyli. 'Spozniony Powrot Waleriana Pidmohylnego.' *Tworczosc* 1989, 9: 125–8.

Bibliography

Nikovs'kyj, Andrij. 'Pro *Misto* V. Pidmohyl'noho.' *Žyttja j revoljucija* 1928, 10: 104–14.

Novyčenko, Leonid. 'Po toj bik spokoju. Poezija Jevhena Plužnyka.' *Ne iljustracija – vidkryttja: Literaturno-krytyčni narysy i portrety*. Kiev: Radjans'kyj pys'mennyk, 1967. 253–326 [vp 257].

*Nykolyšyn, S. 'Ukrajins'ka sovjets'ka proza.' *Probojem* 1941, 8: 150, 152, 155.

[O.S.] Review of Onore Bal'zak, *Horio*, trans. Valerijan Pidmohyl'nyj. *Literaturna hazeta* 13 June 1928.

Oryškevyč, Ivan. Review of *Problema xliba*, by Valerijan Pidmohyl'nyj. *Červonyj šljax* 1928, 4: 211–12.

Paščenko, Vitalij. 'Pryxid.' *Donbass* 1989, 3: 107–108.

Pidhajnyj, L. Review of *Misto*, by Valerijan Pidmohyl'nyj. *Literaturna hazeta* 13 June 1928.

Pinczuk, Jaroslav. 'The Concept of "Rurbanism" in Pidmohyl'nyj's *Misto*.' *Studia Ucrainica 1*. University of Ottawa Ukrainian Studies no. 3. Ottawa: University of Ottawa Press, 1978. 129–32.

Pivtoradni, Vasyl'. *Ukrajins'ka literatura peršyx rokiv revoljuciji (1917–1923 rr.)*. Kiev: Radjans'ka škola, 1968. [vp 48, 93–94, 97].

Poltorac'kyj, Oleksander. Review of Vol'ter, *Kandid*, trans. Valerijan Pidmohyl'nyj. *Komunist* 25 August 1927.

– Review of Gi de Mopasan, *Tvory*, vols. 1 and 2, trans. Borys Kozlovs'kyj and Valerijan Pidmohyl'nyj. *Červonyj šljax* 1928, 5–6: 257–8.

'Pys'mennyky u proletars'koho studentstva (Zbory v INO 2 bereznja 1929 roku).' *Literaturna hazeta* 15 March 1929.

Rabičev. 'Kul'turna revoljucija ta zavdannja profspilok u haluzi kul'troboty.' *IV Vseukrajins'kyj z"jizd profspilok 1–8 hrudnja 1928. Stenohrafičnyj zvit*. Kharkiv, 1929. 332–347 [vp 335–338].

Rodzevyč, Serhij. 'Novyny zaxidn'o-evropejs'koji literatury.' Review of O. de Bal'zak, *Bidni rodyči. Kuzyna Beta*, trans. Valerijan Pidmohyl'nyj. *Žyttja j revoljucija* 1929, 5: 148–56 [vp 149–52].

S. Review of Prosper Merime, *Kolomba*, trans. Valerijan Pidmohyl'nyj. *Žyttja j revoljucija* 1927, 5: 274–5.

Šamraj, A. *Ukrajins'ka literatura*. Kharkiv: Rux, 1927. [vp 181–3].

*Savčenko, Jakiv. 'Žovten' i literaturni uhrupovannja.' *Nova kul'tura* 1923, 11–12.

– 'Problemy kul'turnoji revoljuciji i ukrajins'ka radjans'ka literatura.' *Proletars'ka pravda* 20 June 1928. Reprinted in *Literaturno-naukovyj visnyk* 1929, 2: 154–62.

Savčenko, S. Review of Onore Bal'zak, *Horio*, trans. Valerijan Pidmohyl'nyj. *Žyttja j revoljucija* 1928, 3: 193.

Senyk, Ljubomyr. 'Roman jak žyttja.' *Literatura i sučasnist'. Literaturno-krytyčni statti*. No. 2. Kiev: Radjans'kyj pys'mennyk, 1969. 149–64 [vp 157].

Bibliography

Šerex, Jurij [George Shevelov]. 'Bilok i joho zaburennja.' *Literaturna hazeta* (Munich) 1957, 9: 1–2. English translation: 'A Disturbance in the Protein.' *A Little Touch of Drama*. By Valerijan Pidmohyl'nyj. Trans. George and Moira Luckyj. Preface. Littleton, Colo.: Ukrainian Academic Press, 1972. 9–16.

– 'Ljudyna i ljudy (*Misto* Valerijana Pidmohyl'noho).' *Ne dlja ditej: Literaturno-krytyčni statti i eseji*. New York: Prolog, 1964. 83–96.

Šesternja, Borys [Borys Davydov]. 'Hopakademyky (I recenzija, i fejleton).' *Bil'šovyk* 28 September 1923.

Shevchuk, Valeriy (Ševčuk, Valerij). 'Valerian Pidmohilny: Fame and Oblivion.' *Ukraine* 1988, 10: 28–29.

– 'U sviti prozy Valer"jana Pidmohyl'noho.' Preface. *Misto*. By Valer"jan Pidmohyl'nyj. Kiev: Molod', 1989. 3–13. Reprinted in *Doroha v tysjaču rokiv: Rozdumy, statti, ese*. Kiev: Radjans'kyj pys'mennyk, 1990. 354–60.

Slavutyč, Jar. 'Pidmohyl'nyj anhlijs'koju movoju.' Review of Valerian Pidmohylny. *A Little Touch of Drama*, trans. George and Moira Luckyj. *Ovyd* 1973, 1: 18–19.

Smolyč, Jurij. 'Pidmohyl'nyj.' *Vitčyzna* 1972, 2: 87–99. Reprinted in his *Rozpovidi pro nespokij nemaje kincja*. Kiev: Radjans'kyj pys'mennyk, 1972. 99–120.

Stanyslavs'kyj, Mykola. Review of *Frazeolohija dilovoji movy*, comp. Jevhen Plužnyk and Valerijan Pidmohyl'nyj. *Kul'tura i pobut* 8 August 1926.

Synhajivs'kyj, Mykola. 'Use piznav i perežyv.' *Prapor komunizmu* (Kiev) 28 October 1989.

Tarnavs'kyj, Ostap. 'Parodija na kazku pro popeljušku i vymrijanoho knjazja.' Review of *Nevelyčka drama*, by Valerijan Pidmohyl'nyj. *Lysty do pryjateliv* 5.10 (Oct. 1957): 6–8.

Tarnawsky, Maxim. '"Nevtomnyj Honets v Maibutnie": An Existential Reading of Valeriian Pidmohylny's *Misto*.' *Journal of Ukrainian Graduate Studies* 1979, 2: 3–19. Ukrainian translation: 'Nevtomnyj honec' v majbutnje: Ekzystencial'ne pročytannja *Mista* Pidmohyl'noho.' *Slovo i čas* 1991, 5: 56–63.

– 'Valerijan Pidmohyl'nyj, Guy de Maupassant, and the Magic of the Night.' PhD diss, Harvard University, 1986.

– 'Ostannij tvir V. Pidmohyl'noho.' *Vsesvit* 1991, 12: 174–7.

Tasičko, K. Review of *Jasnoju dorohoju*, by Andrij Xvylja. *Červonyj šljax* 1928, 3: 144–6 [vp 145–6].

Tkačenko, H., M. Sajko, and D. Kosaryk-Kovalenko. Review of *Valerijan Pidmohyl'nyj*, by Petro Kolesnyk. *Žyttja j revoljucija* 1932, 4: 82–5.

[V.Č.] Review of *Tretja revoljucija*, by Valerijan Pidmohyl'nyj. *Zorja* 1926, 20: 31–32.

[V.P.] 'Xiba ce misto?' Review of *Misto*, by Valerijan Pidmohyl'nyj. *Literaturna hazeta* 15 March 1929.

Bibliography

Vasylenko, P. [Petro Odarčenko]. 'V. Pidmohyl'nyj i joho roman *Misto*.' *Svoboda* 3 December 1954.

Xudzej, I., and M. Ovčarenko. 'Iz ukrajins'kyx perekladiv novely A. Fransa *Krenkenbil'*.' *Ukrajins'ke literaturoznavstvo* 39. Lviv: Vyšča škola, 1982. 100–7.

*Xutorjan, A. Review of *Misto*, by Valerijan Pidmohyl'nyj. *Proletars'ka pravda* 1928 no. 120.

Xvylja, Andrij [Andrij Musul'bax]. 'Romantyka Maxnovščyny (*Tretja revoljucija V. Pidmohyl'noho*).' *Bil'šovyk Ukrajiny* 1926, 2–3: 88–100. Reprinted in his *Jasnoju dorohoju (Rik na literaturnomu fronti)*. Kiev: Deržavne vydavnyctvo Ukrajiny, 1927. 104–31.

*Zerov, Mykola. 'Ukrajins'ka literatura v 1923 r.' *Nova hromada* 1924, 17: 29–30; 18: 30–31.

*Zurowsky, Jaroslaw. 'Valerijan Pidmohyl'nyj's *Misto*.' MA thesis, University of Manitoba, 1979.

Zvyčajna, Olena. 'Kryve dzerkalo.' *Avangard* (London) 1955, 5–6: 63–72.

– *Ty: Povist' iz žyttja ukrajinciv u zolotoverxomu Kyjevi v 1927–29 rokax*. Munich: Ukrajins'ke vydavnyctvo, 1982.

Žyla, Volodymyr. 'Kyjiv u literaturi.' *Postup* (Winnipeg) 10 January – 21 February 1960 [vp 7 February].

[Anonymous]. Review of *Misto*. *Literaturna hazeta* 21 June 1928.

*[Anonymous]. Review of *Misto*. *Nova hromada* 1928, no. 9.

Index

alienation, 23, 37, 43, 44, 56, 67, 89, 109, 113, 163, 166, 174, 175, 184. *See also* bad faith; existential philosophy
Andreev, Leonid, 167–9
Antonenko-Davydovyč, Borys, 12, 16
Apollonian, 160, 162
art, 131, 156, 159, 181–3. *See also* music
authorial distance, 71, 76, 78. *See also* consonant narration; dissonant narration; focalization

bad faith, 97, 124, 131–3, 137, 142, 163, 180. *See also* alienation; existential philosophy
Balzac, Honoré de, 4, 51, 70, 73, 107, 108, 116, 140, 169
Barthes, Roland, 69
Bažan, Mykola, 160, 182
Beckett, Samuel, 37
Bel-Ami, 6, 16, 107–11, 113, 114, 120, 124, 125, 131, 132, 136, 138, 141, 149

Besnard-Coursodon, Micheline, 126
Bible, 35, 36
Bildungsroman, 110
Blakytnyj, Vasyl (Ellans'kyj), 11
Bojko, Jurij, 151
Bonnefis, Philippe, 132
Borduljak, Tymofij, 14
Borščak, Il'ko, 16
Brjuxovec'kyj, Vjačeslav, 14
Buddhism, 81, 100, 101
Bulgakov, Mikhail, 51
Burhardt, Osval'd, 12

Camus, Albert, 181
cannibalism, 94
Čapli, 8
Čas, 10, 13, 14
causal sequence, 48, 49, 51, 53, 110, 111, 185
Čerevatenko, Leonid, 12, 13, 17
Červins'ka, Katrja (Pidmohyl'nyj's wife), 10
Červonyj šljax, 11, 12, 103
Chaplenko, Vasyl, 15

Index

Cheka, 66, 101
Chekhov, Anton, 15
Christianity, 81
chronological sequence, 3, 48, 49, 51, 110, 111
Cicero, Marcus Tullius, 20
city: cultural model of, 13, 101, 133, 138; juxtaposed to village, 21, 30, 32, 94, 95, 96, 99, 114, 118, 119, 133, 139, 140, 162; setting for a work, 21, 96; thematic motif, 30, 71–2, 73, 81, 83, 94–7, 140
Cohn, Dorrit, 76
collectivization, 19
Conrad, Joseph, 168
consonant narration, 76–9, 120, 146
contes fantastiques, 148, 169. See also fantastic, the
Čyževs'kyj, Dmytro, 69

Descartes, René, 98
determinism, 78, 174, 177, 181, 185
Dickens, Charles, 51, 52, 70, 116
'Did Jakym,' 24, 25, 35, 36, 65
Diderot, Denis, 17
Dionysian, 160, 162, 165
dissonant narration, 76–8
Dnieper (Dnipro) river, 122, 152, 153, 166
Dnipropetrovs'k, 8, 184
'Dobryj boh,' 24–8, 31, 33, 35, 38, 53, 65, 77, 81, 96, 169
Dolengo, Myxajlo (Klokov), 11, 80, 81, 85, 91, 103, 113
Doncov, Dmytro, 65
Dostoevsky, Feodor, 23, 116
Družba narodov, 18
Duhamel, Georges, 107

existential philosophy, 6, 21, 80, 124, 127, 132, 135, 137, 163, 166, 170, 174, 177, 183, 184

fantastic, the, 6, 18, 23, 34, 82, 91, 169. See also *contes fantastiques*
Fischer, Emil, 145
Fitzgerald, F. Scott, 37
Flaubert, Gustave, 4, 73, 114, 115, 117
focalization, 76, 77, 184, 186
Foster, John Burt, 161, 163, 164
France, Anatole, 4, 9, 16, 17, 106, 107
Franko, Ivan, 71, 99, 188
Freud, Sigmund, 7, 149, 170
Freudian psychology, 14, 22, 23, 89, 125, 127, 129, 149–51, 153, 155, 158
Frye, Northrop, 80

Genette, Gérard, 76
genre, 34, 45, 51, 103, 110, 113, 163, 171, 188
Gide, André, 137, 161
Goethe, Johann Wolfgang von, 181
Gogol, Nikolai (Hohol', Mykola), 17, 23, 166, 167, 169
Grabowicz, George, 167, 169
Gray, Bennison, 69
Gurzuf, 15, 111

'Hajdamaka,' 9, 33, 35–7, 60, 64, 65, 81, 169
Halyč, Maria, 12
Hamp, Pierre (Bourillon), 107
Hamsun, Knut, 106
Hemingway, Ernest, 37
Hončar, Oles', 171
Hrono, 9
Hryn'ko, Hryhorij, 11

Index

humanism, 23, 114

Ibsen, Henrik, 160
impressionism, 71
instinct, 6, 22, 24, 26, 28, 30, 37, 43, 48, 53, 55, 64, 82, 97, 127, 131, 161, 170, 177; juxtaposed to reason, 21, 23, 31, 59, 66, 85, 94, 114, 139, 142, 159, 166; juxtaposed to religion, 26; juxtaposed to repression, 23, 57, 70
intertextuality, 75
irony, 36, 74, 76–9, 102, 117, 131, 147, 181
irrational, the, 5, 6, 23, 82, 83, 85, 178; juxtaposed to reason, 6, 14, 32, 58–9, 139–40, 159, 167–9, 185; in literature, 23, 167–9 (*see also* fantastic, the); and nature, 28; and religion, 26; and sexuality, 28; and the village, 95
'Istorija pani Jivhy,' 96
Istrati, Panait, 14
'Ivan Bosyj,' 25, 29, 78, 80, 85, 89, 90, 91, 94, 95, 169

Janovs'kyj, Jurij, 51, 160, 188
Jefremov, Petro, 9, 30, 77, 82, 106
Jefremov, Serhij, 149
Jews, 66
Johansen, Majk, 51
Joyce, James, 51, 70, 73, 137

Kaniv, 152, 153, 155, 162
Kant, Immanual, 97, 98, 161
Katerynoslav, 8–10, 34, 66, 82
Keyserling, Hermann, 145
Kharkiv, 7, 17, 18, 20, 173, 174, 177, 184–6
Kierkegaard, Søren, 145

Kirov, Sergei, 17
Knyhospilka, 12
Kobyljans'ka, Ol'ha, 71, 160
Kocjubyns'kyj, Myxajlo, 4–6, 23, 70, 71, 188
'Komunist,' 65, 66, 172
Kostjuk, Hryhorij, 105
Kosynka, Hryhorij, 9, 11, 12
Kuliš, Pantelejmon, 167, 169
Kvitka-Osnov"janenko, Hryhorij, 23

Laslo-Kucjuk, Mahdalyna, 107, 119, 131
Lawrence, D.H., 55, 161
Levyc'kyj, Ivan. *See* Nečuj-Levyc'kyj, Ivan
linearity of the plot, 49, 53
Literary Discussion, the, 13, 112
Literaturna hazeta, 17, 171
Luckyj, George S.N., 167, 169

magic of the night, 82–5, 89, 91, 95, 98, 99, 103, 139, 140, 165–7, 169, 170
Malraux, André, 17, 161, 164
Mann, Thomas, 137, 161
Martovyč, Les', 188
Marx, Karl, 35, 36, 65
Marxism, 81, 164
Masenko, Larysa, 14
Maupassant, Guy de, 4, 6, 7, 70, 106, 107–43, 145, 146, 148, 169, 170. *See also Bel-Ami*; *contes fantastiques*
Maxno, Nestor, 15, 37, 57, 79, 85–9, 94–6
Mel'nyk, Volodymyr, 8, 17, 66, 96, 106
melodrama, 50, 53, 60, 77–9, 111, 137, 172

Index

Merimée, Prosper, 107
metaphor, 50, 54, 71–4, 78, 79, 105
Meženko, Jurij, 149
Mickiewicz, Adam, 15
Misto, 6, 13, 15, 16, 27, 30, 33, 45, 52, 53, 57, 95, 97, 105–43, 145–9, 157, 161–7, 170, 185
modernism, 23, 51, 70–3, 161, 163, 165, 188
Moloda muza, 160
Moscow, 16, 174, 184, 185
music, 29, 121, 155
Myrnyj, Panas (Rudčenko), 6, 23, 51, 52, 71, 188

'Na imenynax,' 35, 38
'Na seli,' 28, 30, 31, 34, 35, 37, 65, 81, 82, 96, 161, 169
'Na stepax,' 6
Narbut, Heorhij, 9
narrative technique, 6, 50, 70, 71, 76, 123, 147, 149, 170
Nečuj-Levyc'kyj, Ivan, 4–6, 14, 51, 71, 73, 149–55, 188
Nevelyčka drama, 17, 33, 56, 57, 59, 145–70, 182, 185
Nietzsche, Friedrich, 6, 7, 43, 73, 75, 97, 98, 131, 145, 160–6
Nova Ukrajina, 10, 11
novel, 13, 45, 49, 51–3, 67, 70, 103, 110–3, 145, 160, 171, 187
novella, 45, 49, 111–13, 171

objective method, 6, 7, 114, 116, 120, 145, 146, 170, 186, 187
obsession, 80, 81, 85, 89, 101, 102
Oedipal complex, 14, 149–50, 153
omniscient narration, 7, 76. *See also* authorial distance; focalization

Os'mačka, Teodozij, 11, 12
Ostap Šaptala, 9, 25, 33, 45, 48–65, 72, 77, 80, 81, 103, 110, 111, 113, 114, 127

pathetic fallacy, 120, 121, 146
Pavlohrad, 8, 9
Petljura, Symon, 8, 37
Pidmohyl'na, Natalija, 8
Pidmohyl'nyj, Roman, 15, 18
Plutarch, 18
Plužnyk, Jevhen, 12–14, 111
Poale Zion, 66
poetry, 4, 14, 51, 71, 105, 142
Poliščuk, Valerijan, 9
Postyšev, Pavel, 17
Povist' bez nazvy, 7, 17, 33, 57, 59, 90, 95, 130, 168, 171, 173–87
'Povstanci,' 29, 45–7, 49, 50, 60–2, 64, 65, 80, 82–5, 89, 90, 94, 95, 110, 139, 169
'Problema xliba,' 15, 75–7, 96, 102, 103, 111, 161, 187
'Prorok,' 28, 30, 31, 34, 35, 38, 41, 53, 57, 65, 81, 90, 96, 161, 169
Proust, Marcel, 52, 73
Przybyszewski, Stanisław, 106
Pushkin, Aleksandr, 15
Pylypenko, Serhij, 11

randomness, 82, 174, 176, 181
realism, 67, 73, 115, 116, 117, 142, 169, 187; European, 4, 5, 6, 7, 119, 169; and the novel, 49, 51, 53; psychological, 67, 70, 107, 188; social, 14, 23, 71, 93; techniques of, 20, 187
reason, 14, 33, 46, 53, 126, 137, 159, 160, 161, 165, 169–70, 178–80, 184; inadequacy of, 24;

Index

juxtaposed to instinct, 21, 23,
  31, 47, 59, 66, 85, 94, 114,
  142, 159, 166, 167; and
  mysticism, 31. *See also*
  irrational, the
religion, 25, 33, 75, 83
ressentiment, 163, 166
Robbe-Grillet, Alain, 51
Rux, 12, 17
Ryl's'kyj, Maksym, 14, 142

Šapoval, Mykyta, 10
Sartre, Jean-Paul, 124, 137
Schopenhauer, Arthur, 6, 125, 126,
  131, 145, 163, 168, 170
science, 21, 33, 114, 131, 159–60
science fiction, 15
secondary characters, 57, 108, 154
self-delusion, 85
Ševčenko, Taras, 23, 29, 155,
  167, 169
sexuality, 5, 6, 21, 31, 33, 38, 44,
  59, 78, 101, 108, 125–31,
  153–5, 165, 170; as instinct, 24,
  26, 27, 30, 37, 43, 53–6, 89; and
  other forces, 32, 33, 34, 83, 94,
  114, 185; repressed, 28, 35, 88,
  149; in Vynnyčenko's works, 5;
  of young men, 22, 24, 36, 81,
  168–9. *See also* irrational, the
Shakespeare, William, 18, 70
Shevelov, George Y., 142, 145,
  146
short story, 9, 13, 52, 53, 103, 105,
  106, 171. *See also* genre;
  novella
Skovoroda, Hryhorij, 119
Skrypnyk, Mykola, 17
Škurupij, Geo, 9
Slisarenko, Oleksa, 112
'Smert',' 77–8, 82

Smolyč, Jurij, 17, 106
Sobačyj xutir, 9
'Sobaka,' 9, 94, 96, 97–9, 102, 161
socialism, 31–3, 65, 96, 161
Solovecki Islands, 18, 106
'Sonce sxodyt',' 12, 33
Sosjura, Volodymyr, 145, 182
Spinoza, Baruch, 19
'Starec',' 29, 33, 35, 36, 38, 45,
  71, 73, 74, 77, 81
Stefanyk, Vasyl', 71
Stendhal (Marie Henri Beyle), 129
Storoženko, Oleksa, 23
Šums'kyj, Oleksander, 11
'Syn,' 25, 29, 91–4, 102, 163

thematic parallels, 48, 51–3, 99,
  110, 113
thematic structure, 49–53, 65, 103,
  111
Todorov, Tzvetan, 51
Tolstoy, Lev, 51
topicality, 33, 60, 65, 67, 70, 71,
  173
tragic affirmation, 163, 164
'Tretja revoljucija,' 13, 15, 76,
  78–9, 80, 85–9, 94, 96, 103, 107
Turgenev, Ivan, 17, 150
Tvory: Tom 1, 9, 21–44, 45, 53,
  60, 65, 76, 80–3, 96, 106,
  168–70
Tyčyna, Pavlo, 6, 11

Ukrainization, 11, 117, 119, 157,
  158, 165
Ukrajinka, Lesja (Larysa Kosač), 6,
  24, 160

'V epidemičnomu baraci,' 9, 25,
  29, 45, 47–9, 50, 52, 53, 65, 77,
  82, 103

Index

'Vanja,' 9, 24–6, 28, 34–6, 38–45,
  52, 53, 60, 65, 77, 80, 81, 91,
  148, 169
'Važke pytannja,' 9, 22–3, 24, 28,
  33, 35, 53, 65, 81, 96, 168, 169
'Vijs'kovyj litun,' 11, 12, 33, 73–6,
  78, 80, 96, 99–102, 161
Vitčyzna, 18–20
Voltaire, François, 107
Voroncov-Daškov, Illarion, 8
Vorzel', 10, 17
Vražlyvyj, Vasyl', 106
Vynnyčenko, Volodymyr, 4, 5, 10,
  11, 24, 29, 70, 71, 160, 188
Vyr revoljuciji, 9, 82

Wilde, Oscar, 18, 183
Will to Power, 165
Woodward, James, 168
Woolf, Virginia, 4, 51

Xvyl'ovyj, Mykola, 10, 11, 17, 112

Yalta, 15
Yeats, William Butler, 4

'Z žyttja budynku,' 13, 17, 171,
  172
'Za den',' 66
Zakrževskij, Aleksander, 168
Zan'ky, 17
Zerov, Mykola, 10, 11, 17, 107,
  117
Zola, Émile, 52
Žovten', 9
Zvyčajna, Olena, 15
Žyttja j revoljucija, 12, 14, 17, 107